Sporting Lives

Edited by Dave Day

An MMU Institute for Performance Research Publication

Sporting Lives Edited by Dave Day

First published 2011 by
MMU Institute for Performance Research
MMU Cheshire
Crewe Green Road
Crewe
Cheshire
CW1 5DU
www.ipr.mmu.ac.uk

ISBN 978-1-905476-62-6 paperback

Printed and bound in Great Britain by Manchester Metropolitan University

Frontispiece – Alec Nelson vs Joe Binks, scratch ¾ mile limit race, Reading 26 August 1899 (courtesy of Cambridgeshire Archives)

Table of Contents

Introduction

This collection of short papers on the lives of men and women connected with the sporting world has its origins in a *Sporting Lives* symposium hosted by Manchester Metropolitan University's Institute for Performance Research in December 2010. The contributors come from different backgrounds and include some of Britain's leading sports historians. The one thing they all have in common is an interest in sporting biography and an in-depth knowledge of at least one individual's life course. The work opens with a chapter from *John Bale* that outlines the career of sport scientist Ernst Jokl and explores the difficulty in writing biography especially given the many 'layers of truth' that permeate an individual's narrative. This theme is evident in subsequent chapters on equestrienne Pat Smythe (*Jean Willliams*), the fictional athlete Alf Tupper (*Jeffrey Hill*), footballers The Reverend Hunt (*Dilwyn Porter*) and Patrick O'Connell (*Robin Peake*), football manager Frank Buckley (*Neil Carter*), athletics coach Alec Nelson (*Ian Stone*), swimmer Joey Nuttall (*Keith Myerscough*), Olympic innovator John Hulley (*Ray Hulley*), pedestrian entrepreneur George Martin (*Samantha-Jayne Oldfield*), and eighteenth century boxing entrepreneurs (*Dave Day*). Taken together these papers highlight the richness and diversity of sporting lives as well as demonstrating that these stories can never be entirely finished but will continue to evolve as further sources are uncovered.

Contributors

John Bale is Emeritus Professor of Sports Studies at Keele University. He has authored several books and numerous articles on various aspects of sport. He has a particular interest in written and visual representations, exemplified by his Imagined Olympians (University of Minnesota Press), Roger Bannister and the Four Minute Mile (Routledge), Running Cultures (Routledge) and Anti-Sport Sentiments in Literature (Routledge). He is currently writing a book on Lewis Carroll and his engagements with sports.

Jean Williams is a Senior Research Fellow in the International Centre for Sports History and Culture. After writing two books on women's football A Game For Rough Girls (Routledge 2003) and A Beautiful Game (Berg 2007), she is now working on a research monograph called A Contemporary History of Women's Sport (Routledge Research, 2011) and a history of British women Olympians. The paper discussing the life and career of equestrian Pat Smythe is based on that ongoing research.

i

Jeffrey Hill is Emeritus Professor of Historical and Cultural Studies at De Montfort University where, until 2007, he was Director of the International Centre for Sport, History and Culture. His research interests include the cultural history of sport and leisure, and popular politics in Britain. He has published Sport, Leisure and Culture in Twentieth Century Britain (Palgrave Macmillan, 2002) and Sport and the Literary Imagination: essays in history, literature, and sport (Peter Lang, 2006). Sport: A Historical Introduction is due from Palgrave Macmillan in late 2010. With Anthony Bateman he has edited the Cambridge Companion to Cricket for CUP (to be published March 2011) and he is also working on a study of popular politics and culture in north-west England from the 1880s to the 1930s.

Dilwyn Porter is Senior Research Fellow at the International Centre for Sports History and Culture, De Montfort University. He has written extensively on twentieth century British history and on various aspects of business history. His main work in sports history has focused on Cold War sport, especially football; national and regional identity and sport; amateurism in English football; and entrepreneurship in sports-related business. He was co-editor of *Sport in History* from 2004 to 2008.

Robin Peake holds a Masters of Research from the University of Ulster where his thesis was entitled 'Was Patrick O'Connell a typical professional footballer of his time?' His undergraduate dissertation, for which he won the Donal Conway prize, used association football as a gauge to assess Northern Ireland's involvement in World War Two. He has presented on Irish Sporting Migration and is a contributor in the forthcoming Sports Around the World encyclopaedia, though he hopes to make the transition into Ecclesiastical History for PhD study. Robin is a committed Christian and an avid Northern Ireland supporter, who provides audio commentary at Windsor Park for blind and impartially sighted fans and contributes regularly to the fanzine "Happy Days".

Neil Carter is a senior research fellow in the International Centre for Sports History and Culture at De Montfort University, Leicester. His book, The Football Manager: A History, was published by Routledge in 2006. He has published more recently on the history of sports medicine and was the editor of Coaching Cultures published in 2010 in which he contributed an article on coaching in British athletics. His book on a history of Sport and Medicine is due for publication by Bloomsbury Academic in 2011.

Ian Stone is a Professorial Fellow at Durham Business School, and St Chad's College, Durham University. He is Director of the Policy Research Group at the University and also a Research Fellow at the UK Commission for Employment & Skills. His academic interests are entrepreneurship, business enterprise and labour markets. He has undertaken a large body of research for government departments and agencies, and acted as policy advisor both in the UK and overseas. While his work over the years has included the role of sport in regional development – and his PhD was in history – Ian's involvement in this project arises out of fortuitous contact with Dave Day while researching the life of his great uncle, Alec Nelson. He intends one day to write the definitive work on management failure over the long-term, based upon Newcastle United's experience.

Keith Myerscough is a Senior Lecturer and Curriculum Manager for Foundation Degrees in Sports Studies, Sports Development and Sports Coaching at Blackpool University Centre, an Associate College of Lancaster University. Areas of interest include community sports development and coaching, comparative studies in physical education and school sport, and the historiography of rational forms of recreation. Keith began his career as a teacher of physical education within the State School sector before moving on to manage the UK's first basketball/netball facility in Stockport, Greater Manchester. He returned to teaching in the FE/HE sectors in 1999.

Ray Hulley DMS is a retired senior Home Office official with a management services background in Prison, Police, Fire, Immigration, Magistrates' courts and Forensic Science Services. He has been a family historian for over 30 years and he has written several articles for the Guild of One-Name Studies, the North Cheshire Family History Society and the Manchester and Lancashire Family History Society journals as well as a book covering the history of a Hulley family. He was granted a Fellowship by the Manchester and Lancashire Family History Society in May 2001 for his voluntary work at the Public Record Office in London and at The National Archives at Kew. He has been working on John Hulley's founding role in the 19th century Olympic movement since 2001.

Samantha-Jayne Oldfield is a PhD student and lecturer within the Department of Exercise and Sport Science at Manchester Metropolitan University. Her PhD research is focused on nineteenth century Manchester pedestrianism, constructing biographies of the entrepreneurial publicans who promoted the sport prior to the formation of the Amateur Athletic Association. Recently she has presented work on issues surrounding historical methodology and interpretation, and the use of prosopography as a viable tool in the study of sport, as well as producing further biographies of mid-nineteenth century Manchester sporting publicans.

Dave Day is a senior lecturer in the Department of Exercise and Sport Science at Manchester Metropolitan University where his research interests focus on the history of coaching practice and training and the biographies of coaches and trainers. While his recent published work has been on swimming with a short biography of 1912 Olympic coach Walter Brickett and a paper on nineteenth century swimming professors in London he is currently engaged on illuminating the lives of early nineteenth century pedestrian trainers and the pugilist trainers who preceded them.

Ernst Jokl and Layers of Truth

John Bale

Those who write (auto)biographies tend do so for the same reasons as those who write *per se*. Seeking to categorise the reasons for writing, George Orwell suggested that writers, including biographers, write to seek the 'truth', to change the world, for the pleasure of writing good prose, and for the feeding of ego.[1] However, things are not as simple as this and self-depiction (or simply depiction) poses critical problems. Basic to writing a life is the recognition that writing is about representation: Biographies cannot tell the full story. Jerome Bruner adds that 'an autobiography is not and cannot be a way of simply signifying to a 'life as lived': A life is constrained by the act of autobiography.[2] And consider the words of Philip Roth: 'Memories of the past are not memories of facts but memories of your imagining of facts'.[3] In writing a biography, Vladimir Nabokov notes:

> Don't be too certain of learning the past from the lips of the present. Beware of the most honest broker. Remember that what you are told is really threefold: shaped by the teller, reshaped by the listener, concealed from both by the dead man of the tale.[4]

The hazards facing biographical studies are reiterated in numerous sources. Who could accurately write a complete human life in words? Jonathon Coe, the biographer of the *avant garde* 'sixties novelist B. S. Johnson, wrote: 'If even to condense the details of a comparatively short life … requires grotesque, enormous acts of compression and selection, what hope is there for the whole enterprise?' Presumably then, he suggests that any attempts to represent a *life* results is a pack of lies.[5] In this paper I prefer to grapple with questions of truth and lies by taking the approach of Norman Denzin who writes:

[1] George Orwell, 'Why I Write', in *Decline of the English Essay* (Harmondsworth: Penguin, 1978), 180-87.
[2] Jerome Bruner, 'The autobiographical process', *Current Sociology* 43, no. 2 (1995): 161.
[3] Philip Roth, *The Facts* (New York: Penguin, 1988).
[4] Vladimir Nabakov, *The Real Life of Sebastian Knight* (London, Penguin, 1941).
[5] Jonathon Coe, *Like a Firey Elephant* (London: Picador, 2004).

Lives and their experiences are represented as stories. They are like pictures that have been painted over, and when paint is scraped off and old picture, something new becomes visible. And the stories about it have the qualities of *pentiento*. Something new is always coming into sight. Displacing what was previously certain and seen. There is no truth in the painting of a life, only multiple images and traces of what has been, and what is new.[6]

So, the postmodernist might say, what was fiction becomes truth or, fiction seeps quietly and continuously into reality. Indeed, all [representations] *are* fictions, before in the literal sense of *fictio* – something can be made. And there is no end of ways in which they can be made.[7] It is Denzin's 'model' of representing a life that I adopt in writing some aspects of Ernst Jokl 'fictional' writing but first I think it is worth commenting on sports biographies *per se*.

Biography and Sport.
Are sporting biographies different from any other biographies? It has been suggested that sports biographies are more-de-politicised than others.[8] Also it has been suggested that sports biographies tend to reflect a *career* rather than a *life*. The perfect biography is impossible and the quality of literary representation various massively. For example, many sports biographies are hagiography, ghosted by journalists and written by a writer whose name differs from that on the cover. On the other hand, returning to Orwell's categorisation, a 'sport autobiography' that seeks to 'change the world' is, I suggest, *Pretty Good for a Girl* by Leslie Heywood - an autobiography that illuminates the world of women's long distance running and the brutal relationship between athlete and coach. This work could have ended up in the 'muck-raking' tradition of many sports books but partly because Heywood is a professor of English the book emerges as a committed study of modern sport.[9] An example of a 'revisionist' approach to biography is Brett Hutchins's work on Donald Bradman

---

6 Norman Denzin, *Interpretive Biography* (Beverley Hills, Sage, 1985), 81.
7 Derek Gregory, 'Areal Differentiation and Post-Modern Geography', in *Horizons in Human Geography*, in (eds.) Derek Gregory and Rex Walford (London: Macmillan 1994), 78-112.
8 Gyöngyi Szabó Földesi, 'The use of Autobiographies in Sport Sociology', in Otmar Weiss and Wolfgang Schultz (eds.), *Sport in Space and Time* (Vienna: Universität Verlag, 1995), 147-56.
9 Leslie Heywood, *Pretty Good for a Girl* (New York, The Free Press, 1998).

in which he presents a revisionist view rather than an attempt to represent the conventional wisdom.[10] For elegant writing, there are few autobiographies than Roger Bannister's *First Four Minutes*. [11] However, few studies have applied the ideas of Norman Denzin and my objective in this essay is to employ his idea of a 'layers of truth' or 'traces' while exploring part of the life of Ernst Franz Jokl.

Jokl: A Brief Overview

Ernst Jokl was born in Breslau (now Wrocław) in 1907 and died in Kentucky (USA) in 1997. I first encountered Jokl *via* his co-authored work on the 1952 Olympic Games in which he analysed quantitatively the athletes competing in the Games from a geographical perspective with the aim of correlating the performance of the nations and athletes represent. [12] I was impressed with this study and subsequently discovered other works that he had authored. Some years later he published what amounted to a repetition of his earlier work but added two somewhat gratuitous chapters on 'Sport and Culture' and 'Sport and Human Development'[13] I recognised in Jokl a man with an eclectic range of interests and was intrigued by the subjects he chose to study.

Over the years he was acknowledged as a 'father of American sports science'. He undertook medical training at the universities of Breslau and Berlin and in 1928 it seems that he assisted in some way in a study of the medical assessment of the athletes participating in the 1928 Olympic Games. In 1933 he married Erica Lessman, Lutheran Christian but his Jewishness led the Jokls to migrate to South Africa. There he became a lecturer at Witwatersrand Technical College and later a director of Physical Education at Stellenbosch and a physical education consultant to the South African Defence Corps. While in South Africa he developed a national programme of sports science and authored many articles on kinesiology, physiology, and sports.[14] His research output ranged across a dazzling array of subjects, from 'aviation medicine' to comparison of the physical efficiency of various

---

[10] Brett Hutchins, *Donald Bradman: Challenging the Myth* (Cambridge, Cambridge University Press, 2002).

[11] Roger Bannister, *First Four Minutes* (London: Putnam, 1955).

[12] Ernst Jokl, M. J. Karvonen, J. Kihlberg, A. Koskella and L. Noro, *Sports in the Cultural Pattern of the World*, (Helsinki: Institute of Occupational Health, 1956).

[13] Ernst Jokl, *Medical Sociology and Cultural Anthropology of Sport and Physical Education*, (Springfield: Charles C. Thomas, 1964).

[14] Van de Merwe, 'Ernst Franz Jokl as the Father of Physical Education in South Africa?', Paper presented at the annual conference of the North American Society for Sports History, Banff, (1990).

South African ethnic groups. He also acted as trainer for the sprinters in the South African team taking part in the 1938 British Empire Games (Figure 1).

Figure 1. Ernst Jokl (in black vest) training with the South African sprint team for the 1938 Empire Games.

Following the Second World War the Jokls returned to Germany but Ernst was unable to find work and migrated to the USA, finding a job in the University of Kentucky at Lexington where he stayed for the rest of his life. However, he made many trips abroad, attending numerous conferences and being an active member of numerous sporting organisations. He worked in a variety of fields, ranging from rehabilitation, dance, exercise, sports medicine, anthropology, psychology and many more. In 1952 he led a substantial study of the Helsinki Olympics, aided by Finnish colleagues which sought to explore the geographical variations of sporting success.[15] Jokl's life was one of energy. He was recalled as a brilliant lecturer. He was a major figure in the establishment of the American College of Sports Medicine and Physical Education (ICSSPE). He continued writing on various subjects, contributing a preface with the Duke of Edinburgh, on *Drugs and Performance Horses*. In his later years he received an honorary professorship at the universities of Berlin and Frankfurt and as a gesture of reconciliation Jokl Strasse in Cologne was named after him. In 1993 he received the Distinguished Service of the United States Sports Academy for his contribution to sports medicine.

This is a bland account of a life, the sort that is often found in an obituary or encyclopaedia. It is time now, however, to return to Denzin, his traces and his layers of truth.

---

[15] Jokl et al, *Sports in the Cultural Pattern of the World*.

Jokl – Sports Anthropologist
I now turn to a small though contentions point in Jokl's academic career which raises questions about his career and the ways in which he has been represented. In his *Reminiscences*, a slim, self-published memoir in 1988, he recalled some of his work while living in South Africa. I was attracted to his reference to an alleged expedition that he had 'organised' to Rwanda. He wrote:

> With the financial support of Sir Ernest Oppenheimer, I organised a research expedition to Ruanda-Urundi to study the traditional jumping ceremonies for young Watussis. The ceremonies had been described in 1906 (sic) by Adolf Friedrich, Duke of Mecklenburg, who visited Ruanda Urundi on behalf of the German Colonial Administration. … The Watussi jumpers took off from a mound one foot high. The best jumpers cleared 2.0 meters (6'7"). The sketches of them [Figure 2] were drawn from films by Ernst Ullman.[16]

And that was all his *Reminiscences* had to say about the 'traditional jumping'. It is in the above paragraph that I have to question the reliability of his writing.

As far as is known, the first written and photographic record of this form of jumping was indeed taken by the photographer attached to the expedition led by the Duke of Mecklenburg in 1907.[17] The configuration of Rwandan jumping, which differed from the European form in various ways (Figure 2), was subsequently represented in written and photographic form by many explorers and tourists during the first half of the twentieth century. It was usually attributed to Tutsi (who Jokl called 'Watussi') people, a group that made up about fifteen percent of the population but politically the most powerful.[18] Jokl authored at least four publications, each very brief, in which he alluded to the 'Rwandan high jumpers'. The first and longest was a quasi-technical paper published in 1941 in an obscure Scottish source, *The Journal of Physical Education and School Hygiene*.[19] Jokl was an avid advocate of 'developing' the sporting potential of African peoples and

---

[16] Ernst Jokl, *South African Reminiscences* (Lexington, Jokl, 1988), 13.
[17] Adolf Friedrich Mecklenburg, *In Central Africa* (Cassell: London, 1910).
[18] John Bale, *Imagined Olympians* (Minneapolis: University of Minnesota Press, 2002).
[19] Ernst Jokl, 'High Jump Technique of the Central African Watussis', *The Journal of Physical Education and School Hygiene*, 33, (1941) 145-151.

Figure 2. Typical representation of Rwanda high-jump.

argued that the Rwandan high jumpers should be admitted to the Olympic games, despite the fact that their body-culture was neither sportised nor carried the same ideological baggage as Olympic high jumping. It can be reasonably assumed that his written references to the Rwandan jumping were the result of the Oppenheimer-funded visit, though Jokl does not acknowledge this benefice in his paper but does do so in his *Reminiscences*. However, anyone with the most rudimentary knowledge of Rwanda would recognise that there were several qualities in Jokl's writing about the 'Watussi' jumpers that were mysterious to say the least. These can be catalogued as follows.

First, Jokl made the basic factual error of describing the majority of the population of Rwanda as being Tutsi. The most cursory knowledge of the composition of the Rwandan population would include the fact that at the time of Jokl's visit, as noted above Tutsi counted for about 15 percent of the Rwandan population and that Hutu were the numerically dominant group. How Jokl could have made such a simple mistake is difficult to understand? Perhaps it was a slip of the pen which the copy editor failed to spot.

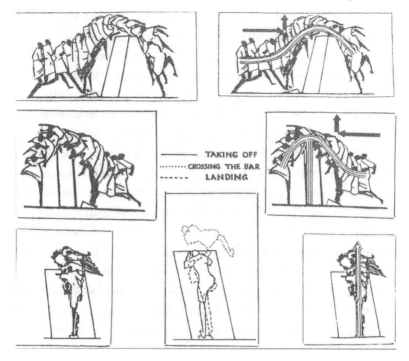

TAKING OFF
CROSSING THE BAR
LANDING

Figure 3. Generalising Tutsi.

Secondly, in his references to the Rwandan high jump, Jokl included diagrams that summarised the run-up, take-off and landing of the jumpers and served as a kinesiological model of their technique. The diagrams were made from a movie that, according to his 1941 paper, had been made by Professor J. H. Wellington but over forty years later, in his *Reminiscences* he attributed the movie to Ernst Ullmann who almost certainly drafted the diagrams of the jumping[20] (Figure 3). Perhaps this confusion was the result of Jokl's advanced age when he wrote his reminiscences.

Thirdly, it cannot be said with any certainty that Jokl travelled to Rwanda and in his *Reminiscences* he states that he 'organised', rather than actually travelled to, Rwanda with the expedition. However, whether he went or delegated others to explore Rwandan body-culture, it seems reasonable that a 1930s traveller with anthropological interests would have taken a camera on his travels, especially to photograph the objects of the research - the Rwandan jumpers. However, in each of the published accounts of the high jump it was the

---

[20] Jokl, *South African Reminiscences*.

Mecklenburg image of 1907 that was the only photographic illustration (Figure 4), an image that has been reproduced in many sources since.

Figure 4. Untypical (Mecklenburg) representation of Rwanda 'high-jump'.

Yet this is arguably the *least typical* of the many photographs of the jumping phenomenon that I have seen. Invariably, photographs of the jumping are shown by the much more typical configuration in Figure 2. Why didn't he include a photograph by a member of his expedition in the late 1930s rather than rely on the Mecklenburg image of 1907? The Jokl archives at the University of Cologne reveal that there is no record of the visit made by Jokl to Rwanda.[21] It is, nevertheless, conceivable that no material from the visit were placed in the archive or/and no member of 'his' expedition took a camera with which to record the visit.

Fourthly, in one of his papers on the Rwandan jumping Jokl described the apparatus consisting of a *hemp rope* with *weights* at each end, placed between two *upright* over which the athlete jumped.[22] The only illustrations of this kind of apparatus (i.e. rope placed in notches, crudely cut uprights from branches of trees) that I have seen is taken

---

[21] W. Sonnenscheim, quoted in Bale, 'The mysterious Professor Jokl'.
[22] Ernst Jokl, *Physiology of Exercise* (Springfield: Charles C. Thomas, 1964).

from that on the 1907 expedition (Figure 4). In all other early photographs of the high jump, two upright reeds with another reed (Figure 2) placed over the top with the upright reeds sloping away from the on-coming jumper. There are neither 'hemp rope' nor weights. Indeed, Jokl contradicted himself by showing the configuration of the equipment in his Figure 2 – based on the movie noted above – which are not based on the Mecklenburg photographs but on other (non-Mecklenburg) images.

Finally, and perhaps the most serious, in none of his brief allusions to Rwanda did Jokl do anything other than quote secondary sources of the Rwandan jumpers. There is no suggestion in his writing that he 'witnessed', 'observed' or 'recorded' anything to do what he was writing about. Instead, for example, the heights achieved by the jumpers 'are said by reliable observers' to be around 7'2".[23] It seems that he had not read Mecklenburg's popular book in which it is claimed that the athlete in the photograph had cleared 2.50 metres (about 8'2"). Depending as he does, upon what he was told or witnessed on film and photograph, it is if he had never actually witnessed the jumping - or, perhaps, he did not regard the Mecklenburg photograph and the staggering statement of the 2.50 metres jump as unreliable.

I now return to Denzin's observations on 'traces' of truth. Two simple traces can be seen in the 'story' of Jokl's study of the high jump. First, Jokl presented himself as an expert on Rwanda by publishing his 'research' in an 'academic' journal. Secondly, a layer is scratched away to revel him as an ignoramus. One can speculate that he had never visited Rwanda – and what happened to the 'financial support'?

Jokl – Athlete
Jokl was not only a student of body cultures. In his youth he was an athlete, a good sprinter (Figure 1) and his wife was a gymnast. Jokl recalls that in 1924 he ran the final leg of his university's 4 x 400 metres relay team in 'under fifty seconds at the age a seventeen.[24] If true, this would have been an impressive performance. He also competed in the 400 metres hurdles, his best time being apparently 58.0 seconds, made in a race in Berlin in 1927 in which he finished third.[25] According to

---

[23] Jokl, 1941, 'High Jump Technique' p. 146.
[24] Ernst Jokl, 'Indisposition after running', in E. Jokl and E. Simon (eds.), *International Research in Sport and Physical Education*, (Charles C. Thomas, Springfield, 1960), 682-692.
[25] Arnd Krüger, quoted in Bale, 'The mysterious Professor Jokl'

ranking lists collected by the Association of Track and Field Statisticians, this ranked him as the 44th fasted in the world for this event that year. He also competed in the shorter sprints and the high and long jumps in which he achieved more modest results.[26]

A number of written accounts state that Ernst Jokl was a member of the German track and field team which competed in the 1928 Olympics in Amsterdam. Jokl was, according to at least two sources, 'an outstanding 400-meter and hurdler for the German Olympic team in 1928'.[27] In an interview as part of a study of the P.E. department at Stellenbosch, it is reported that Jokl himself stated that he had competed in the 1928 games in the 400 metre hurdles and that he had won German titles (Hy het later as baanatleet bedenheid in Duitsland verwerf en by twee geleenthed nasionale titlesverower. In 1928 was hy lid von de Duutse atletekspan spele in Amsterdam, waar hy aan die 400 metres hekkies deelgeenen het). However, an obituary notice records that [28] Jokl 'made the 1928 Olympic team as an alternate in the 400 metres hurdles, but did not compete'.[29] That he was an alternate of substitute for the team was supported by an email communication from Jokl's daughter.[30]

A further trace of 'the truth' can be exposed exploring the statistical records of the results of, and participation in, the 1928 Games. A careful reading of all Olympic results, the names of all entrants for the 1928 games, all the athletes who have ever competed for Germany in the Olympics, the German Olympic Committee's list of Olympians and several other gazetteers, fail to reveal the name Jokl, Jockl, or Joekl. One of the most eminent track and field statisticians in the world, with a specialist interest in the Olympic Games, is adamant that Jokl never competed in the Olympics.[31] Nor does it seem that he was an alternate

---

[26] A. Boshoff, 'Die geskiedenis van die Department van Liggaamlik Opvoed-kund aan die Universiteit van Stellenbosch', (Unpublished master's thesis, University of Stelenbosch, 1981), 3.

[27] D. Williamson, 'Life saving Dr. Mueller selected to get sports medicine aware', http:www.unc.edi/news/newserv/research/muell6 (accessed 1998).

[28] J. Kane, 'Ernst Jokl's 85th Birthday', *ISCCPE Bulletin*, 16, (1993) 22-23;1993; S. Bailey, *Science in the Service of Sport and Physical Education*, (Chichester: Wiley, 1996) 17; M. Hebbelink, 'Prof. Dr. Ernst Jokl', *ICSSPE Bulletin*, 23, (1997) 16-17.

[29] F. Litsky, 'Dr. Ernst Jokl, a pioneer of sports medicine, dies at 90', *New York Times*, November, (1997).

[30] Ball, quoted in John Bale, 'The Mysterious Professor Jokl' in *Writing Lives in Sports*, ed. John Bale, Mette K. Christiansen, and Gertud Pfister, (Aarhus: Aarhus University Press, 2004), 25-40.

[31] Mallon, quoted in Bale,'The Mysterious Professor Jokl'.

(reserve). He did not take part in the 1928 German championship, nor achieved a performance that ranked him in the top thirty in German in any event. Arnd Krüger and Karl Steinnmetz, leading track and field scholars, dismiss the idea that he could have been a reserve, the latter laughing it off as being 'utterly ridiculous'.[32] Yet another trace of Jokl's life seems to have been removed. Nor does it seem that he ever won any German titles. He never finished in the first six in any event at the German championships – except, that is, as a member of the VfB track club's 4 x 400 metres relay team which finished second in the 1927 National championships.[33].

In passing, it can be mentioned that Erica Jokl was named as a member of the German track and field team and a gymnastics 'gold medallist in the 1928 Olympics[34], a view seemingly supported by Jokl himself.[35] Jokl's daughter informed me that her mother won a group medal for a collection of sporting activities which included discus, jumping, javelin, and a group gymnastic performance.[36] Jokl's grandson reported a more or less identical story.[37] Yet , as with the case of Ernst Jokl, there is no record of any Olympic participation for Erica Jokl or Lestmann in the 1928 Games. Indeed, there was no German team in the gymnastics events of the 1928 games. The most that can be said is that she awarded a medal for one of several unofficial and little-known exhibitions or demonstrations events that took place alongside the Olympics but not officially part of the Games.

Attempting to write even part of the life of Ernst Jokl perfectly exemplifies Denzin's notion of something new always becoming visible in biographical work. Likewise, Nabokov's caution about oral evidence, even from members of the biographical object's family and himself, is shown here as being fraught with uncertainty and, apparently, untruth. It might also be worth returning to the words of Jerome Bruner: 'Perceiving and remembering are themselves constructions and reconstructions'.[38] In attempting to write Jokl's

---

[32] Quoted in Bale, 'The mysterious Professor Jokl'.

[33] Ibid.

[34] P. Schneider, 'Technology ambassador', Healthcare Information on Line, http://healthcare-informatics.com, (accessed 1998).

[35] Boshoff, 'Die geskiedenis van die Department', 1981, p. 35.

[36] Ball, quoted in Bale, 'The Mysterious Professor Jokl' (2003).

[37] Ball , quoted in Bale, 'The Mysterious Professor Jokl' (2003).

[38] Quoted from D. McCooey, *Artful Histories: Modern Australian Autobiography* (Cambridge; Cambridge University Press, 1996), 8.

engagement with the 1928 Olympics, it appears that it was almost all rhetorical (Table 1).

Layers	Layers of 'truth' about Jokl and the 1928 Olympics.	Source, e.g.
1	Competed in the Olympic 400 m and 400 m hurdles.	Williamson, 1998
2	Competed in the Olympic 400 hurdles	Boshoff, 1981
3	Did not compete in the Olympic games.	Krüger, 2000
4	Was a reserve for the Olympic team.	Litsky 1997
5	Neither competed nor was a reserve for the Olympic team.	Krüger, 2000

Table 1. 'Traces' of truth about Jokl's 1928 Olympics

Representing Ernst Jokl

The ambiguous nature of the two events (the Rwanda and Amsterdam episodes) illustrates clearly some of the hazards of writing both history and biography. But how many more layers of truth could be exhumed? What do these two cases tell us about Jokl as a scholar and, perhaps more importantly, as a human being? In response to these questions I explore Jokl as a 'placeless' person and secondly as a 'trickster', practicing perhaps not a life of sport but one of disport.

Jokl's life gives the impression of being focussed around work and sport. But he was central to neither. He was characterised by his fluidity and marginality rather than rootedness and centrality. He was a man at the margins, placeless, socially, professionally and as a sportsman. Let me elaborate. Coming from Breslau, he was born at the margins of Germany and Poland. He was known to be a Jew on his father's side and can also be seen as being marginal of, successively German, South African and American society. He seemed to be Jew-ish than Jewish. To be sure, he was sufficiently Jewish to represent the Kochba (Jewish) track club while in Berlin and leave Germany in 1933. On entry to South Africa he described himself as a 'German refugee'[39] and he was recognised as Jewish by both the editor of *South African*

---

[39] Jokl, *Reminiscences*, (1988), 180.

Jewry[40] and by his obituary writer in the *New York Times*[41] though members of his family felt that 'the German part of his family felt that 'the German part of his identity was far more dominant'.[42] There is more than a suggestion that he did not project his Jewishness while in South Africa and Jews or Jewishness is not mentioned in his *Reminiscences*. One of my informants told me that her family knew Jokl well while in South Africa but they never regarded them as Jewish and were amazed when they told he was. Another informant, a friend and colleague of Jokl wrote:

> Concerning his Jewishness … this is a rather complex question. He often told me that he was half-Jewish since his mother was not … As far as I know in the Jewish cemetery in Wrocław there was his father's grave … When we were together in Israel on the occasion of several scientific seminars he occasionally told me that his ancestors were indeed Jewish, but that he felt to himself to be a Christian!

Others who knew him also felt that he was more a German than a Jewish stereotype. Yet the ambivalence of his Jewishness is revealed by his 'on and off' affiliation to the local synagogue during his life in Lexington[43] and the fact that on occasions he seemed to urge non-practicing back into the faith.[44] 'Feeling Jewish' is at one definition is at least one defining of being Jewish.[45] Jokl's personal identity was ambivalent to say the least. His placelessness, being neither one thing nor the other, could be put into operation when the need arose. He seems to me to be reminiscent of Woody Allen's *Zelig*, a 'chameleon man' who could adopt the guise of anyone he liked, at a moment's notice. In the academic world Jokl's vast range of publications leads to the problem of categorisation. Where can he be placed academically?

He was apparently not allowed to practice in Kentucky, not being a qualified medical doctor (or, more accurately, not having any proof that he was). So, he was not a 'proper' medical doctor. Nor was he a

---

[40] A. Goldman, 'The World of Sport', in M. Arkin (ed.), *South African Jewry*, Cape Town, (1984).
[41] Litsky, 'Dr. Ernst Jokl, a pioneer of sports medicine'.
[42] Ball, quoted in Bale, 'The Mysterious Professor Jokl'.
[43] Ibid.
[44] A. D. Munrow, *A. D. Munrow's Travel Diary and Commentary*, (unpublished typescript, Centre for Olympic Studies, University of Queensland, 1956), 73.
[45] George Eisen, 'Jews and sport: A century of retrospect', *Journal of Sport History*, 26, (1999), 225-39.

qualified anthropologist but this did not prevent him publishing quasi-anthropological studies, calling his co-authored study of the 1952 Olympics a 'medical anthropology'. He was not a central player in any academic discipline and therefore ran the risk of interdisciplinarity with its shallowness and lack of digestion. The fact that he had no training in dance, veterinary science, and anthropology did not stop him publishing papers in these subjects. He refused to be 'placed' and being placeless Jokl might be seem to have transgressed the norms of 'the specialist' in academic life.

Jokl, Joker / Jokl-Sokal?

Another way of (perhaps more speculatively) reading Jokl is to see him as a joker or trickster who not only blurred distinctions of academic disciplines but also between truth and fiction. He carnivalised sporting discourse by transgressing disciplinary norms. For example, careful reading by specialist in a variety of subjects would be needed to scrutinise his writing with great care before one could be sure he was not an imposter. Is it taking things too far to suggest that he was a (modest) forerunner of Alan Sokal, an American physicist who submitted a nonsensical spoof paper to the trendy journal, *Social Text* – and whose editors published it, assuming it to be a serious paper?[46] Like Sokal's hoax article, Jokl's Rwanda paper (and how many others?) was 'liberally scattered with nonsense', even though it 'sounded good'.[47] It may have flattered the editor of a now defunct, little known, modest journal of physical education. A possible difference between Jokl and Sokal is that the latter's spoof was deliberate while Jokl was simply sloppy. Or *was* Jokl trying to hoax his readership, most of whom were hardly experts on Rwanda and its body cultures. Or was it simply that the editor or reviewer was insufficiently *au fait* with the subject of the paper? Did Jokl really care whether his facts were right or wrong? Was he submitting yet another paper to be published on his route to become a polymath?

A final reading of Jokl is that he was a clown – the dialogical 'other' of official academic culture, contaminating the supposedly monological voices of the powerful when he ventured into the world of sports anthropology? Jokl the jester could be seen as a representative of the carrnivalesque, or a writer of 'sport' – the word being used in

---

[46] A. Sokal and J. Bricmont, *Intellectual Imposters* (London: Profile Books 1999).
[47] R. T. Carroll, 'The Sokal Hoax', *The Skeptics Dictionary*, http://skepdic.com/sokal.html (accessed 13/3/02.).

nineteenth century literary circles to describe a work that cannot be satisfactorily categorised.[48]

---

[48] Robert Polhemus, 'Lewis Carroll and the child in Victorian Fiction', in *The Columbia History of the British Novel*, (ed. John Richetti), (New York: Columbia University Press' 1994), 579-606.

2

The Immediate Legacy of Pat Smythe: The Pony-Mad Teenager in 1950s and 1960s Britain

Jean Williams

Introduction

Equitation has been prized as an art, leisure pursuit, work technology and a means of war for thousands of years. Though women have ridden, raced, hunted and fought with horses since well before the formation of the Jockey Club in the 1750s, access to the best livestock has always been an indicator of social class. Brailsford, for example, has horse races with nine un-named women riders in Newcastle in 1725 and Ripon in 1734, perhaps suggesting a north-east bias.[1] Just as male royalty and aristocracy patronised the sport, by 1797 Ladies' Plates had been established at Guildford, Lewes, York and Egham races and a Ladies' Purse at Chester. While we know about some wealthy individual women equestrians in eighteenth and nineteenth century Britian, we generally know less about the lower classes who had fewer material resources at their disposal. Pierce Egan, for example, made Alicia Thornton famous in his 1832 *Book of Sports*, because of her beauty, access to thoroughbred stock and the notorious side bet of her husband, Colonel Thomas Thornton. It is unclear whether she died shortly after her racing feats or whether the title 'Mrs' was a courtesy, as her husband is said to have married again in 1806.[2]

As the collections of the British Library in London and the National Sporting Library in Middleburg Virginia show, women's equestrian participation has long been combined with literary representation. The mythologising of Lady Godiva riding naked through Coventry in protest of taxes imposed by her husband, first recorded two hundred years after it supposedly happened in 1236, is part of a longer tradition. It includes Chaucer's *Wife of Bath*, who symbolically rode her

---

[1] Dennis Brailsford *A Taste for Diversions: Sport in Georgian England* (Cambridge: Lutterworth, 1999), 146.

[2] Pierce Egan Pierce *Egan's Book of Sports and Mirror of Life: Embracing the Turf, the Chase, the Ring, and the Stage Interspersed with the Original Memories of Sporting Men etc.* (London: T.T.& J Tegg, 1832), 346-47 British Library Collection.

horse astride and, later, the brilliant horsewomanship of Lucy Glitters written by R. S. Surtees, said to be based on real-life huntress Lady Lade. Two women made riding particularly fashionable to the urban elite between 1850 and 1880 and the national press helped spread their fame. The first was Catherine 'Skittles' Walters, an elegant courtesan who rode in Hyde Park in a costume so tight that a letter to *The Times* in 1862 complained that the traffic in both directions was halted by the spectacle. However, the Liverpool-born Queen of the Chase was eclipsed in 1876 by Elizabeth, Empress of Austria and the number of women hunting rose dramatically. By 1880 women increasingly wrote about their experiences, as much for readers as for riders: Mrs Power O'Donoghue; Edith Somerville; Violet Greville; Belle Beach and Mrs Stuart Menzies became prominent authorities before the First World War.[3] Susan, Countess of Malmesbury, in her book on *Cycling*, for instance, drew links with commanding a horse and taking charge of a bicycle.[4] Meanwhile, Lady Georgiana Curzon's chapter on 'Tandem Driving' dismissed those critics of women's ability to control a carriage and pair as themselves lacking the necessary technical skills of proper harnessing or suffering from 'want of nerve.'[5] However, hunting aside, the militaristic links of equestrian sport before 1945 have tended to be documented at the expense of women's history.

The British are notoriously sentimental, and cruel, towards animals, so the stereotype goes. The White Horse at Uffington, Berkshire is thought to be a 400 foot representation of Epona, goddess of the horse and a site of sacrifice. The carnage associated with Boadicea, the widow of the king of the Iceni, in AD 61 is re-told in schools and has been the subect of numerous television and film programmes, both

---

[3] Nannie Power O'Donoghue *Ladies on horseback. Learning, park-riding, and hunting, with hints upon costume, and numerous anecdotes* (London: W. H. Allen & Co., 1881); Nannie Power O'Donoghue *Riding for ladies: with hints on the stable* (London: W. Thacker, 1887); Edith Somerville *Through Connemara in a governess cart* (London: W. H. Allen & Co., limited, 1893); Violet Greville *Ladies in the field, sketches of sport* (New York: D. Appleton and Co., 1894); Belle Beach *Riding and driving for women* (New York: C. Scribner's Sons, 1912) and Mrs Stuart Menzies *Women in the hunting field* (London: Vinton, 1913) National Sporting Library Collection, Middleburg Virginia.

[4] Susan, Countess of Malmesbury, G. Lacey Hillier and H. Graves *Cycling* The Suffolk Sporting Series (London: Lawrence and Bullen, 1908) British Library Collection.

[5] Lady Georgiana Curzon 'Tandem Driving' in His Grace The Duke of Beaufort K.G. (with contributions by other authorities) *Driving* (London: Longman, Greens and Co. 1889), 147 British Library Collection.

popular and documentary.[6] In more recent times, it is now generally accepted that in the second Boer War (1899-1902) the British forces alone lost over 300,000 horses, whilst campaigns during World War One cost the lives of around a half a million horses. Michael Morpurgo's *War Horse*, a novel for children written in 1982 has recently been a success as a play at the National Theatre, and continues to attract much popular attention, most recently as a Steven Spielberg film adaptation.[7]

Yet surprisingly very little academic research exists on equestrian sport in the twentieth century beyond horse racing and hunting. Female equestrianism is an historically important, but underacknowledged, sporting phenomenon therefore, and particularly after 1945. Not least, the International Olympic Committee (IOC, founded in 1896) and Fédération Équestre Internationale (FEI, founded in 1921) gradually admitted women to the three disciplines at the Games, beginning with dressage in 1952, show-jumping in 1956 and three-day eventing (combining dressage, jumping and cross-country) in 1964. There was some precedent it seems, as, at the 1900 Olympic Games, Elvira Guerra competed for France on Libertin in the 'Hacks and Hunter combined' section. There remains some dispute, though, about whether this was an Olympic event. Helen Preece similarly tried to compete in the 1912 Modern Pentathlon competition (shooting, cross-country, fencing swimming and horse riding) but was declined the opportunity by the Swedish Olympic Committee at the instigation of Pierre De Coubertin.[8] Outside of the Olympic conmpetition, Lady Wright, Marjorie Avis Bullows, became the first woman to ride astride at Olympia; the first to win the show-jumping championship there in 1928 and later ran a prestigious riding school at Metchely, Edgbaston with her husband Robert. The innovation of 'working pupils' developed a career-path for young women such as 'Pug' Verity and Tinka Taylor later to be replicated at other riding schools. The first

---

[6] Gilliam Newsum (foreword by Pat Koechlin-Smythe) *Women and Horses* (Hampsire: The Sportsman's Press, 1988), 14-16.

[7] Michael Murpurgo *Warhorse* (London: Kaye and Ward Ltd, 1982 reissued by Egmont UK Ltd 2007); Michael Murpurgo (adapted by Nick Stafford in association with the Handspring Puppet Company) *Warhorse* http://www.nationaltheatre.org.uk/warhorse 2007 accessed 30 November 2010.

[8] Stephanie Daniels and Anita Tedder '*A Proper Spectacle*': Women Olympians 1900-1936 (Dunstable, Bedfordshire: Priory Press, 2000), 25-6. Helen Preece had already won the $1000 Gold Cup at the Madison Square Horse Show in 1912, suggest Daniels and Tedder, referencing the *Louisville Herald* 7th July 1912.

youth gymkhana was held in 1928, a forerunner to the formation of the Pony Club in 1929 which had 8,350 members in 1934.[9] Recovering from a fractured pelvis in 1936, Wright won the *Daily Mail* Cup at Olympia on Jimmy Brown to set a new Ladies' record of 7ft 4 inches. However, World War Two saw the mechanisation of cavalry battalions which weakened the military links with the Olympic versions of the sport which had been reserved until that point for officers. In British post-war civilian life, more people used cycles or motor transport for and so the horse increasingly became linked with leisure, rather than work.

This article focuses on the life of Britian's Pat Smythe (22 November 1928 - 27 February 1996), particularly the autobiographies *Jump For Joy* (1954); *Jumping Round the World* (1962) and *Leaping Life's Fences* (1992) to explore the part that equestrianism played in her life as leisure, work and as cultural practice. Pat Smythe's win at the 1949 Grand Prix in Brussells and her dominance in national British championships between 1952 and 1962 helped to develop a tradition of horse-riding as a widely televised post-war 'open' sport; even the three-day event.[10] While equestrianism was to have an important place in Olympic competition, Pat Smythe and other female riders were to popularise it in Britain after 1948 as a wider cultural practice. Equestrianism (like motor racing) draws our attention to the gendered nature of access to sporting resources. Pat Smythe's career as an Olympian began later than that of her horses which were required to be available for British team (but were not used) at the 1948 London Games at which women were not allowed to compete. The 1950s and early 1960s were, then, important times for a swift change in the image of horse riding.

The thesis of this work concerns the 'immediate legacy' of Smythe, who is argued to have been a founding figure in creating a recognisable stereotype of the pony-mad British teenager by the time of her first Olympic appearance at Stockholm. While the influence of women like Marjorie Wright should not be underestimated, in 1956 Smythe and and Brigitte Schockaert of Belgium were present at the Stockholm Olympic Games and Smythe helped to win a team bronze. Smythe had already been made an OBE the same year and was a published author. This show-jumping first nevertheless marked a change in the militaristic nature of Olympic equestrian competition and more people from a wider range of backgrounds began to take

---

[9] The Pony Club History http://www.pcuk.org/About-Us/History accessed 27 January 2011.
[10] Jeffrey Hill, Smythe, Patricia Rosemary 1928-1996 Oxford dictionary of national biography OUP 2004-11.

part in more events in Britain and abroad.[11] Like the athlete Mary Rand in the 1960s, Pat Smythe was conflicted by media interest in her private life, but she was also one of several postwar British sports personalities to have a profilic career as a writer and columnist on a number of subjects from horse care and management, to ski-ing, conservation and adventure stories for children. The style of writing, for children and adults, was a particular brand of plucky glamour. This contrasts with the more derisive depiction of pony-mad girls in the work of Norman Thelwell who was to become 'the unofficial artist of the British countryside' and one of the nation's most popular cartoonists. Thelwell's first pony caricature was published in *Punch* in 1953. The 'Thelwell Pony' and its rider became a recognisable cultural type: his first book *Angels on Horseback* was published in 1957, and was inspired by his observations of two hairy ponies - 'small and round and fat and of very uncertain temper' - who grazed in a field next to his house. In Thelwell, it is always the pony, not the human companion, who is in charge. Smythe's Three-Jays series of children's books articulated an altogether different world where pony-ownership faciliated modesty in victory, equanimity in defeat, adventure and teamwork.

A short biography of Pat Smythe: From *Jump For Joy to Leaping Life's Fences*

Patricia Rosemary Smythe was born 22nd November 1928 at 24 Shotfield Avenue East Sheen to join elder brother Ronald, already three and a half, and in her words 'as a replacement for elder brother Dickie who had died of a heart complaint two years and a day before'. Her father noted in his diary 'Patricia born 10.05 am, Monique splendid! Dull wet morning. To office after lunch. Aunt Isobel died today.' [12] Monique, her mother, had been brought up with three brothers at Cromhall Rectory in Gloucestershire, riding farmer's hunters and point to pointers. At St Swithin's School Winchester she was captain of the cricket XI and head of house so this seems to be where Pat's love of sport came from. Monique was married at nineteen to Eric Smythe. The second son of an electrical engineer, Eric and his brother Gordon were taken to Davos when their father contracted Tuberculosis. This meant that both sons became fluent in German, French and English, going to school in Lausanne. Eric then went to

---

[11] At Berlin in 1936 only 29 riders from eleven countries had competed while the 1948 Games had 46 entrants; subsequent to 1952 the top 25 competitors in each discipline compete for the Finals.
[12] Pat Smythe *Leaping Life's Fences* (Wiltshire: the Sportsman's Press, 1992), 1.

Heidelberg University and qualified as a Civil Engineer working in the military, before becoming the youngest staff officer in the Intelligence Corps. This seems to be where Pat got her internationalist perspective from. A precarious kind of upper middle class upbringing followed as the family briefly owned a £2000 house called Beaufort, by Barnes common before becoming 'homeless'. While at Beaufort Pat therefore grew up close to the Roehampton Club with its roller skating rink, swimming pool, golf course, tennis and polo matches but also within reach of plenty of open space. Monique Smythe was often sent horses to break-in and school and Pixie was such a pony, having been kicked and blinded in one eye. With 13 as her lucky number Pat won equal first prize on Pixie at the Richmond horse show in 1939 and came to national prominence.[13]

Eric Smythe's rheumatoid arthritis meant that his health was fragile and he was advised to go for a dry cure in North Africa, effectively leaving the family homeless and Pat was sent to boarding school at Seaford, Ronald to Newquay and their mother joined the Red Cross in London. The experience was to persuade Pat never to send her own children to board. It was also to affect her fiction, as the children's adventures were not nostalgic depictions of her peers, based in educational institutions: there were to be no school-stories.

A large part of the Smythe mythology was borne out of the combination of an innate ability to 'bring on' horses, especially those considered frail or flaky, an entrepreneurial 'can-do' spirit and a matriarchal family structure. A lot of this was necessity: Eric was to die 19 January 1945 having tried a range of therapies from gold injections to psychic healing. It helped of course to have family friends such as the Drummond-Hay family, daughters of the Duchess of Hamilton who invited the Smythes to their Ferne Gymkhanas, society and sporting events which were photographed for *Tatler*. But Pat Smythe, though an Olympic-class name dropper, was not a total snob. She had much to say in praise of circus families and their empathy with animals in using the psychology of each character as part of their training, for example. In the holidays both the children and the ponies worked on local farms and this ethic of hard-graft in the face of adversity also became a Smythe trademark. Miserden House for

---

[13] Pat Smythe *Jump For Joy* (Watford: The Companion Book Club, 1955), 42 is more straightforward on this issue saying 'Pixie tied for first place with another pony' than *Leaping Life's Fences* p. 10 where it is mentioned the other two riders who shared first place were Dougie Bunn, a future master of Hickstead, and Fred Winter, later to be a famous jockey and trainer.

example, looks like a country pile, but it was paid for by a combination of teaching children to ride and speak English, as well as being a guest house and term time lodging for students at Cirencester College of agriculture. It was launched as such on Pat's twenty-first birthday and it is from here that the Three Jays journey on their competitive adventures to Olympia and further afield.

Because of space it is not possible to outline the development of each horse the family owned, but, as an example, the unschooled Finality was to be an important purchase. Bought for £40 each with Johnnie Traill (the Polo and golf Pro), Finality was the product of a Thoroughbred stallion and a milk cart pony who had been honourably retired to stud for kicking the cart to pieces in Tunbridge Wells High Street.[14] It seemed initially that Finality had inherited her mother's sense of humour: the horse endured strangles and injury from a barbed wore fence before Monique Smythe healed it in time for the inaugural White City competition. Against the odds, Pat and Finality won the show jumping event at the White City in 1947. Financially, as well as in terms of prestige, entering a horse how for shillings and winning pounds became an important means of supplementing, then forming, the family income. It also meant a life of travel, as Smythe was selected for the British Team travelling to Belgium in 1948, no mean feat given the number of Army riders and horses in post-war competition. It also meant Traill wanted to sell the horse for £1,500. Finality was sold by the time of the post-Olympic competition in 1948 but as a loan, it won Smythe the George VI Cup. The next year a Princess Elisabeth Cup for Ladies was introduced to save male rider's egos.

The show-jumping event at the London 1948 Olympics was not open to women but the Smythe's were obliged to lend Finality to the team. There was no compensation, which deprived them of an important means of income for six weeks, and in any case the horse was declared 'unsuitable' for Olympic competition. The British were to come third. Harry Llewellyn, who dominated pre and post war British Show jumping seems nevertheless to have been of help to Pat at a distance. More tangible though, were changes to the British media. The First Horse of the Year Show in 1949 was therefore another nationally important breakthrough event for Smythe overseen by Colonel Mike Ansell who used the White City to provide an indoor show. On a

---

[14] Pat Smythe *Jump For Joy* p. 66 is much more tender and dramatic in writing about Kitty the milk horse than the brief summary of this in *Leaping Life's Fences* p. 18.

loaned Finality, Smythe won the Leading Show Jumper of the Year. She then won the French Ladies cup on novice Leona and the Belgian Grand Prix on another loaned horse called Nobbler. This so surprised the International Equestrian Federation that they did not have rules in place to prevent a woman from winning. Smythe's reputation in Europe helped her domestic fame in Britain. This developed in 1950 when she bought a bay for £150 at the National Hunt meeting and retitled him Prince Hal. She paid a similar price for Tosca. The television public were again entertained by the Horse of the Year duel in 1950 between Smythe on Finality tying equal first with Llewclyn and Foxhunter. As Sportswoman of the Year in 1952 (with Len Hutton as sportsman) at the Savoy presented by the Marquis and Marchioness of Exeter (Lord David Burghley had won the hurdle Gold medal for Britian in the 928 Amsterdam Olympics), Smythe was effectively among Fifties Britain's sporting elite. Madame Tussads made a waxwork.

However, 1953 was to see both the worst of times and personal success: Monique Smythe was killed in a road accident in January. The bank manager phoned on the same afternoon to ask for the repayment of £1500 on the house. Leona was sold immediately to raise the funds. Later that year the seven foot high bank at the Nice show would injure Pat, Tosca and Prince Hal. All three were to recover and Tosca in particular won £1542 in 1952 and £1350 in 1953 before a tour of America supplemented this income. Later Roy Plumley invited Pat onto *Desert Island Discs*. She was a household name. This she amplified and extended by her writing. The bibilography of her autobiographical/ equestrian/ travel/ conservation writing was to become *Jump For Joy* (1954); *Pay Smythe's Book of Horses* (1956); *One Jump Ahead* (1958); *Tosca and Lucia* (1959); *Florian's Farmyard* (1960); *Horses and Places* (1961); *Jumping Round the World* (1962); *Leaping Life's Fences* (1992). Her children's books were to include *Jacqueline Rides for a Fall* (Cassel, 1956); *Three Jays Against The Clock* (Cassel, 1958); *Three Jays On Holiday* (Cassel, 1958); *Three Jays Go To Town* (Cassel, 1959); *Three Jays Over The Border* (Cassel, 1960); *Three Jays Go To Rome* (Cassel, 1960); *Three Jays Lend A Hand* (Cassel, 1961); 'What a Night!' in John Canning (ed.) *Adventure Stories for Girls* (Octopus: London, 1978 reprinted 1979, 1980, 1981 and 1982). This does not include her journalism for the *Daily Express*, forewords to numerous books and other writing.

As has been said above, Britain won won team bronze in 1956 behind Germany in gold medal place. Smythe described the occasion, 'Olympic Games. What a vista of glory and supreme effort those words conjure up! In a flash return the memories of training, falls, fun. Disappointments and achievement all leading to the goal of any sport, the Olympic Stadium, with the hope of a place on the rostrum, the centre place.'[15] But success was interspersed by more misfortune: in 1957 Prince Hal was to die suddenly, a fact announced on the late *BBC News*. From this period on, Smythe spent more time travelling than at home. At the 1960 Rome event the gender politics of show-jumping still affected selection policies. Four British show jumpers were selected for the team though only three were allowed to ride in the team competition. Dawn Wofford (nee Palethorpe), the other female British rider had come third in the individual event on Hollandia in the first round, but had a disasterous second round to finish in twentieth place (Smythe came eleventh overall on Flanagan). David Barker was selected with Franco and with three refusals, the British team was disqualified by 8am. Smythe was nevertheless required to jump a round with Flanagan to entertain the public. It was a dispiriting end to Olympic competition passed over with considerable restraint in all Smythe's writing.

The question of amateurism and equestrian Olympic sport is one of considerable complexity, given what has been said about the military nature of participation in the first half of twentieth century. Officers were assumed to be amateurs, other ranks were not. Smythe apparently relied on Lucozade for her energy though, as a magazine dedicated to amateur values, *World Sports* was keen to ensure readers that her fee to endorse the fact benefited the British Equestrian Fund.[16] While a prize of a Rolex watch in 1955 might attract the accusation of professionalism from the IOC president Avery Brundage, writing, so long as it was suspended for the duration of Olympic competition, did not seem to trouble him quite so much. He may have been aware of the problem of the employment of at least one male participant at the pretigious Spanish Riding School. By the early 1960s Smythe had contributed six titles to an established genre of girls' adventure stories: both riding and writing were lucrative, prestigious and self-promoting work. With eleven books on the market and two more to be published in 1961, Smythe could afford to buy Sudgrove in the Cotswolds with 150 acres and a pig farm. It also became clear that in spite of avoiding relationships with male equestrian colleagues, she had fallen for, the then married, Sam Koechlin, father of three small children (Catherine,

---

15 Pat Smythe 'Olympic Arena' *Jumping Round the World* (London: Cassell, 1962), 1.
16 'Pat Smythe…Another Lucozade Enthusiast' *World Sports* September 1955: 10.

Sibylle and Dominick). They married in September 1963, had two daughters, Monica and Lucy, and spent their time between Switzerland and Sudgrove. This was hardly a retirement to the domestic sphere though.

Joining the World Wildlife Fund in 1961, Pat Smythe also saw that there are things that are more important than sport. She used her international fame to draw attention to the need for conservation of animals and natural resources. This green agenda has become a belated aspect of Olympic competition but there is a fundamental paradox here. As many commentators have pointed out, there is a flaw in hosting a mega event designed to draw large numbers of international tourists to a particular host country, using huge amounts of natural resource, in order to stage something as unimportant as a nationalistic sporting contest. There is also a questionable brand of conservationist thinking, now much practised by music industry stars and criticised in the popular press, in flying around the globe to try and save the planet. The only person who can have collected as many air-miles as Pat Smythe would be Condoleeza Rice and that would be much later.

In 1947 the Pony Club had a membership of seveteen thousand, by 1962 this was over thirty thousand, in 1972 forty thousand and, after a peak of forty three thousand in 1982 it current membership stands at around thirty two thousand.[17] Having spent from 1948 until 1963 in top level sport, Pat Smythe was to dedicate the rest of her life to conservation projects until her death in 1996. She continued her links with domestic events, and served from 1983 to 1986 as President of the British Show Jumping Association. We could argue that over the period in Olympic history since Rome 1960 the global market forces of commercial sport have predominated over the ethical concerns of our planet. Have 'green-Games' become part of a corporate social responsibility agenda designed to shield the Olympics from the worst criticisms that environmental protesters might level at the degree of expense, waste and consumption? Smythe was an incredibly successful entrepreneur as a writer, equestrian, expert and transnational public figure before and after her Olympic medal. It is very tempting to say that she was a global figure: conservation, travel and tourism had growing importance in women's lives in the 1950s and 1960s and, unlike Steve Wagg's girls next door in British athletics,

---

[17] The Pony Club http://www.pcuk.org/About-Us/History accessed 27 January 2011.

Smythe was a rather glamorous and cosmopolitan figure.[18] Readers could vicariously travel through her books and the theme of going 'on holiday,' 'over the border' and more exotically 'to Rome' is evident here.

If travel was part of her commercial activities, it was also part of her political life though I suspect she was a conservative in every sense of the word. This is an important issue that academics have overlooked to the detriment of their analysis of the Games and its competitiors. Jennifer Hargreaves has somewhat dismissed female participation as a rather one-sided story:

> The history of the Olympics could be rewritten as a history of power and elitism, obsessions and excesses, divisions and exploitation. Certainly, the modern Olympic movement has been imbued with male chauvinism and domination over women. The position of women in the Olympics does not depend only on their relationship and struggles with men – it varies historically and is different for women from different nations and with different backgrounds. [19]

Hargreaves further suggests that female competitors have been 'seduced' by the Games, but reading Pat Smythe caused me to re-think this rather sneering attitude that has developed since *Five Ring Circus* was published in 1984. There is more to participation in the Olympic Games than being the sporting equivalent of a bad boyfriend. How balanced then, are views that there is little good to say about participating in the Games? As one example of this, Smythe was an enduring icon and the sporting culture of Britain was changed by pony-mad girls (and, in my experience in the 1960s and 1970s boys too). Not least, the rate of youth engagement in this non school sport is interesting for all kinds of reasons. For example, the Riding for the Disabled Association (RDA incorporating Carriage Driving) was established in 1965 to provide exercise, therapy and fun. Originally the Advisory Council on Riding for the Disabled it became the Riding for the Disabled Association in 1969 when membership had grown to 80

---

[18] Stephen Wagg '"If you want the girl next door…": Olympic sport and the popular press in early Cold War Britain' in Stephen Wagg and David Andrews (eds.) *East Plays West: Sport and the Cold War* (London: Routledge, 2007), 100-121.

[19] Hargreaves, Jennifer 'Women and the Olympic Phenomenon' in Alan Tomlinson and Garry Whannel (eds.) *Five Ring Circus: Money, Power and Politics at the Olympic Games* (Sydney: Pluto Press, 1984), 52.

member groups. It is one of the most successful of the sporting charities, with 18,000 volunteers facilitating 430,000 rides and drives for 28,000 participants.[20] This and autistic response to horse therapy are whole other issues too big to develop here.

With Smythe's writing career and popularity as a public figure, along with that of Dawn Palethorpe and other contemporaries, the 1950s right through to the mid 1980s saw one after another of talented British female riders. In 1965 Marion Coakes (later Mrs Mould) had such success with Stroller that she won the Sportswman of the Year award at nineteen. At the 1968 Olympics she won silver to become the first women to win an individual medal in show jumping. Ann Moore on Psalm went on to also win a silver medal in Munich in 1972. Wales' Debbie Johnsey became, at nineteen, the youngest competitor in a show jumping contest at Montreal in 1976, narrowly missing out on a medal. Caroline Bradley was never an Olympian because she was not selected for the 1972 Olympics and had been ruled a professional by 1976. Though she could not afford to own Tigre, she was the outstanding woman rider of her generation on the borrowed horse and died of heart failure in 1983 at the age of thirty four. Four years later the rules regarding professionalism were reclassified and equestrianism became an 'open' sport. Liz Edgar, who took sponsorship with Everest Double Glazing in 1970 and therefore could not compete in the Olympics, gave up her chance to ride in the 1964 Tokyo Olympics, opting instead to lend her horse Jacapo to her brother David. Eventing was popularised by HRH Princess Anne (now the Princess Royal) in 1972. Others also became household names, Lucinda Green (nee Prior-Palmer) for instance, won Badminton (for the second of a record breaking six times) in 1976 on her horse Wideawake, which collapsed and died during the prize-giving. By the 1980s the 'golden girls' of British equestrianism were epitomised by Virginia Leng (nee Holgate) who nearly suffered an amputation as a result of her arm being broken in twenty three places but recovered to go on to win an Olympic bronze individual medal and shared a team silver with Green (plus Tiny Clapham and Ian Stark) in the 1984 Los Angeles Games. Ginny Leng would go on to win the individual World Championships with Gawler in 1986, to write several books and to manage the Irish equestrian team as part of her public profile.

---

[20] http://www.riding-for-disabled.org.uk/about-us/ accessed 27 January 2010.

For a time from the mid-fifties to the mid-eighties, when most of the British public bought their first television set, and then their first *colour* television set, equestrianism became a staple of the media 'menu' of sport. Unlike other 'popular' indoor activities that became redefined by, and widely mediated to more homes, such as snooker, wrestling and darts, the television enabled viewers to 'follow' a sport in which most ordinary people could not afford to participate. While male riders, such as Harvey Smith, felt no compunction to behave properly, equestrian women were generally aspirational figures. Might Smythe's pioneering conservation work be viewed, like that of yachtswoman Ellen MacArthur more recently, as drawing attention to issues which transcend sport? As compassionate and engaged environmental ambassadors, long before slogans about the 'greenest games ever' became commonplace, Smythe and her co-equestrians deserve more recognition.

Conclusion

With current media interest on the Royal Wedding of Prince William and Kate Middleton, and speculation as to who will succeed the current Queen, it is easy to forget that at her Coronation on 2 June 1953 Elizabeth was the world personality who most embodied the hope of the times. She was young and beautiful, so in spite of post-war austerity, to have a twenty seven year old take the throne seemed to herald enthusiasm and optimism. It is worth remembering that the Coronation was the first significant public event to be televised in lavish Technicolor. Royalty collaborated in the process of becoming uber-celebrities, from being photographed by the likes of Cecil Beaton and Dorothy Wilding the women wearing Hollywood-inspired designs by Hardy Amies and Norman Hartnell.[21] Whatever Elizabeth did was fashionable and the Queen has become a well-known horsewoman, race-patron and judge of breeding. While attending Wimbledon and other events of the Season are often delegated to lesser royals, equestrian events are seldom missed so lightly. That Princess Anne, rather than any of her three brothers, has been the lone Olympic competitor of the present Royal family, to date, perhaps draws our attention to female equetrianism as being part of the expression of Elizabeth's sporting monarchy. The issue over the injury to Toytown, owned by Princess Anne's daughter Zara Phillips, and her possible exclusion from Olympic competition in 2012 as a result, raises perhaps facetious questions over whether the rider should be given the medal or the horse. Pat Smythe's glamour was of a somewhat down-to-earth, outdoorsy kind that nevertheless seemed to translate into

---

[21] Stephen Gundle *Glamour: A History* (Oxford: Oxford University Press, 2008).

evening receptions wearing 'posh' frocks with ease. A homogenous middle or upper class 'reading' of the sport is therefore to be resisted.

Meanwhile in contemporary Britain, the recreational variants of equine sports have a very active female base, as British popular culture from Thelwell and Giles cartoons and *Only Fools On Horses*, a more recent BBC's celebrity show jumping contest as part of Sport Relief, depict. However, chubby little girls in earnest but hopeless endeavour on scruffy ponies, supervised by bossy blazeratti are not really representative of our sporting past. The British Horse Society (BHS) survey in 2005-6 indicated that forty three percent of British households have a household member with some form of interest in equestrianism (including racing); 4.3 million people have ridden in the previous 12 months (that is, seven percent of the population); one third of equestrian participants are under sixteen and almost half under twenty four and of the total numbers 75 percent of horse riders are female.[22] Equestrianism, as this paper has argued is a sport in which multiple kinds of femininity across classes combine quite happily with fashion and spectacle. It would also be interesting, but now difficult, to know what girls who read about Pat Smythe and other women equestrians made of their writing. With millionaire glamour model and author Jordan (Katie Price) attempting to become part of the British equestrian team for 2012, mostly wearing shocking pink clothes, the combination of high and low culture in our equestrian sport looks set to remain part of a very British way of doing things.

---

[22]   British Horse Society Equestrian Statistics 2005-6 https://www.bhs.org.uk/About_Us/Equestrian_Statistics accessed 27 January 2011.

3

Alf Tupper – 'The Tough of the Track' and the Class Struggle in British Athletics

Jeffrey Hill

In 2008 the *Independent on Sunday* ran a feature on a leading British middle-distance runner of the late 1940s and early 1950s.[1] He was Bill Nankeville, a milkman's son from Woking who ran in the final of the 1500 metres at the 1948 Olympics. Between 1948 and 1952 Nankeville won the Amateur Athletics Association (AAA) mile title on four occasions. Asked by the newspaper about the social relations in athletics in his day, Nankeville said: yes, there was class distinction, but you didn't seem to worry much about it. 'It was just wonderful to be able to represent your country, especially for someone like me, coming from where I did.'[2] Nankeville was aware of a class divide in athletics, but like many sportsmen of his generation, in games such as cricket and rugby as well as in athletics, he was prepared to accept the established order of things rather than kick against it.

Not so another leading runner of the day, Alf Tupper – the Tough of the Track – the comic-book hero whose popularity reached its peak in the 1950s and 1960s. Tupper was the creation of the writer Gilbert Dalton, and made his first appearance in the D.C. Thompson publication *Rover* in 1949. In 1961 he was given comic-strip form and moved to another Thomson title, *Victor*. Here he ran for some thirty years, though as the world of athletics changed his appearances became less and less frequent. As a working man and a committed amateur Tupper was something of an anachronism in an age when top athletes had become highly-paid professionals. In 1992 Alf was quietly retired.[3]

---

[1] *Independent on Sunday*, February 17 2008, 76-7.

[2] *Ibid.*, 76.

[3] On Tupper see: Jeffrey Hill, '"I'll Run Him": Alf Tupper, Social Class, and British Amateurism', *Sport in History* 26, 3 (December 2006): 502-19; 'Alf Tupper: Real Worlds and Imagined Heroes' in Stephen Wagg and Dave Russell, *Sporting Heroes of the North: Sport, Region and Culture* (Newcastle: Northumbria Press, 2010), 71-86; '"I Like to Have a Go At the Swanks": Alf Tupper and English Society 1945-90', in Philip Dine and Sean Crosson, *Sport, Representation and Evolving Identities in Europe* (Bern: Peter Lang, 2010), 79-100;

Tupper was presented to his readers – mainly working-class secondary schoolboys – as a truculent individualist with a supreme talent for running: middle-distance, of course, since the stories came onto the market at the same time as Britain's greatest achievements in this event. Tupper was the fictional equal not only of runners like Nankeville but of the yet more celebrated athletics stars of the period – people like Bannister, Chataway, Pirie and Ibbotson. Unlike any of them Alf actually won an Olympic gold, in Helsinki in 1952. His demeanour both on and off the track, however, compared with 'rebel' athletes like Gordon Pirie rather than university-educated runners such as Bannister and Chataway. [4] More than *middle* distance separated Alf from them, who were worlds apart from him socially. But it was Alf's humble origins and his championing of ordinary men and women that kept the relationship with his readers alive. Alf was 'real'; more so, for example, than his fictional comic-book contemporary Wilson, who appeared in *Wizard*. Wilson's astonishing athletics achievements had a magical quality about them. Tupper's triumphs on the other hand seemed achievable, at least for someone with outstanding abilities. Wilson's were more than extraordinary, they were unbelievable. He lived in a cave on the moors and had subsisted for over a hundred years on a diet of berries.[5] Alf's food was fish and chips and his environment was unambiguously urban. Realistic too were the places Alf inhabited: the towns of Brassingford and Greystone, down-to-earth Midlands industrial towns with important engineering factories, part of the beating heart of the British post-war economy. The stories even contained an element of 'technical' detail about workshops, work routines, and machinery, all of which, we might suppose, would strike a chord in the minds of the many readers anticipating an engineering apprenticeship on leaving school.

The stories, told in a third-person voice, were at one level simply exciting sport dramas written to a predictable formula. Alf was an outstanding runner and a particularly fierce competitor. 'I'll run him' was his trademark challenge to any rival who sought to better him. A race with Alf promised a draining physical and mental contest calling upon all the resources of the human body. Alf was able to draw upon a deep resilience – ''I just don't like being beat' he would say when

---

Brendan Gallagher, *Sporting Supermen: The True Stories of Our Childhood Comic Heroes* (London: Auram Press, 2006), 47-75.

[4] Pirie's 'rebelliousness' was expressed in his appropriately titled autobiography *Running Wild* (London: W.H. Allen, 1961).

[5] On Wilson see Gallagher, *Sporting Supermen*, 17-43.

asked to explain the secret of his success[6] – and in many races when apparently losing he summoned up a reserve of energy to pip his rivals to the tape. Each story would climax in a thrilling race, but interspersed with the athletics theme would be a *challenge* of some kind that needed to be met *before* the race itself began. It was usually work-related and always involved strenuous physical exertion on Alf's part. The effort of achieving a solution either explained Alf's failure to win (though he himself never sought excuses) or made his ultimate victory the more remarkable for its having been won in unfavourable circumstances. A frequent test came in the form of the 'rush job'. Alf, a welder by trade, would be faced with a critical order demanding two or three days of unremitting toil, forcing him frequently to work throughout the night. The job would be completed by about midday on the Saturday of an important athletics event, with Alf delivering the finished work (usually in a handcart in the early stories, thus adding to his physical burden) before catching a bus or hitching a lift to the track. Often, as he made his way to the stadium, he would see his rivals cruising past him in a luxury motor coach – a symbol of contrasting life experiences. Here is encountered the central moral theme of the stories. Nothing came easily for Alf; everything had to be struggled for through hard, disciplined work. The contrast between 'haves' and 'have nots' was a constant feature in the life of Alf Tupper.

Tupper's athletic determination carried through into his social relationships, giving the character a political quality not usually present in juvenile fiction. It is manifested in Alf's aggressive quest for fairness and justice for people like himself who have nothing, and is directed in the main against supercilious members of the upper class. Although the publishers, D.C. Thomson, were a politically conservative firm the figure of Alf has obvious links with the ethos of 'fair shares for all' that had been formulated during the war and enshrined in the Labour Party's 1945 election manifesto *Let Us Face the Future*.[7] In the Tupper stories it is brought out in relation to both work and sport. Work and workplace relations form an important part in the stories. Alf's welding skills are instilled not by book learning but – as in the tradition of the millwrights of old – by diligent observation of the 'mysteries of the trade'. He has an almost *intuitive* understanding of machinery. Allied to this is a prodigious capacity for hard work. At one aircraft factory, he is taken on after impressing the works manager with his steely determination to see the task through. 'Offer him a job', says the manager to his foreman:

---

[6] *Victor*, March 9, 1968, 22.
[7] Hill, '"I Like to Have a Go at the Swanks"', 83-5.

> That's the kind of worker we want, the kind of fellow who can work all night and all day in order to get a rush job done, then turn out in a mile race, win it, pass clean out, and, on being taken home, start at once to his work. What a lad![8]

In this respect Alf might seem a model employee. But, at the same time, he retains many of the traditional attributes of the skilled worker: pride in his status, a defiant guarding of his skills, control over the carrying out of his work, and a complete lack of reverence for authority. Men of whatever position are invariably addressed as 'mister', shown no deference, and judged by their competences not by their background or social position. Alf's 'toughness' is a mark of his sense of individualism and independence.

His chosen sport has a particular significance. While there were many British clubs with a relatively humble membership and location athletics was, as Bill Nankeville's reminiscences suggest, a sport controlled by a social elite.[9] The ruling body, the AAA, was Oxbridge-dominated and had conducted a long (and largely successful) struggle to turn the sport away from the taint of gambling and money-making with which it had been associated in the Victorian period. Athletics was therefore keenly amateur in spirit, and equally hostile to any suggestion of professionalism. All athletes, of whatever social class, were amateur, and none more so than Tupper. He rejected offers to run for money, and while he loved his sport he always gave priority to his job: '[r]unning's my sport, mister, but welding is my work, and work comes first'.[10] Upper-class amateurs – the 'toffs' as Tupper called them – were freer to devote time to athletics, and it was such people who were to be found in the leading positions of the sport. It was this presence and the influence it wielded that Alf Tupper fought. In his running there was always a streak of class conflict: 'I like to have a go at the swanks', he says, as if his mission is to prove that given the opportunity working men can achieve as much as those from a more privileged background.[11] Many of his opponents, though excellent athletes, are snooty: the Hon. Piers Mornington, for example, a Cambridge sprinter known as 'the light blue streak'; Jerrard Tarne, a hurdler who trains in the United States; and the haughty Lew Murdoch, who travels from meeting to meeting in a customised motor

---

[8] *Rover*, April 22, 1950, 69.

[9] Ross McKibbin, *Classes and Culture: England 1918-1951* (Oxford: Oxford University Press, 1998), 358.

[10] *Rover*, April 24, 1954, 70.

[11] *Rover*, April 29, 1950, 66.

caravan provided by his rich father and driven by Lew's own personal masseur. Nor is snobbery and privilege is confined to British athletes. Overseas adversaries are equally as likely to offend Alf's sense of common decency. Skimba Ru, for example, the son of a Zulu chief, and the American Lash Lanigan, represent 'toffee-nosed types' from abroad. It is remarkable how often the 'toffs' encountered in the Tupper stories are also 'swanks' and 'snobs'. Moreover, in spite of the ethos of fair play they will resort to cheating if they cannot prevail by acceptable means. All come from families able to support their athletics without the need for them to do a 'proper' job. Thus, while amateurs in name, they are in effect full-time runners who embrace the professionalism denounced by the governing body – 'shamateurs' as the press was beginning to call them in the 1950s. The fictional world of athletics is riddled with such hypocrisy and unfairness. The sport seems to exist for the benefit of the rich. Readers are left in little doubt that these representatives of the British establishment occupy their position at the expense of those who, either lacking the financial means or the exceptional ability possessed by Tupper, suffer from missed opportunities, their potential talent and contribution to sport thereby unfulfilled. Thus within the text of the stories lies a discourse of modernisation that questions the status quo.

As a symbol of a popular animus against the well-to-do, Alf was also in many ways a loner with a personal autonomy comparable to many contemporary heroes of crime fiction and the western. He is poor, and on occasions verges on poverty. In one of the last series, which appeared in 1990, Alf declares: 'times are hard and work is scarce. Gotta hunt up a few jobs or I don't eat next week.'[12] Notwithstanding his skills, Tupper operates on the margins of the labour market, oscillating between states of waged- and self-employment and rarely staying in the same job for very long. He has few possessions, and what he owns has usually been purchased second hand. He has no home; often he lives where he works, sleeping on the floor and washing at the works tap. In a series of 1952, when Alf is working on the railways in a locomotive depot, he inhabits a disused platelayers' hut at the side of the track. In none of the stories does Alf have a car, nor even aspire to owning one. His meals consist of fish and chips, his love of which constitutes his only known pleasure, aside from the pleasure of running. His 'best' clothes are an old sports jacket and trousers, but his usual attire is a pair of workman's overalls. His running kit is moth-eaten, and his vest mysteriously carries the monogram 'MHC', which (readers are eventually informed) stands for

---

[12] *Victor*, April 12, 1990, 3.

'Moontucket Hunting Club': it is a cast-off, discarded by some wealthy American, and picked up by Alf for half a crown (12.5 p.) at a jumble sale. At the start of a crucial mile race the narrator wryly observes: 'All stripped off tracksuits except Alf, who didn't have one.'[13] Tupper has no family, and rarely operates within a strongly established social network. As an athlete he is not a club man, preferring on most occasions to enter races as an 'unattached' competitor. As a workman his pride ensures that Alf stands up for his rights, but there is little of the class solidarity we might otherwise associate with the skilled worker's outlook, historically expressed in independent trades unionism and the labour movement. No matter where readers might place him on the political spectrum, Alf's own preferences are unspoken. He follows a lone path, solving problems by individual effort.

Work and running, however, represent twin aspects of a certain kind of masculinity, always a central motif of the boys' comic hero. The American critic Michael Oriard, in creating a typology of fictional sport heroism from American literature, has noted that: 'the athlete-hero is primarily a 'prowess hero" ... He is always handsome, generally medium in size, and in all ways *manly*.'[14] As a model of masculinity in the 1950s Tupper exhibits conventional qualities of strength, determination and honesty but in other respects is something of an oddity. In a period often described as 'the age of affluence' he actually *contradicts* much of the reader's contemporary social knowledge, experience and aspirations – undermining the 'common sense' about growing up. You have to read against the grain to believe in him. There is no indication of contemporary consumer behaviour in Tupper's material circumstances. Nor is *appearance* important to him. His hair is a mess, and it is frequently remarked in the early stories that he does not wear socks, because they 'make his feet sweat.'[15]

There is too a great silence in the stories. If, as Richard Hoggart has claimed, sex and sport were the two major topics of interest in the mid-twentieth century male workplace,[16] the Tupper stories give the reader plenty of the latter but of the former there is no sign. In his work on

[13] *Rover*, April 24, 1954, 56.

[14] Michael Oriard, *Dreaming of Heroes: American Sports Fiction 1869-1960* (Chicago: Nelson Hall, 1982), 30.

[15] *Rover*, June 14, 1952, 42.

[16] Richard Hoggart, *The Uses of Literacy: Aspects of Working-Class Life, with special reference to publications and entertainments* (London: Chatto and Windus, 1957), 91.

Tupper Brendan Gallagher has pointed out that 'sex and emotional turmoil were not to be acknowledged or spoken about'[17]. Gallagher attributes this to the times, when young men who had come through the war were expected to be stoical and not tangle with 'feelings'. There is a suggestion in this that masculinity – and especially perhaps working-class masculinity – involved an unknowingness about intimate relationships, a theme taken up and explored with great sensitivity in David Storey's fine novel of northern working-class gender relations *This Sporting Life*.[18] For Alf, women scarcely featured in his life. His mother had died when he was young, and thereafter the opposite sex was represented either by vile harridans like his appallingly alcoholic and devious Aunt Meg, or grumpy landladies. When we consider that readers of the stories would have been experimenting in one form another with sex – 'exploring their sexuality' to use a modern phrase – and that even that other great fictional schoolboy hero Biggles was known to have had one or two dalliances (chaste, to be sure) the omissions seem surprising.[19] But they were not confined to Tupper. In all the D.C. Thomson comics the emphasis was on male society and camaraderie: war and sport provided the dominant subjects of the story lines, and although school stories were rare there was a residual trace of fictionalised school culture. While Tupper was in many respects far removed as a character from the public-school figures in the *Gem* and the *Magnet*, especially the egregious Bunter, there is a similar monosexual – should we say even *misogynist*? – tone about both sets of stories. At a time when youth (and especially male youth) was creating for itself a cultural space through distinctive *styles* – even the 1960s skinheads fashioned out of their apparent *anti*-style a stark persona of stripped down menace – Alf Tupper remained the antithesis of contemporary models: completely resistant to fashion, music, cars, sex and all the other temptations which Mark Abrams in his classic 1959 study of youth culture observed as being the badge of the teenage consumer.[20] And when such behaviour gave rise to notions of 'embourgeoisement' and the decline of social class Tupper stood as an unregenerate representative of an older and more austere working-class lifestyle.[21]

---

[17] Gallagher, *Sporting Superman*, 50.

[18] David Story, *This Sporting Life* (London: Longmans, 1960).

[19] See 'Affaire de Coeur' in W.E. Johns, *The Camels Are Coming* (London: John Hamilton, 1932), 227-43.

[20] Mark Abrams, *The Teenage Consumer* (London: London Press Exchange, 1959).

[21] Many of the new ideas about 'embourgeoisement' and the 'end of ideology' appeared in the discipline of sociology in the 1950s and early 1960s. For a contemporary critical appraisal see J.H. Westergaard, 'The Withering Away of

Conclusion

Gilbert Dalton had created Tupper in the aftermath of the 1948 London Olympics, where British athletes had met with little success. His aim was to inspire the younger generation to take up athletics. It is, of course impossible to measure the impact the stories might have had in this respect, though D.C. Thomson was selling close on half a million copies when Victor was launched in 1961, which meant that Tupper was reaching a nationwide audience.[22] Running was presented as a sport that anyone with determination could take up. No special resources were needed apart from time, which was available before and after school and work. Clubs were there if people wished to join them, though Alf usually didn't. They were where the chief obstacle to working people's enjoyment of athletics was likely to be found – in the form of snobbery. Alf's success on the track was explained by individual talent and resolve. He had received no coaching; in fact he remained averse to anything that smacked of 'schooling'. Nobody told Alf how to run or train. As with work, his sporting knowledge and technique were intuitive. Several stories make fun of scientific training regimes, especially where diet is concerned. Fish and chips provide the necessary fuel to run fast. In the end the approach was simple. As Alf always said when asked about his method: 'I ain't got one – I just run as fast as my legs will carry me.'[23]

What about the political undertones of the stories? How might contemporary readers have responded to them? Before answering, we must first of all be clear that Tupper is not an unambiguous symbol of anything. The character of Alf is a contradictory and elusive one that defies simple pigeon-holing.[24] For one thing the Tupper stories bear some similarities with that older form of schoolboy tale to be found in the *Gem* and the *Magnet*. George Orwell, in a famous essay written at the outbreak of the Second World War, found these weeklies to be fixated with public-school mores embodied in 'good' boys who upheld ideas of fair play. Ideologically they purveyed a nostalgia for an

---

Class: A Contemporary Myth', in P. Anderson and R. Blackburn, *Towards Socialism* (London: Fontana, 1965), 77-113.

[22] By the mid 1950s *Rover*'s circulation was over 250,000, but had dropped to 52,000 by the time of the final issue in 1973. When Tupper moved to *Victor* at its lunch in 1961 the comic's circulation was just short of half a million. In 1970 it was 384,00, and 135,000 ten years later. (I am grateful to Mr Bill McLoughlin of D.C. Thomson for supplying me with this information.)

[23] *Rover*, June 8, 1957.

[24] See Hill, 'I Like to Have a Go At the Swanks ...' in Dine and Crosson, *Sport, Representation and Evolving Identities*, 91-4.

England of the pre-First World War, and were (as Orwell put it) 'sodden in the worst illusions of 1910'. He was especially struck by the prevailing tone of somnolent conservatism, and this led Orwell to conclude that the comics were a ploy by the owners of the large press organisations to focus boys' reading on the kinds of values and priorities that served the interests of the 'ruling class'.[25]

The Tupper stories certainly do not serve this purpose, though at the same time do not entirely reject other aspects of their fictional legacy. For example, without being overtly jingoistic they nonetheless indulge in an Anglo-centrism that creates conventional stereotypes of Americans (ostentatious and boastful), east Europeans (unimaginative and bureaucratic), and Arabs (lazy and deceitful). There is also a similar moral earnestness, brought out through the same kinds of fictional devices used in older weeklies, where the good/decent is counterpoised to the obviously shady. Stock characters invite the reader to form easy associations and identifications from predictable, formulaic situations. Lew Murdoch and the other snobs in the Tupper stories perform a role similar to that of Billy Bunter in the *Magnet*, bringing forth from Tupper a basic decency and rough-hewn morality that readers might share.

By contrast, however, the Tupper stories assume a critical stance towards the contemporary social order. They can, I would suggest, be read as subversive of dominant British discourses of the period, even the one to which the stories partly subscribe and which argued for a process of 'modernisation' to forge a new, post-imperial form of capitalism.[26] Tupper diverged from this in three ways: by rejecting consumerism, by providing a statement of class at a time when the relevance of this social identity was being questioned, and thirdly by creating an oppositional ethic that sat uneasily with contemporary notions of social and political consensus. This is symbolised in the races that form the narrative climax of the stories. Because of circumstances that placed him at a disadvantage Tupper needed to draw upon deep reserves of energy and determination if he was to succeed. We are asked to believe that Alf's victories were forged in adversity and motivated by a desire to triumph over injustice. Jason Cowley has reminded us that this was a key function of the comic book text: 'you didn't read the *Victor* for a realistic representation of

---

[25] George Orwell, 'Boys' Weeklies' in George Orwell, *The Penguin Essays of George Orwell* (Harmondsworth: Penguin, 1984), 106.

[26] See Kenneth O. Morgan, *The People's Peace: British History 1945-1990* (Oxford: Oxford University Press, 1992), 199-203.

contemporary society; you read it to be inspired [...]'.[27] There are two ways of looking at this. In one sense the fictional race might be equated with the race of life, and the *moral* lesson conveyed in the stories might therefore be the simple one of sticking to your task and seeing it through by playing fair. In this reading Tupper's race represents a personal challenge which, when approached with determination, allows for an individual solution. But this is a reading in which the broader and bigger issues of society – those outside the scope of individual influence and requiring collective action – are obscured. The stories might therefore seem to be saying put up with the system, make the best of it, and console yourself with specific individual honours. There is, however, an alternative reading related to the material and social conditions of the text's production. D.C. Thomson's commercial imperative of selling realist fictions to working-class readers dictated that a particular layer of *class* sensibility should be present in the stories. Part of the popularity of Alf as a character was that he seemed 'real' to readers: he captured, to an extent, their own experiences and mentalities. In this sense there is a powerful suggestion in Tupper that the system is not perfect, or even the best available; it is unequal and often unfair, and this demands that the individual be prepared at times to kick against the pricks. This is not a revolutionary ethos, but it does proclaim a spirit of stubborn independence.

---

[27] Jason Cowley, 'We Can Be Heroes', *New Statesman*, August 23, 2004.

4

The Reverend K.R.G. Hunt, Muscular Christian and Famous Footballer

Dilwyn Porter

Ordained clergymen have not made much of a mark in professional football. Of the 16,151 players listed as having appeared in English Football League matches between 1888 and 1939, only four were ministers of religion.[1] The most famous of these was the Reverend Kenneth Reginald Gunnery Hunt ('K.R.G.') who played 61 league and cup matches for Wolverhampton Wanderers, mainly between 1906 and 1909, making his last appearance for the club at the age of 35 in 1919. Hunt, an uncompromising half-back who retained amateur status throughout his playing career, was capped twice by England at full international level, appearing against against Wales and Scotland in 1911. He also made at least twelve appearances for England in amateur international matches and was a member of the teams that represented Great Britain at the London Olympic Games in 1908 and at Antwerp in 1920.[2]

Though we will begin with a brief account of his playing career, our chief concern here is with Hunt as a writer on football. His achievements as a player gave him credibility as an author and this was augmented by the moral authority derived from his status as a cleric. As far as publishers were concerned, it was an attractive combination. He first outlined his views on how the game should be played in three articles for the *Boy's Own Paper* in 1915-16 entitled 'How to Become a Football Star'. In 1922-23, he followed this up with three more, in the form of letters to the 'Captain of Footer' at the imaginary 'Severn Side School'.[3] By then, Hunt had written his first

---

[1] Michael Joyce, Football League Players' Records 1888-1939 (Nottingham: SoccerData Publications, 2002), 5, 124.

[2] The most comprehensive biographical source for Hunt is Patrick A. Quirke, The Reverend Kenneth Hunt: 'Wolves Footballing Parson', http://www.localhistory.scit.wlv.ac.uk/genealogy/KennethHunt.htm (accessed 26 November 2010).

[3] K.R.G. Hunt, 'How to Become a Football Star', Boy's Own Annual, XXXVIII, (1915-16), 20-1, 106-7, 163-4; 'Captain of Footer. Being Letters from his Uncle to

book, *Association Football*, published as part of a series comprising 'Popular Handbooks on Athletic Sports' in 1920 and reproduced in a slightly expanded second edition three years later. Another book, *First Steps to Association Football*, followed in 1924.[4] *Football: How to Succeed*, a 32-page pamphlet with a preface by the secretary of the English Schools Football Association (ESFA), was published in 1932.[5]

Hunt's career as a footballer c.1904-20

Hunt achieved a distinctive profile as a player on account of his prominence at the highest levels of both professional and amateur football. He first attracted attention when representing Oxford University, where he was a regular at wing-half between 1904 and 1908, playing in four varsity matches and finishing on the winning side in three.[6] It was while he was at Oxford that Hunt first appeared for the elite Corinthians club, making his debut against Woolwich Arsenal on Boxing Day 1905 and later joining them for a continental tour in 1906 which ended with a victory over the Dutch national side.[7] Hunt, even at 21, was regarded as an outstanding footballer and made his first appearance for the England amateur representative team in 1907 while still an undergraduate. Selection for the Olympic squad that won the tournament at the White City in October 1908 was a natural progression.

By then, however, it was what Hunt had achieved while playing alongside professionals at Wolverhampton Wanderers that seemed more significant. His father had become vicar of St Marks, Wolverhampton in 1898 and Hunt was educated at the local grammar

---

James Macalister Brown, of Severn Side School', Boy's Own Annual, XLV, (1922-23), 34-5, 129-30, 190-1.

[4] K.R.G. Hunt, Association Football (London: C.A.Pearson Ltd, 1st edn., 1920; 2nd edn., 1923); First Steps to Association Football (London: Mills and Boon, 1924).

[5] Football How to Succeed (London: Evans Brothers Ltd, 1932). Recent evidence suggests that this was first published in 1931 in association with the National Union of Teachers; see http://mirror football.co.uk/opinion/blogs/got-not-got/How-to-put-some-crunch-in-your-tackle-by-Wolves-star-the-Rev-K-R-G-Hunt-article161036.html (accessed 27 November 2010).

[6] Colin Weir, The History of Oxford University Association Football Club 1872-1998 (Harefield: Yore Publications, 1998), 28-9; see also Ian M. Sorenson, 'Oxford and Cambridge', in A.H. Fabian and Geoffrey Green (eds), Association Football (London: Caxton Publishing Co., 1960), vol. 2, 151-2.

[7] Rob Cavallini, Play Up Corinth: a History of the Corinthian Football Club (Stroud: STADIA, 2007), 85-6, 244.

school before leaving in 1902 to become a boarder at Trent College. The local professional club, then in the Second Division of the Football League, was delighted that a player of his calibre was sometimes available for selection and he was able to play a major part in the campaign that led to victory in the Football Association (FA) Cup Final in April 1908. Wolves' 3-1 win over Newcastle United, a powerful First Division side and clear pre-match favourites, owed much to Hunt, who opened the scoring with a speculative shot from 40 yards. Seasoned observers attributed Wolves' success to 'the overpowering character of their first class half-backs'.[8] By 1908, the FA Cup Final was a sporting fixture of national significance and Hunt became something of a celebrity. In his home town he was feted as a hero, with Wolves loyalists eager to point out that he had 'learnt his craft as a footballer at the Grammar School and not at Trent College'.[9] In this respect Hunt seems to have been representative of an era 'when provincial towns produced and cherished their own great men'.[10]

Figure 1. Wolverhampton Wanderers at the start of Hunt's great season, 1907-8. Hunt, back row, fourth from left, adopts the casual pose characteristic of the gentleman amateur, hands in pockets. (Wolverhampton Archives and Local Studies, DX-212/1/2)

---

[8] Sir Frederick Wall, 50 Years of Football 1884-1934 (Cleethorpes: Soccer Books Ltd, 2006), 159; first published in 1935; see also J.A.H. Catton ('Tityrus'), The Story of Association Football (Cleethorpes: Soccer Books Ltd, 2006), 89; first published in 1926.

[9] See Quirke, Kenneth Hunt, chapter 4. Hunt's caps, medals and other memorabilia are on display at the Molineux Stadium; see Tony Matthews, The Legends of Wolverhampton Wanderers (Derby: Breedon Books, 2006), p.113. For the blue plaque commissioned by the Wolverhampton Civic Society, see www.cityofwolverhampton.com/ Plaque%20Book%202009.pdf (accessed 27 November 2010).

[10] See John Arlott, Jack Hobbs: Profile of the Master (London: John Murray and Davis-Poynter Ltd, 1983), 20.

make a living from the game at which he excelled. A few months after his success with Wolves, he embarked on a conventional career for a young man of his social and educational background when he took up a teaching post at Highgate School in London. In 1909 he entered Holy Orders, following his father into the Anglican ministry, but did not seek a parish and was content to remain at Highgate until his retirement in 1945. Though he continued to turn out occasionally for Wolves, he chose to play most of his football in the years before the First World War for Leyton, then a professional club in the Southern League. Charles Buchan, who played for the East London club before moving on to Sunderland, Arsenal and England, later recalled Hunt's influence on him as a young player: 'It was Hunt who instilled in me the art of positioning. In his quiet voice he would tell me where to go when he had the ball, or where to position myself when we were on the defensive'.[11]

Figure 2. Local hero: FA Cup winner with Wolves, 1908. (Wolverhampton Archives and Local Studies, DX-1036/3/3)

Like many gentleman amateurs, Hunt was noted for his robust play. Buchan remembered that he liked to make use of 'an honest shoulder charge, delivered with all the might of his powerful frame'. The convention in English football before 1914 was for wing-halves, rather

---

[11] Charles Buchan, A Lifetime in Football (London: Pheonix House Ltd, 1955), 23. Leyton ('The Lilywhites') are not to be confused with Leyton Orient ('The Os'), a different club, then playing as Clapton Orient.

than full-backs, to mark wing-forwards, and Hunt's physicality undoubtedly made an impression. Billy Meredith, an outstanding winger for Manchester City, Manchester United and Wales, later told Buchan, 'I never ran up against a harder or fitter half-back. It was like running up against a brick wall when he charged you'. [12] It is possible, however, that Hunt came to rely rather too much on this aspect of defensive play. After leaving Leyton, he played for Oxford City, members of the Isthmian League, assisting them in their run to the FA Amateur Cup Final in 1913. It was reported that the referee for the replayed final against South Bank 'took exception to the Rev Hunt's persistent shoulder-charging', and this may have contributed to City's defeat.[13] Hunt may have had this unhappy experience in mind years later when he was 'delighted to see signs that referees are becoming more friendly to charging than they were'.[14]

Hunt seems to have liked the idea that he was free to accept invitations to turn out for any side and played for Eccleshall Comrades at Christmas 1918, presumably while staying with his father who had by then moved to the Staffordshire village. He appeared for both Wolves and Crystal Palace in 1919-20, the first full season after the war, but mainly for the Corinthians, though both he and they were past their best by this time. His retirement from senior football seems to have come after he had played for the Great Britain side that was eliminated in the first round of the 1920 Olympic tournament.[15] Thereafter, he pursued his interests in the game mainly as master-in-charge of football at Highgate, where he assembled a succession of teams that dominated English public schools soccer in the 1920s and 1930s. Highgate's old boys team, the Old Cholmelians, also enjoyed considerable success in this period.[16] Hunt's playing days were over before the offside rule was reformulated in 1925 and he was unhappy with some of the tactical changes that followed but his credibility as an authority on how to play the game remained intact. Under the direction of Stanley Rous after 1935, the FA began to take coaching seriously, establishing training courses for coaches. Rous claimed that 'this was a new idea for any sport'. Hunt had a part to play in this

---

[12] Ibid.

[13] Bob Barton, Servowarm History of the F.A. Amateur Cup (Newcastle-upon-Tyne: privately published, 1974), 69.

[14] Hunt, How to Succeed, 17.

[15] See http://www.eccleshallpast.org.uk/eccleshall (accessed 11 December 2010); Joyce, Players' Records, 124.

[16] Geoffrey Green, 'The Romantic Driving Force of the Public Schools', in Fabian and Green (eds), Association Football, vol, 2, 101-3.

initiative and was used as a technical advisor for at least one of the FA's instructional films.[17]

Hunt's advice to young footballers

The *Boy's Own Paper*, founded in 1879 and published by the Religious Tract Society, was the perfect vehicle for Hunt's first efforts as an author. Its contents – improving tales of pluck and derring-do alongside features on hobbies, scouting and sport – were designed to appeal to a core readership of public schoolboys and also to their parents, who often bought the magazine for them. The monthly issues, attractively bound as the *Boy's Own Annual*, made an acceptable Christmas or birthday present. By the early twentieth century, as the impact of the 1870 Education Act on mass literacy became increasingly apparent, its readership had expanded and 'B.O.P.' (as it was known to its readers) began to attract boys from grammar and state schools with pocket-money to spend.[18] Though Hunt always had the public schoolboy in mind when he wrote, he seems to have been aware from the start of this wider audience.

Hunt was one of a number of sporting celebrities who contributed to 'BOP' and his credentials - 'by the Rev KRG Hunt (English International, 1906-13)' - were prominently displayed at the head of each article. 'How to Become a Football Star' appeared in three parts from November 1915 to January 1916. The first, entitled 'Captaincy – Coaching Hints – Play in General', comprised advice to the captain of a school team, a literary form to which Hunt would return. It opens with Hunt's musings on the captain's role. 'An ideal boy skipper' was 'very hard to find', he conceded, but perhaps this was because the qualities required were so many and so varied:

> ... for your school skipper must be a many sided person. He must of course be a sound performer himself, but in addition to this he must know the game thoroughly, and by this I mean that he must not only know his own duties as a centre-half or full-back, or whatever he may be, but he must know what each member of his side individually, and what the whole team collectively, should do and *can* do.

---

[17] Sir Stanley Rous, Football Worlds: a Lifetime in Sport (London: Faber and Faber, 1978), 58-9; Quirke, Kenneth Hunt, ch.6.
[18] See Mary Cadogan, Frank Richards: the Chap behind the Chums (London: Viking, 1988), 40.

The 'boy skipper' was also expected to study the strengths and weaknesses of opponents and to plan accordingly.[19] Taken as a whole, this was the kind of thinking to which junior officers undergoing staff training in the armed forces were routinely exposed and it is difficult to separate Hunt's ideas on captaincy from their wartime context, or indeed from his role as Lieutenant of Highgate's Officer Cadet Corps attached to the Third Volunteer Battalion of the Middlesex Regiment.[20] Though Hunt advised captains of football not to push their teams too hard in training, he valued exercises that would encourage boys to develop their ball skills. 'Perhaps the most valuable practice that a boy can get', he advised, 'is to take a tennis-ball into an old fives court', before noting that the Eton fives court, which incorporated a buttress, was 'almost useless' for this purpose. At this point, Hunt risked losing an important part of his audience - boys with no experience of public school life who would never have seen a fives court - but he rose to the challenge.

> At many schools will be found an asphalt playground bounded on at least one side by a brick wall. Like the fives court, this may be a valuable asset in teaching the game to a school side. No better idea of the perfection of forward play as practised by the Corinthians can be given than when a boy tries to dribble along such a playground, passing the ball to the wall, receiving it as it rebounds, and immediately passing it back again.[21]

Even a working-class boy could thus aspire to play like the cream of gentlemen amateurs.

Hunt's first series of articles introduced other themes that were to feature in the books he wrote later. His Christian faith was of the muscular variety that underpinned the ideology of sport emanating from the public school system. As Richard Holt has argued, this was connected with a redefinition of masculinity as English public schools and the grammar schools that imitated them sought ways of shepherding adolescent boys safely through puberty. Games played an important part in distracting boys from 'impurity' in its various forms

---

[19] Hunt, 'How to Become a Football Star', 20-1; first published in the Boy's Own Paper, November 1915.
[20] Quirke, Kenneth Hunt, ch.6.
[21] Hunt, 'How to Become a Football Star', 20-1.

while simultaneously building 'character'.[22] As far as sport was concerned, the 'give and take' attitude that it was said to foster was a significant learning outcome, a key stage in the process of converting a boy into a man, or more specifically, an Englishman. The objections raised at the first meeting of the FA in 1863 to those who opposed 'hacking' (i.e. shin-kicking) come to mind here. 'If you do away with it', a representative of the Blackheath club had argued, 'you will do away with all the pluck and courage of the game, and I will be bound to bring over a lot of Frenchmen who would beat you with a week's practice'.[23] In his article on the art of defence, published in December 1915, Hunt's advocacy of the 'honest shoulder-charge', seems rooted in the same set of beliefs. It was 'not only legitimate, but has done very much to make the game the manly sport that it is'. If it was eliminated, he added mysteriously, 'something far less harmless will creep in'.[24]

'Captain of Footer', Hunt's second series for *Boy's Own Paper*, published between November 1922 and January 1923, covers similar territory. Just as it is possible to read some of the preoccupations of a nation at war into Hunt's first series, these letters from an 'affectionate uncle' are indicative of anxieties arising from the political and social tensions that characterised Britain in the 1920s, the decade of the General Strike. The first is mainly devoted to Hunt's thoughts on relations between the middle-class amateur and the working-class professional. 'James Macalister Brown', the boy skipper at Severn Side, to whom the letters are addressed, had been invited to sign as an amateur for 'the Rovers', his local professional club. Hunt's comments focus on the soul-searching that would inevitably ensue. 'Now Jim', he wrote, '... I fancy this invitation is flattering to your soul, but that while inclination prompts you to accept, you fear you may lose caste with some of your fellows if you play with the pros'. He urged him, however, to put his doubts aside.

> You and I know, of course, that there are things in pro footer that we don't like, but if fellows who have had the good fortune to be born under a lucky star, and to go to a public school like Severn Side, and afterwards to Oxford ... are going to give

---

[22] See Richard Holt, *Sport and the British: a Modern History* (Oxford: Oxford University Press, 1989), 86-98; see also David Winner, *Those Feet: a Sensual History of English Football* (London: Bloomsbury Publishing Ltd, 2005), 9-29.
[23] Cited in Geoffrey Green, ''The Dawn of Football', in Fabian and Green (eds), *Association Football*, vol.1, 52.
[24] Hunt, 'On the Defence', 107; first published in Boy's Own Paper, December 1915.

themselves airs and think themselves above playing with the pros, then who can wonder if pro-football *is* dirty.

For Hunt, it was clear that young James had much to offer the professional game, notably moral leadership and brains. 'You will teach these fellows something of the Public School spirit', he argued, 'just as they will certainly teach you something of football'. 'Candidly', Hunt continued, 'I don't think they will teach you much as to tactics, but I shall be surprised if they do not speed you up a great deal'.[25] In all this, it is possible to detect an effort to reach across the social and political chasm then separating the middle-class from the working-class. While we know little of Hunt's politics, we do know that he was quick to distance himself from middle-class footballers who looked down on their working-class counterparts. He had, after all, preferred to mix with the professionals at Wolves and Leyton in the period of English soccer's 'great split' between 1907 and 1914 rather than play for a socially-exclusive amateur club such as the Corinthians.[26] Later, during the 1930s, while serving on an Amateur Football Alliance committee, he made a point of disassociating himself from a colleague who talked down to the secretary of a working-men's club.[27]

This is not to say that Hunt ever detached himself from his class and the public school system in which he felt comfortable. The books and pamphlets that he wrote in the 1920s and early 1930s were addressed to schoolboy footballers – principally those at public schools – and to those who continued to play as young men. Though he was no snob, there was an underlying assumption that the game as played by public schoolboys, varsity men and gentlemen amateurs before the Great War, represented football at its best. In *Association Football*, for example, he acknowledged that it was now unfashionable for wing-haves to mark wing-forwards, as he had once marked Meredith, but noted that it was still favoured in 'the best type of amateur football'.[28] As far as Hunt was concerned, there was no doubt as to where this was to be found.

---

[25] Hunt 'Captain of Footer', 34-5; first published in Boy's Own Paper, November 1922.

[26] For the social basis of the schism see Dilwyn Porter, 'Revenge of the Crouch End Vampires: the AFA, the FA and English Football's "Great Split", 1907-14', Sport in History, 26, no. 3 (2006), 406-28.

[27] Walter Greenland, The History of the Amateur Football Alliance (Harwich: Amateur Football Alliance/Standard Publishing Co., 1965), 74.

[28] Hunt, Association Football (1923), 31-2; see also First Steps, 34.

Much of Hunt's advice to defenders related to the importance of 'combination' play, with team-mates adjusting their positions so as to frustrate oncoming forwards, but he tended to look to the gentlemen amateurs of the pre-war era, rather than the professionals of the post-war era for inspiration. Defensive combination, he argued, had been developed to perfection by A.M. and P.M. Walters, while playing at full-back for the Corinthians in the 1880s. One would always play a little in front of the other, making the initial challenge that would cause an opponent to lose control of the ball, thus allowing his partner to step in and clear. 'I am afraid', Hunt added ruefully, 'that the Walters' play would be too vigorous to suit modern players or referees, which is a pity, for their hefty charging did a great deal for the game'.[29] With full-backs assigned to the last line in defence, the centre-half was free to join the attack; he was 'the only player who can roam practically all over the field, and yet be doing his job properly'. As late as 1932, when 'stoppers' like Herbie Roberts of Arsenal, had became commonplace in English football, Hunt was still arguing that the centre-half should have a creative role – 'because your centre-half should be the flywheel of the whole team and around him the whole team should revolve'.[30]

As far as attacking play was concerned, Hunt favoured the long ball, making strategic use of diagonal passes to demoralise the opposing defence. 'Nothing discourages a back ... so much', he noted, 'as to chase out some forty yards or so after a wing forward, only to find the latter slinging the ball across just before he can be tackled'.[31] On a more pragmatic level, he argued that attacks which relied on combinations of short passes were more likely to break down, especially in English conditions. Moreover, the short-passing style required players with above average technique if it was to be played successfully, and these were in short supply. 'On the whole', he wrote

---

[29] Hunt, Association Football (1923), 20. Significantly, the Walters brothers were noted – and sometimes criticised - for their vigorous shoulder-charging. See Neil Carter, 'Football's First Northern Hero? The Rise and Fall of William Sudell', in Stephen Wagg and Dave Russell (eds), Sporting Heroes of the North (Newcastle-upon-Tyne: Northumbria Press, 2010), 135.

[30] Hunt, How to Succeed, 26. For details of the new offside rule and the tactical innovation that followed see Jonathan Wilson, Inverting the Pyramid: the History of Football Tactics (London: Orion, 2009), 42-51; Matthew Taylor, The Association Game: a History of British Football (Harlow: Pearson Education Ltd, 2008), 221-2; Dave Russell, Football and the English: a Social History of Association Football in England, 1863-1995 (Preston: Carnegie Publishing, 1997), 84-5.

[31] Hunt, First Steps, 67-8.

of the long-ball game, 'it is an easier game to play, for there is not the same need of accuracy, and against some types of defence it pays all along the line'.[32] One senses that Hunt's ideas on tactics would have been sympathetically received by Stan Cullis, manager of the successful Wolves teams of the 1950s, who also preferred a direct approach. 'Tip-tap, tip-tap', Cullis would murmur in frustration, when his players knocked the ball around in midfield.[33]

Hunt's views on passing would strike observers of the modern game as eccentric: he thought that there was far too much of it and regretted that dribbling with the ball, which allowed a player to express his individuality, was becoming a lost art. Though he would have adopted a different formation to that employed by the Corinthians, he would certainly have approved of their method of attack 'with long sweeping passes usually into space, for a colleague to run onto'.[34] There was, however, a moral viewpoint lurking behind these observations. In *Association Football*, he had insisted that the forward who spurned an opportunity to shoot in favour of a pass was guilty of 'moral cowardice'.[35] He later developed this idea in *First Steps to Association Football*. 'Passing', he advised his readers, 'is only a means to an end, and that end should never be – as it so often is – the shifting of your own responsibility onto someone else's shoulders'.[36] There is a slight but significant pre-echo here of some contributions to the debate regarding the respective merits of 'individualist' as opposed to 'collectivist' football that surfaced when Moscow Dynamo came to Britain in 1945 and again when England played Hungary in 1953.[37]

The most explicit statement of Hunt's muscular Christianity is to be found at the start of *Football: How to Succeed*, which was targeted at 'youngsters just starting the game'. Winning, was important – ('You will want to win - we all do') - but not at all costs.

---

[32] Hunt, Association Football (1923), 59-60.

[33] See Ronald Kowalski and Dilwyn Porter, 'England's world turned upside down? Magical Magyars and British football', Sport in History, 23, no.2 (2003-4), 44.

[34] See Tony Mason, Association Football and English Society 1863-1915 (Brighton: Harvester Press, 1981), 216.

[35] Hunt, Association Football (1923), 54.

[36] Hunt, First Steps, 78-9.

[37] See Ronald Kowalski and Dilwyn Porter, 'Political Football: Moscow Dynamo in Britain, 1945', International Journal of the History of Sport, 12, no.2 (1997), 110.

How often, especially in Cup-ties, we see a side that is leading by one goal kicking the ball into touch, and resorting to other tactics of this sort calculated to waste time. If you are sportsmen you will find small satisfaction in a victory won by such means.

Figure 3. When tackling, Hunt favoured a technique he had learned from M. Morgan-Owen of the Corinthians in the early years of the twentieth century. This involved blocking the ball with both feet while leaning into an opponent. Reverend K.R.G. Hunt, Football: How to Succeed (London: Evans Brothers Ltd, 1932), 16-17.

Playing the game in the right spirit was what really counted and this meant avoiding the various temptations that would inevitably arise over the course of 90 minutes. A defender, for example, who might be tempted to block a goal-bound shot with his hands, was urged not to yield. Though his action might save the match,'he [would lose] his reputation as a sportsman'. Hunt was bringing to a wider audience the kind of advice that he might have given a public schoolboy who had let himself down by misabehaving in a house match. 'It is a great thing to play in a successful side', he continued, 'but it is a far greater thing to play in a side that has a reputation for sportsmanship and fair play'.[38]

Football, it seemed, could supply the kind of testing environment in which character was formed. 'Observe the spirit of the game as well as the letter of the law, and learn to be undiscouraged by defeat', wrote Hunt, 'just as I hope you will be chivalrous in victory'.[39] Hunt's reputation as a footballer – his England caps and FA Cup winner's medal – lent authority to this neat restatement of the Corinthian ideals with which every public schoolboy would have been familiar. But he was also writing as 'Rev. K.R.G. Hunt' and this added a spiritual dimension to his thoughts on how football should be played. This was underlined by T.P. Thomas of the ESFA in his foreward to *How to Succeed*. 'So when you leave school and become a Junior or even a Senior player', he urged, 'remember that the "straight game", as the Rev K.R.G. Hunt says, is the only game to play'. Here was soccer's equivalent of learning how to play cricket with a straight bat, a moral compass that would serve a chap well as he made his way in life.

Conclusions

This essay has supplied a preliminary assessment of Hunt's contribution to English football. Though his articles and books provide clues, further research is required to reach an understanding of what Hunt was like as a coach. Yet it is possible to draw some provisional conclusions regarding the historical significance of his published work. Perhaps the most obvious is that Hunt's observations confirm the impression that gentleman amateurs – especially defenders – were often very physical in their approach to football. The application of muscle, however, did not preclude thinking strategically about the game. Even though Hunt favoured the the long ball, he made it clear that there was little to be gained from the hopeful punt upfield. 'Always remember', he warned, 'that there must be just as much method in the long passing as in the short passing game'.[40] Hunt's advice to defenders – that they should maximise their strength by pivoting simultaneously to meet the point of a developing attack – owed something to science. There was more to defending than the manly shoulder charge and an uncompromising method of tackling that Hunt had learned from Morgan-Owen of the Corinthians 'in the very early years of [the] century '.[41] Football required both brawn and

---

[38] Hunt, How to Succeed, 3.
[39] Ibid.
[40] Hunt, First Steps, 68.
[41] Hunt, How to Succeed, 16-17.

brains and it was the the role of the well-educated, middle-class player to provide the latter. Writing in 1924, at the end of a season in which England had finished last in the Home International Championship , he reminded his readers – 'especially the Public School element' – that 'the brainy player is needed more than ever if the game is to be restored to its old place'.[42]

Restoring soccer to 'its old place' had become especially important for Hunt and other advocates of the association game in the 1920s and 1930s when there was a discernible 'rush to rugby' in the public and grammar schools. Ross McKibbin has argued that this was 'an overt statement of deliberate class-differentiation', part of 'the middle class reaction to an apparently politicized and aggressive working class'. [43] Whatever the causes of this trend, it was clear that many headmasters now believed that rugby union was 'unequalled by any other game as a school of true manhood and leadership'.[44] As far as Hunt was concerned, this was regrettable for two reasons. At the peak of his powers, he had been one 'of a small and dwindling number of exceptional amateurs' playing at the highest level.[45] If this pool of middle-class talent dried up, he feared for the future of English football 'for the old Public Schoolboy has invariably provided that spice of originality which may yet lift the game from that mediocre level to which it appears to have sunk'.[46] This was the important contribution which young James Macalister Brown could make by playing with the 'pros' at the Rovers.

Underpinning this concern, however, was an issue of wider importance. 'If Rugby', Hunt argued, 'is to become the game of the Public Schools and Soccer is to be left entirely to the working classes, we are deliberately severing one of the chains which still serve to hold the classes and the masses together'.[47] As Tony Collins has indicated, this idea was to be powerfully restated by defenders of public school soccer at the Headmasters' Conference in 1925.[48] It is important to read his advice to young footballers in this context. Maintaining social

---

[42] Hunt, First Steps, 11-13.

[43] Ross McKibbin, Classes and Cultures: England 1918-1951 (Oxford: Oxford University Press, 1998), 350-1.

[44] See Taylor, Association Game, 122-3; also Rous, Football Worlds, 45-8.

[45] Russell, Football and the English, 45.

[46] Hunt, First Steps, 11-13.

[47] Ibid.

[48] See Tony Collins, A Social History of English Rugby Union (London: Routledge, 2009), 65-8.

cohesion seems to have been as important for Hunt as ensuring that boys acquired technical skills and tactical awareness. By restating the values of nineteenth-century muscular Christianity and realigning them with twentieth-century soccer, Hunt sought to ensure that the people's game would survive in the top people's schools.

5

Patrick O'Connell, an Irishman Abroad

Robin Peake

Fabio Capello, Louis Van Gaal, Johan Cruyff, Leo Beenhakker and Terry Venables. Thus reads an illustrious list of names; some of the

Figure 1. Patrick O'Connell in Hull City gear (*Sports Express* (Hull), January 10, 1914)

men who have won the Spanish *La Liga* Championship as a coach. Irishman Patrick O'Connell, who led Betis Balompie to the title in 1935, has earned his place amongst this select group. His feat has not been repeated at the Andalucian club, making his triumph all the more notable, and his place in the club's folklore all the more secure. O'Connell had played as a half-back in the English and Scottish first divisions in the years enveloping the First World War, before coaching in Spain's premier league competition. He captained Manchester United and was given the same honour to lead his country in their historic victory over England in February 1914, as Ireland won their first ever Home International Championship. As a coach he won twelve major and minor trophies in Spain, including winning the regional *Lliga Mediterrania* with FC Barcelona when football was disrupted by the Civil War.

Though a handful of white-haired men can recant his achievements in some of Andalucia's bars, sporting stardom has begot O'Connell no legacy either in his homeland or in England, where he spent most of his playing career.[1] There is no statue or plaque commemorating his achievements, and few football fans, even those who keenly follow the clubs he played for, have ever heard of him. Today he is little more than a footnote in the game's history, a statistical anomaly featuring in the appendix pages of the histories of the clubs he played for, and even then, sometimes misnamed.[2] Yet were he to have played in today's intensely media saturated milieu, he would be a regular feature on the front pages as well as the back. As a young man, O'Connell married the woman he got pregnant, and would later leave his wife and four children. When he bigamously married in Spain, neither of his wives apparently ever knew of his deceit.[3] However, whilst he deserves no accolades as a father or husband, his successful coaching career abroad deserves attention. An Irish coach with a British pedigree, O'Connell's success in Spain was measured both by the trophies that he won, and the extent to which he adapted and stayed in the country in comparison with both his peers and the stay-at-home British coaches of today.

Patrick Joseph O'Connell was born in Dublin on 8 March 1887 to Patrick and Elizabeth, one of nine children and the eldest son.[4] He grew up in the Drumcondra area in the north of the city, and by 1899 the family was living in a four roomed house in Jones Terrace, a street whose predominantly Roman Catholic populace reflected the religious identity of the city.[5] Patrick O'Connell senior was a clerk at Boland's Corn Mill; junior was said to have worked there as well, though the 1901 census lists him as a glassfitter, at age fourteen.[6] His social class was fairly typical for a would-be footballer. On Jones Terrace, there was a family of bricklayers, a plumber, a few carpenters and an

---

[1] See Richard Holt, 'The legend of Jackie Milburn and the life of Godfrey Brown', in *Writing lives in sport: Biographies, life-histories and methods*, ed. John Bale, Mette Christensen, and Gertrud Pfister (Aarhus: Aarhus University Press, 2004).

[2] Padraig Coyle, *Paradise lost and found: The story of Belfast Celtic*, (Edinburgh: Mainstream, 1999), 25.

[3] Sue O'Connell, in discussion with the author, St. Helen's, 27 Nov. 2009.

[4] 1901 Irish Census.

[5] Thom's Dublin Street Directory, 1899; 1901 Irish Census.

[6] 1901 Irish Census.

unemployed sanitary officer; the street consisting mainly of members of the skilled and semi-skilled classes three and four.[7] O'Connell's early years ran in tandem with the development of association football in Ireland. The Irish Football Association was formed in Belfast in 1880, some seventeen years after their English counterparts. By the time O'Connell was born, football was being played in an organised setting in Dublin and a priority of the IFA was to encourage the growth of the game outside of Belfast and Ulster.[8] In 1892 the Leinster FA was established in Dublin to promote the game in the province. The LFA grew from a membership of 11 clubs in 1899, to 65 just two years later.[9] This extraordinary growth can in part be attributed to the dissolution of the Army FA, but was also probably a response to the creation of a number of pitches for the association code across Dublin, and the location of the Ireland v England match of 1900 at Lansdowne Road.[10] This decision was part of the IFA's 'missionary work' which aimed to encourage the growth of the sport in the south, despite international matches in Dublin taking a financial loss.[11] Thus by the time O'Connell entered his teenage years, football was becoming an increasingly attractive leisure pursuit in Dublin. Furthermore, he lived just fifteen minutes' walk from the pitches at Fairview Park where he could play the sport, and though as a youngster he lived in three different houses, O'Connell and his family were never more than 100 metres from the Jones Road playing fields, now Croke Park and home to the Gaelic Athletic Association. Bohemians had played matches there, as did Tritonville AFC in the early 1900s.[12] By the time the GAA had purchased the playing fields in 1908, ninety soccer clubs were

---

[7] 1901 Irish Census; See W.A. Armstrong, 'The use of information about occupation: I. As a basis for social stratification', in *Nineteenth Century Society*, ed. E.A. Wrigley (Cambridge: Cambridge University Press, 1972), 191-214.

[8] Tony Reid, *Bohemians A.F.C. official club history 1890-1976* (Dublin: Tara, 1976), 9.

[9] Irish Football Association minutes of Committee 1898-1902, minutes for 1899 and 1901 AGMs.

[10] Irish Football Association minutes of Committee 1898-1902, minutes for 1899, 1900 and 1901 AGMs; Neal Garnham, *Association football and society in pre partition Ireland* (Belfast: Ulster Historical Foundation, 2004), 12.

[11] Irish Football Association minutes of Committee 1898-1902, minutes for 1900 AGM; Irish Football Association minutes of Committee 1903-9, entry for 9 May 1908.

[12] Reid, *Bohemians A.F.C.*, 11-13; Irish Football Association minutes of Committee 1903-9, entry for 5 June 1906.

registered with the Leinster FA.[13] Patrick O'Connell played for two of them.

His first known team was Frankfort, a small club who played in the minor cup competitions and who were probably located in Phoenix Park.[14] He then played for Strandville, a club who were formed around the turn of the century and who played just a twenty minute walk from his home. With them, O'Connell won the Leinster Junior Cup in May 1908.[15] There was double cause for celebration when he married Ellen Treston that same month though it was probably forced upon him; she was three months pregnant with his child.[16] By September, he had moved north to senior side Belfast Celtic, with Strandville acting as a 'feeder' club for them at that time. At Belfast Celtic he was a regular starter as a centre-forward but by the end of the 1908-9 season, he was spotted by the manager of Sheffield Wednesday and was signed and converted to a half back, as English and Scottish teams stepped up their pursuit of Irish players.[17] Though he travelled with the club as part of their 14 man playing staff on their first continental tour, to Scandinavia in 1911, O'Connell was largely a fringe player who made only fleeting appearances when others were injured.[18] After only twenty-one appearances in just over three seasons at Wednesday, he dropped down a league to Second Division Hull City in May 1912 for a transfer fee of £350.[19] At Hull he was a first team regular, known as a 'sound and judicious' player who was 'as amusing on the field as he is off' by the local press who knew him affectionately as 'Patsy'.[20] When Davy Gordon was unable to lead the side, it was O'Connell who was appointed temporary captain and

---

[13] Irish Football Association minutes of Committee 1903-9, minutes for 1908 AGM.

[14] *Sport*, September 5, 1908.

[15] Ibid. May 9, 1908.

[16] Sue O'Connell, in discussion with the author, St. Helen's, November 27, 2009.

[17] Football League registration book for Division 2, 1908-9; *Irish News*, March 29, 1909; See Robin Peake, 'Irish sporting migration c.1890-1925' (paper presented at the annual meeting of the Irish History Students' Association, Trinity College Dublin, 20 Feb. 2010).

[18] Richard Sparling, *The romance of the Wednesday, 1867-1926* (1926; Wiltshire: Desert Island Books, 1997), 201.

[19] Football League transfer list, 1912-13; *The Week and Sports Special*, 11 May 1912.

[20] *Sports Express*, January 31, 1914; September 20, 1913.

showed 'splendid leadership'.[21]   His consistent and capable play
during the 1913-14 season, attracted the attention of the Irish selectors
as it had done two years previous.   On Valentine's Day 1914 he
captained Ireland to a memorable 3-0 triumph at Middlesbrough, only
their second victory over England in more than thirty attempts, their
first on the opposition's patch. A month later, O'Connell picked up his
fifth cap as part of the team which drew against Scotland where he
finished the game despite picking up a serious elbow injury.[22] The
game finished a goal apiece, meaning that Ireland won the Home
International Championships for the first time in over three decades of
trying.

Perhaps it was his international fame, coupled with his league form
that led to him signing for Manchester United in May 1914.
Undoubtedly there were other reasons.   According to the *Sports
Express*, O'Connell had requested a transfer having desired to leave
Hull for some time, with Liverpool, Chelsea and Newcastle United all
interested.[23] However closer examination reveals more, exemplifying
what Bale terms 'layers of truth', a model outlined by Denzin, which
argues that something new always becomes visible in biographical
work.[24] It transpired that O'Connell had felt in a sufficiently strong
position to ask the club for a new three year contract and permission to
live twenty miles away in Hornsea owing to Ellen's now 'delicate state
of health', a version initially stifled by club sources.[25] Whilst they were
losing one of their best players, the club would also benefit from a
transfer. Hull City were struggling to remain solvent as a result of
their high wage bill. They were paying half what Manchester United
were on wages despite attendances being around a fifth and were
predicted to be upwards of £2,000 in debt at the beginning of the 1914-
15 season owing to summer wages and an absence of gate money.[26]
Furthermore, on Easter Monday 1914 Hull's Anlaby Road ground was
seriously damaged by a fire. To carry out the repairs the club took a

---

[21] Ibid. October 25, 1913.

[22] *Irish News*, March 16, 1914; *Eastern Morning News*, March 18, 1914.

[23] *Sports Express*, April 4, 1914.

[24] John Bale, 'The mysterious Professor Jokl' in *Writing lives in sport*, ed. Bale,
Christensen, and Pfister, 31-4.

[25] *Sports Express*, May 2, 1914.

[26] Ibid. May 31, 1913; March 21, 1914; April 11, 1914; December 21, 1915; Steven
Tischler, *Footballers and businessmen: The origins of professional soccer in England*
(New York: Holes and Meier, 1981), 84.

loan of £1,000 from a local businessman.[27] Within two weeks of the fire, O'Connell was bought by Manchester United for the same amount, and became their second most expensive signing, £400 paid up front and two cheques of £300 to follow.[28]

Figure 2. Moving from Hull to Manchester United (*Sports Express* (Hull), May 16, 1914)

[27] Mike Peterson, *Century of City: The centenary of Hull City AFC, 1904-2004* (Harefield: Yore, 2005), 19.
[28] Manchester United minutes of Board of Directors 1912-22, entry for April 22, 1915.

It is said that Pat O'Connell brings out his best form when a wee bit angry!

Figure 3. O'Connell's anger was noted by at least one cartoonist (*Manchester Football Chronicle*, Sept. 18, 1915)

It was at Old Trafford that he reached the pinnacle of his playing career, playing regularly for a leading club. The press recognised him as the club's best half-back, 'brainy and skilful', 'industrious and clever', though accusations of poor ball distribution continued to be levelled against him, as had been noted during his days with Belfast Celtic.[29] In early 1915 he was described by *Athletic News* as 'a much more finished and restrained player than he was years ago with Sheffield Wednesday. Then he was merely a wild Irishman, but experience has made him a calculating man.'[30] Yet the hot temperament alluded to here must still have followed him, his anger being characterised by one cartoonist and it was noted that during one match he caused a referee to limp when he 'accidentally' kicked him on the ankle.[31] O'Connell was the sixth Irishman to play for Manchester United, the first from outside Ulster, and in January 1915 he became the first Irishman to captain the club.[32]

By this time the war which was supposed to be over by Christmas was intensifying and many of O'Connell's peers and teammates had signed up. A Footballers' Battalion had even been created, and forty of the staff at Clapton Orient registered from the off.[33] Eight of Manchester United's 1914-15 team would sign up; Sandy Turnbull would later be

---

[29] *Athletic News,* January 4, 1915; January 18, 1915; January 25, 1915; March 29, 1915.

[30] Ibid. January 4, 1915.

[31] *Manchester Football Chronicle,* September 18, 1915; February 13, 1915.

[32] Manchester United minutes of Board of Directors 1912-22, entry for January 14, 1915.

[33] Steve Jenkins, 'Clapton Orient's brothers in arms', *Soccer History,* 3 (2002), 10.

killed at Arras.[34] In reality though, the experiences of Burnley centre half Tommy Boyle, who admitted to trying to avoid military service, were probably more representative.[35] The Footballers' Battalion only attracted around 7% of the League's professionals.[36] It was much more common to find footballers engaged in alternative employment, heeding the call of future Football League chairman Charles Sutcliffe, who said that those illegible or unable for active service were 'to seek and engage in employment of military service and significance'.[37] Patrick O'Connell, along with teammates Enoch West, George Anderson, and a handful of others from Manchester United, found war supplies work at the Ford Motor Works in Trafford Park where O'Connell became a foreman.[38]

Clubs found the first wartime season a difficult period to operate in financially with contractual obligations to fulfill despite a considerable fall in gate receipts. Manchester United had to delay the installments of O'Connell's transfer fee for a full twelve months.[39] On 29 March 1915, the expected announcement was made that owing to the ongoing war effort, there would be no summer wages for three months, and that upon the resumption of payments, the basic maximum wage would drop from £4 to £3 per week.[40] Shortly after this news which limited their earnings, the footballers of Manchester United and Liverpool were brought into serious disrepute, as it was alleged and later proven that some of them had been involved in squaring a match between the two teams, and placing money on the correct score. The match in question was at Old Trafford on 2 April 1915, Manchester United winning by two goals to nil. It was a result that many punters had betted upon, and one which particularly helped United in their battle against relegation. Patrick O'Connell, captain of the home side, curiously missed a penalty in the second half when the score was 1-0.[41]

[34] *Athletic News,* December 27, 1915; *Topical Times,* March 8, 1930.
[35] *Topical Times,* April 26, 1930.
[36] Derek Birley, *Playing the game: Sport and British society, 1910-1945* (Manchester: Manchester University Press 1995), 73.
[37] *Athletic News*, April 26, 1915.
[38] *Manchester Football Chronicle,* April 17, 1915; Simon Inglis, *Soccer in the dock* (London: Willow Books, 1985), 47.
[39] Manchester United minutes of Board of Directors 1912-22, entries for May 22, 1914; January 14, 1915, November 9. 1915.
[40] Football League minutes of Management Committee 1913-19, entry for March 29, 1915.
[41] *Liverpool Daily Post,* April 2, 1915; *Manchester Daily Dispatch,* April 3, 1915.

His shot was so extravagantly wide, that it is reported the referee consulted his linesman, convinced that something was amiss.[42] The fix insufficiently subtle, the sporting press and the authorities demanded to know who was involved. The commission set up to investigate the match, involving both the FA and the Football League, issued their findings at Christmas. It found five of those who played, including just one of the United team, Enoch West, guilty of pre-arranging the result for the purpose of betting and winning money thereby and permanently suspended them from taking any part in football.[43] As *Athletic News* commented, 'It is beyond the power of human credibility to assume that only one of the [United] players was "in the know"'.[44] O'Connell had been interviewed by the Commission, but was not deemed guilty. As captain, he was probably never thought of as being entirely innocent either.

Under relaxed registration rules, O'Connell spent the last wartime years playing as a guest for Rochdale Town and Clapton Orient when it became clear that he was surplus to requirements at Manchester United.[45] In August 1919 Scottish side Dumbarton signed him for £200.[46] O'Connell was by now, growing estranged from his wife, Ellen, and their four children. It seems that they followed him to Scotland for a while, only to return to Manchester.[47] After a fairly uneventful year in Dumbarton, he returned to England. Responding to an advert offering 'good wages to experienced men', he signed for Ashington in May 1920 and moved to the North Eastern League side without his family.[48] A year later, he was appointed as player-manager of the club, now elected to the newly formed Third Division

---

[42] Graham Sharpe, *Free the Manchester United one* (London: Robson Books, 2003), 51, 90.

[43] Minutes of FA council 1914-20, minutes of the proceedings from July 13 1915 to December 31, 1915.

[44] *Athletic News*, December 27, 1915.

[45] *Sporting Chronicle*, December 30, 1916; Manchester United minutes of Board of Directors 1912-22, entry for August 24, 1917.

[46] Manchester United minutes of Board of Directors 1912-22, entry for August 19, 1919.

[47] Daniel Treston, interviewed by Raidió Teilifís Éireann (undated) re-broadcast on 'Bowman on Sunday', July 18, 2010; Sue O'Connell, in discussion with the author, St. Helen's, November 27, 2009.

[48] *Athletic News*, April 19, 1920; April 26, 1920; May 3, 1920; Football League transfer list, 1922-3.

North.[49] He helped the club to tenth place in the league, but with a four figure loss sustained, the better and higher paid players at the club had become a luxury.[50] At the end of the 1921-2 season he was offered for sale.[51] However, with no bids forthcoming, he was released on a free transfer by the club in June and embarked upon a coaching career in Spain which would span three decades and four different systems of governance.

Academics have drawn various conclusions as to the occupations that many early professional footballers took up upon retiring from playing, though solid evidence regarding the spectrum of employment of former sportsmen has been hard to locate, even for contemporary sociological studies.[52] The consensus, drawn from a range of sources and much of it impressionistic, is that footballers at the lower end returned to their previous trades, while many of the footballers who made it to the top of their profession ventured into a new trade as publicans and owners of small businesses, or advanced in their current trade, working with football clubs as managers, trainers or scouts.[53] This is neatly captured by the legendary Manchester United half-back line of Duckworth, Roberts and Bell. Charlie Roberts, who had been O'Connell's predecessor at United, ran a successful tobacconist's business, even creating a cigarette brand called 'Ducrobel' named after the famous trio.[54] Of the other two, Bell became a football trainer and Duckworth a publican.[55]

An attempt to offer something more like quantitative data can be made by collecting some information from a popular source. From January to May 1930, *Topical Times* ran a series entitled 'Cup Heroes of other days and what has happened to them'. Presenting information on a

---

[49] *Blyth News*, May 19, 1921.

[50] Garth Dykes, Ashington AFC in the Football League (Nottingham: SoccerData, 2011) 45-6.

[51] Football League transfer list, 1922-3.

[52] Peter Hill and Benjamin Lowe, 'The inevitable metathesis of the retiring athlete', *International Review for the Sociology of Sport*, 9 (1974): 5-32.

[53] Dave Russell, *Football and the English* (Preston: Carnegie, 1997), 49-50; Nicholas Fishwick, *English football and society, 1910-1950* (Manchester: Manchester University Press, 1989), 82; Tischler, *Footballers and businessmen*, 99-100.

[54] Tony Matthews and John Russell, *The complete encyclopedia of Manchester United Football Club* (West Midlands: Britespot, 2002), 276.

[55] *Topical Times*, March 8, 1930.

player-by-player basis, it details the post-playing exploits of those footballers who appeared in FA Cup finals from 1898 to 1914, covering most of the winning sides and a few of the losing finalists.[56] However, the series neither mentions every job each player held after his career, nor gives much of an indication as to how long they were engaged in their various jobs. It must also be remembered that given the range of teams selected, any chronicling of these details can only be said to be representative of the game's elite.

The *Topical Times* Cup Heroes series provides information regarding the post-playing employment circumstances of 155 unique players. As shown in Table 1, some 5% of players took manual jobs in factories; the same number worked in the mines.

A considerable number were self-employed. 41% of our sample of players operated their own business. Of these, some ran shops as butchers, grocers, confectioners and tobacconists. Ten managed their own hotels but the largest grouping of those who ran their own business were publicans who made up 19% of the total sample. That almost one in five players was in the licensed trade adds substance to the stereotype of the ex-footballer as a pub landlord. Yet we need to remember that this is a sample of FA Cup finalists, players who were more likely than their less successful counterparts to have both the money to establish a business, and the fame to attract the punters. One would expect that a sample taken from less successful teams would produce more manual workers and fewer publicans. Nevertheless, it is clear that a large number of footballers at the top of the ladder ran their own business after hanging up their boots, and many of these were licensees.

A sizeable number too remained in football. The series mentions turnstile operators, groundsmen, directors and scouts. Many more were employed in a more hands on role, as managers, trainers and coaches, the latter term likely to denote the role now commonly referred to as manager.

---

[56] It covers the FA Cup winning teams of 1898, 1901, 1903 to 1912 and 1914, as well as the losing finalists of 1903, 1904 and 1912. I am grateful to Matthew Taylor, whose work pointed me to this valuable source.

Table 1. Post-playing occupations of FA Cup finalists, 1898-1914

Role / Industry	No. Of men involved[57]
Self-Employed	41% (64)
Football Coach	30% (46)
Publican, Licensee	19% (29)
Hotelier	7% (10)
Collier, Mineworker	5% (8)
Mine Host	5% (8)
Factory Employee	5% (8)
Tobacconist, Confectioner	5% (7)
Mechanic	3% (5)
Finance, Insurance	3% (4)
Football Scout	3% (4)
Dock worker	3% (4)

Source: *Topical Times*, January 18 to May 19, 1930

Topical Times lists 15 men as trainers, and 35 as football managers or coaches, a combined unique sample of 46, just one short of the number of all the publicans, hoteliers and colliers combined. Although it is recognised that – even amongst the elite – only a small number of footballers remained in the game in a variation of the coaching role, that 30% do is a significant number. And whilst our data is far from infallible, it is clear that Patrick O'Connell's post-playing role as a coach was not a surprising choice of career. It is even less surprising when one considers that O'Connell had been the on field captain at Ashington, as he had been at Manchester United and intermittently at Hull. Fishwick has commented that a 'player with a reputation for

---

[57] The sample also included 29 other occupations, ranging from a clergyman to a strongman, but they are too numerous to tabulate here.

maturity, reliability, good judgment and leadership might attract directors as potential management material'.[58] Selectors evidently thought O'Connell fitted these criteria when they chose him as captain for club and country, as did the press who variously called him a him a 'commanding figure' and 'something of a leader'.[59] As well as the leadership qualities which others had pinpointed, his industrial management experience would also have made him a choice candidate for managerial posts. Carter has argued that the development of the football manager was in line with similar developments throughout industry. He contends that the earliest football managers held duties not too dissimilar to those who managed in factories and industrial sites.[60] O'Connell's experience as a foreman at the Ford Motor Works in Trafford Park further strengthened his candidacy.

Of the 46 men from our sample who went into coaching or management, 12 of these took their trade abroad. Popular destinations were Canada, Holland and Germany. Others like Alf Spouncer and Vincent Hayes went to Spain.[61] Thus when Patrick O'Connell - an Irishman, but through his pedigree effectively a British coach - went to Real Racing Club de Santander in the summer of 1922, he was not the first to make the journey. Jack Greenwell was in charge of FC Barcelona since before the war ended, as was Arthur Johnson at Madrid and William Barnes at Athletic Club de Bilbao. Another Englishman, Fred Pentland, who had been interned during the First World War while coaching in Germany and then coached the French National side in the 1920 Olympics, was in charge of Santander for the two seasons previous to O'Connell. Many were hired because of their background in British football which had a reputation par excellence on the continent. Steve Bloomer probably benefitted from networks with former teammates Pentland and Ted Garry who were coaching in the north of Spain when he was hired as coach at Real Irun.[62] Others

---

[58] Fishwick, *English football and society*, 82.

[59] *Athletic News*, February 22, 1915; *Dumbarton Herald and County Advertiser*, December 24, 1919.

[60] Neil Carter, *The football manager: A history* (Oxford: Routledge, 2006), 48.

[61] *Topical Times*, April 12, 1930; David Hunt, *The history of Preston North End Football Club* (Preston: PNE Publications, 2000), 123.

[62] Peter Seddon, *Steve Bloomer: The story of football's first superstar* (Derby: Breedon, 1999), 162; Matthew Taylor, 'Football's engineers? British coaches, migration and intercultural transfer c.1910-c.1950s', *Sport in History,* 30 (2010): 149.

got jobs through more official networks like the FA or the employment bureau of the Association of Football Players' and Trainers' Union.[63] Still others replied to adverts posted in the British sporting press. In May 1922, O'Connell replied to an advert in *Athletic News* on behalf of a Spanish club who were seeking a 'first class trainer coach'. [64] Applicants were invited to reply to R. B. Alaway, a former amateur with Middlesex Wanderers who had built up a number of contacts in Spain through organising footballing tours there.[65] The advert only appeared for one week, when most stayed for at least a fortnight, and three weeks later there was a notice from the Spanish club thanking all those who had applied, stating that there were too many applicants to reply individually. [66] Managerial posts were keenly sought after, whether at home – 58 had applied for the Preston job in 1925 – or abroad with many footballers, like other entertainers and sportspeople, keen to remain in a trade which they knew well.[67]

In Spain, the 1920s was the decade when football's popularity took off. Introduced at the end of the nineteenth century by British sailors and engineers, the springboard from which the sport launched itself into the wider public's enthusiasm was the national team's surprise success at the 1920 Olympics, when they won the silver medal.[68] Many clubs, such as Santander, Betis and Irun enjoyed royal patronage, indicated by the prefix *Real*. Between 1920 and 1930, attendance at football matches quadrupled in some areas.[69] In 1926, professionalism was legalised, and two years later a national league had been established.[70] As if to illustrate the great strides the game had made during this

---

[63] Taylor, 'Football's engineers?, 146-7.

[64] *Athletic News*, May 22, 1922.

[65] R.B. Alaway, *Football all around the world* (London: Newservice, 1948).

[66] *Athletic News*, June 12, 1922.

[67] Preston North End minutes of Directors meetings 1921-6, entry for May 5 1925; Joan Jeffri, 'After the ball is over: Career transition for dancers around the world', *International Journal of Cultural Policy*, 11 (2005): 346.

[68] D. Shaw, 'The political instrumentalization of professional football in Francoist Spain, 1939-1975' (PhD diss., University of London, 1988), 14; Andrew McFarland, 'Ricardo Zamora: The first Spanish football idol', *Soccer & Society*, 7 (2006): 1-13.

[69] John Walton, 'Reconstructing Crowds: The rise of association football as a spectator sport in San Sebastian, 1915-32', *International Journal of the History of Sport*, 15 (1998): 48.

[70] Liz Crolley and David Hand, *Football and European identity* (London: Routledge, 2006): 98.

decade, in May 1929 forty thousand Spaniards watched their national team defeat England by four goals to three, humbling the country which, in the words of one journalist, 'exported the goods, [but] lost the knack of making them.'[71]

O'Connell's reign at Santander lasted until 1929, where he was relatively successful, leading the club to seven successive wins in the local *Federación Cántabra*, though never achieving much success in the cup. It was during these years that he met and bigamously married Ellen O'Callaghan, a red headed Irish girl.[72] Whilst his separation from his first wife had increased his range of mobility, his marriage in Spain, albeit not to a native, increased the likelihood of him settling permanently. [73] Other notable coaches from Britain who were successful in Europe were Pentland and Jimmy Hogan, who were said to be fluent in Spanish and German respectively.[74] Some did not settle just so well. Athletic Bilbao's first foreign coach, a Mr Shepherd, returned home after only a few months in 1910, and Steve Bloomer noted the difficulties of being apart from his wife who remained in England.[75] By 1932, O'Connell moved to the city of Seville, via a stint at Oviedo, to take over as coach of Betis Balompie, their royal prefix removed under the rule of the Second Republic. It is at Betis where he is most fondly remembered. In 1935 he guided the club to their sole *La Liga* championship. Only promoted to Spain's premier division four years previously, it was a fantastic footballing achievement, one recognised by the municipality who gifted the club a new stadium.[76] At Betis, O'Connell had twice guided his side to victories over FC Barcelona in the cup. This, coupled with his recent success at Betis, made him an ideal candidate for the vacant post at Barcelona. In the summer of 1935, Patrick O'Connell became the coach of arguably Spain's biggest club, at a time when the country was on the cusp of civil war.

---

[71] Ivan Sharpe, *Forty years in football* (London: Sportsman Book Club, 1954), 125.

[72] Sue O'Connell, email message to author, August 10, 2010.

[73] Jacob Mincer, 'Family migration decisions', *Journal of Political Economy*, 86 (1978): 753; Pierre Lanfranchi and Matthew Taylor, *Moving with the ball* (Oxford: Berg, 2001), 53; Stephen Castles and Mark Miller, *The age of migration*, 4th ed. (Basingstoke: Palgrave, 2009), 33.

[74] Seddon, *Steve Bloomer*, 167; Sharpe, *Forty years in football*, 49.

[75] Phil Ball, *Morbo: The story of Spanish football*, 2nd ed. (Guildford: WSC, 2003), 68; Seddon, *Steve Bloomer*, 163.

[76] Ball, *Morbo*, 153.

At Barcelona, Patrick O'Connell won the *Campeonato de Cataluña* in his first season, securing a bonus of 1,000 pesetas to add to his 1,500 pesetas monthly wage.[77] After guiding the club to 5th in the league that same season, he led them to the final of the Spanish Cup, in June 1936. There his team met Real Madrid, the first time these two great rivals had met on Spain's greatest stage. Madrid won by two goals to one,

an ominous victory for the club who would become known as Franco's team against a Catalan side who would consistently oppose the regime. A month later, with the team on holiday and O'Connell back in Ireland, General Franco and his men took control of the Canary Islands and Spain lurched into civil war. As a club, Barcelona suffered heavily during the conflict; its stadium was bombed and its President was shot dead by Falangist troops loyal to Franco.[78] Under threat financially and politically repressed, they were presented with a lifeline in April 1937. Mexican businessman Manuel Mas

Figure 4. *El Entrenedor:* **O'Connell at Barça c. 1936 (FC Barcelona)**

Soriano got in contact with the club and offered them 15,000 US dollars plus expenses to embark upon a footballing tour of Mexico. The club agreed readily and a six match tour over two months was arranged, commencing in June.[79] O'Connell oversaw the trip, which saw a two month long tour extend into four and twelve of the sixteen players enter exile in Mexico and France.[80] O'Connell returned with the

---

[77] FC Barcelona minutes of Board of Directors and Workers Committee, entries for November 7, 1935, May 22, 1939.

[78] Jaume Sobreques i Callico, *Historia del F.C. Barcelona: De la crisi al gran creixement, 1931-1957,* Vol. II (Barcelona: Editorial Labor, 1993), 24-5.

[79] Ibid., 23.

[80] *New York Times,* September 21, 1937; Jimmy Burns, *Barça: A people's passion,* 2nd ed. (London: Bloomsbury, 2000), 120.

reduced party of players and staff but by the closing stages of the conflict, he had left the country along with the rest of the coaches from the British Isles, staying with his brother Larry in London.[81] Whilst the conflict and reduced wages that accompanied the Civil War drove out O'Connell, Pentland, and their peers, the reality was that coaches with a British pedigree had lost the aura which had accompanied them in the early part of the 1920s. While touring teams once seemed invincible, now even the national team could be defeated. Though five different Englishmen had won the Spanish Cup in the 1920s, by the early 1930s, the British coach was becoming increasingly expendable as coaches from Hungary, Germany and Austria grew in stature. Jimmy Hogan claimed in 1933 that English coaches were no longer in demand in Europe, with the exception of the Netherlands.[82] In Spain, Hungarians such as Lippo Hertza and Franz Platko, South Americans like Enrique Fernandez Viola and a plethora of national talent steadily replaced coaches from England, Scotland and Ireland. Over twenty British coaches have been identified as working there in the 1920s, but as Tables 2 and 3 show, the top clubs were no longer looking abroad for guidance.

Following Franco's victory, O'Connell was corresponding with Barcelona who were evidently expecting him to return.[83] However he declined to return to the club, and instead went back to coach Betis once more. In doing so he became the only coach from the British Isles to return to Spain after the conflict, perhaps aided by a nationality and religion not deemed threatening to the Regime. In 1942 he made the short journey to CF Seville where he led the club to the runners up spot in *La Liga*, at that time their joint highest ever position. Eventually his coaching career petered out, coaching Betis and Santander once more before carrying out some scouting work for teams in the south of Spain. That even during these years he didn't take his second Irish wife back to their homeland or to England shows just how settled he was in his adopted country; that he continued to find work, defied the decline of the British-educated coach abroad.

---

[81] FC Barcelona minutes of Board of Directors and Workers Committee, entry for May 22, 1939.
[82] *Topical Times*, March 18, 1933.
[83] FC Barcelona minutes of Board of Directors and Workers Committee, entry for May 22 1939.

Table 2. Nationality of coaches in charge of teams who finished in the top two in La Liga

Seasons	Spain	Britain and Ireland	Elsewhere
1928/29 – 1935/36	5.5 (34%)a	9.5 (59%)	1 (6%)
1939/40 – 1949/50	17 (77%)	1 (5%)	4 (18%)

a. Athletic de Bilbao were led by both Jose Maria Olabarria and William Garbutt during their 1936 title winning season

Table 3. Nationality of coaches in charge of teams who reached the Spanish Cup Final

Seasons	Spain	Britain and Ireland	Elsewhere	Unknown
1918/19 – 1935/36	10 (28%)	20 (56%)	1 (3%)	5 (14%)a
1938/39 – 1949/50	23 (96%)	1 (4%)	-	-

a. Credible information was unavailable concerning Real Club de Irun and Arenas de Guecho; it is possible that these teams were managed by a group of directors.

Sources: Official Club Websites, Correspondence with clubs.

In the 1950s, he was tracked down by Daniel Treston, his son from his first marriage, who had abandoned the O'Connell name in favour of his mother's maiden name. O'Connell had adopted a 'Ne'er the twain shall meet' stance and neither of his two families knew the other existed. He cannily introduced Daniel as his nephew, further embittering his son, who was open about his hostility towards his father.[84] This charade over, he remained in Seville, save for when he went to London to be with his brother in his final days. Patrick O'Connell died on 27 February 1959, in St. Pancras, aged seventy-one.[85]

The direction of Patrick O'Connell's career upon ending his playing days was not altogether unusual. His experience in leading men both on the field and in the factory, combined with his pedigree in British football eased his path into coaching. That he coached abroad was certainly uncommon but not altogether rare, and his initial move to the north of Spain was in keeping with British coaches who took up positions there. However, O'Connell does stand out from the other coaches in Spain due to his staying power. No other British coach had a career which straddled both sides of the Civil War. That Patrick O'Connell achieved not just success, but longevity in his coaching career in Spain, marks him out among both his peers, and the modern British manager.

---

[84] Daniel Treston, interviewed by Raidió Teilifís Éireann (undated) re-broadcast on 'Bowman on Sunday', July 18, 2010.
[85] Register of deaths for England and Wales, January to March 1959.

6

Monkey Glands and The Major: Frank Buckley and Modern Football Management

Neil Carter

Introduction

On 22 December 1964, the main headline on the back page of the Wolverhampton *Express and Star* read simply, 'The Major is Dead'. For the paper's readers no further explanation was deemed necessary. Frank Buckley had been the manager of Wolverhampton Wanderers from 1927 to 1944. During this period, Wolves had become one of the most feared and respected teams in the country. However, during this time he never won a trophy, although Wolves did nearly win the Double in 1939. Indeed, the Golden Era of Wolves was in the 1950s under one of his protégés, Stan Cullis. Yet it is clear, that over 20 years after he left Wolves, Buckley's presence and his legacy was still firmly fixed in the memories of the fans of Wolves and of the people of Wolverhampton in general.

In addition, in *The Times*, together with two internationally renowned scientists and an important Scotland Yard policeman, there was also an obituary for Buckley. This was significant for a number of reasons. First, it reflected football's position as the national game. It also highlighted not only the importance now ascribed to the position of the manager within football but also its growing visibility within popular culture more generally. And of course, it illustrated the importance of Buckley himself. Percy Young has stated that 'Modern [football] management is based largely on the pioneer work of [Herbert] Chapman and Buckley'.[1] In *The Times* obituary, Buckley was described amongst other things as 'a pioneer in modern training methods' and someone who had 'an uncommon flair for public relations'.[2] So, why was he considered such an important figure within football and in what context did his managerial career develop?

Frank Buckley – A Sporting Life

First, while this essay is mainly concerned with Buckley's career at Wolverhampton Wanderers, it would useful to provide some brief

---

[1] Percy Young, *A History of British Football* (London: Arrow, 1968), 254.
[2] *The Times*, December 24, 1964, 11.

background to this main focus. Franklin Charles Buckley was born in Urmston, Manchester in 1883. After attending St. Francis Xavier College in Liverpool and then working as an office clerk, he joined the army in 1900. He excelled at sport, especially football, and later represented his regiment, the 2nd Battalion of the King's Liverpool. After playing for them in the Army Cup final in 1903, Aston Villa persuaded him to buy himself out of military life. Buckley enjoyed a relatively long career as a professional with a number of clubs but he played his best football for Derby County (1911-14). As a result, this gained him international recognition and he won one cap for England (albeit in a famous 3-0 defeat to Ireland at Middlesbrough's Ayresome Park in 1914).[3]

Managerial Background

Buckley took his first managerial position at Norwich City (1919-20) on the advice of FA secretary, Frederick Wall.[4] For Buckley and other managers at this time, there were no models of football management to follow. Training was learned on the job. To what extent, therefore, could his background, in addition to his playing days, have shaped his career in football management?

First, during the inter-war period the growing number of men who were employed as football managers increasingly represented the first generation of professional footballers: Frank Buckley belonged to this group. Early football clubs generally employed secretaries who generally had clerical experience but little on the football side. Through their knowledge of the professional game, directors believed that ex-players would 'know the ropes' and understand players from a practical sense, such as detecting malingerers. But directors also looked for other qualities such as leadership. In this sense, through his military background, he fitted some of these specifications. While he did not see any active service during his military career between 1900 and 1903, Buckley reached the rank of lance sergeant. In addition, he qualified as a Gymnastics Instructor, which gave him an

---

[3] He played for Aston Villa (1903-1905); Brighton (1905-06); Manchester United (1906-07); Manchester City (1907-09); Birmingham (1909-11); Derby (1911-14); and Bradford City (1914). The onset of war ended his professional playing career.

[4] *Guide and Ideas*, May 29, 1937, 8; See Patrick J. Quirke, *The Major: The Life and Times of Frank Buckley* (Stroud: Tempus, 2006), 52-9. After Wolves, he would also manage Notts County (1944-46); Hull City (1946-48); Leeds United (1948-53); and Walsall (1953-55).

understanding of training and physical fitness as well as ideas about instruction and handling men.

In the First World War he joined the Footballers' Battalion, although he was wounded at the Somme and later discharged. Because of his previous military experience, Buckley was awarded a commission and eventually reached the rank of 'Major', although it was actually only a temporary title.[5] Nevertheless, he retained it for the rest of his life. It became a kind of sobriquet, but one that virtually everyone – including his wife – referred to him by. The title of an army officer still carried much social status, especially in the inter-war years, as it allowed one to be regarded as a 'Gentleman'. Army life was generally based on hierarchy and run through strict discipline, and this was later reflected in how Buckley ran his football clubs. In addition to his army background and officer bearing, Buckley owned a farm in partnership with his brother Chris. He dressed like a farmer, wearing a tweed suit with plus fours, although he may also have been trying to cultivate an image of a country gent. By the time he became Wolves manager, it was claimed that he had lost his Manchester accent, indicating a propensity for social climbing.[6] Pat Carter, however, later the wife of Raich saw another side to Buckley. She worked at Hull when Buckley was manager. Although she acknowledged his strict manner with the players, she also described him as a gentleman who was 'a very charming man to his ladies [secretaries], he was very, very charming.'[7] These social qualities were useful for his next job as a commercial traveller, rather than in football. Between 1920 and 1923, he worked for Maskell's Ltd, a London confectionary manufacturer. It also indicates that Buckley had or at least acquired good verbal skills, which were another important skill that football managers required. In 1923, he was back in football and appointed the manager of Blackpool FC.

Management Culture

Buckley's career also needs to be seen in light of football's prevailing management culture. Initially, football managers were the secretaries, then later secretary-managers of clubs. They combined responsibilities for the team with administrative duties but, importantly, a secretary-manager deferred to his directors on playing matters. During the inter-war year though the stature of the manager began to rise. This process can be largely attributed to one man: Herbert Chapman. His success at Arsenal pointed towards the future model for managers who had the

---

[5] Quirke, *The Major*, 41.
[6] Quirke, *The Major*, 60.
[7] Interview with Pat Carter, December 30, 1998.

power to pick the team, decide tactics and to buy players. Of course, Chapman was assisted because Arsenal was a unique club as it was located in prosperous London, while much of the country suffered during the Depression. The emergence of the football manager also reflected the growing technocratic middle classes of the inter-war years, whose scientific and technical skills allowed them to bring new expertise and techniques to industry and government administration.[8]

Frank Buckley was appointed manager of Wolves in 1927 although it is difficult to assess the extent his appointment marked a change in the culture of the club's management. Previously, between 1885 until his death in 1922, the club's first and only secretary-manager had been a former Wolves player, Jack Addenbroke. However, it was the club's directors who had the final word on team selection and recruitment. This policy continued with Addenbroke's three successors. Buckley's immediate predecessor, Fred Scotchbrook was never given full control. Speaking at the club's AGM following his resignation, Scotchbrook claimed that he had been unfairly made a scapegoat for the team's poor fortunes. He asked if the directors were going 'to allow Mr Buckley to be manager? What is the use of me or any other man spending my time riding day and night to find a man if three directors come along and turn the man down?'[9]

The appointment of Buckley, however, did not mark a complete break with this past. While Buckley was given greater powers over team building, he had to defer to the directors on the matter of team selection. It was not until 1933 when the team was having a poor run of results, together with changes in the boardroom, that he was accorded full powers to select the team.[10] Initially, the Wolves directors had expected their manager to keep a tight rein on its finances. Unlike Arsenal, Wolves was a provincial club and lacked the Gunners' financial clout. When the post was advertised in the *Athletic News*, it was unequivocally stated in capital letters, that 'A SPENDTHRIFT IS NOT NEEDED'.[11] And this set the tone both during Buckley's tenure and the club's long-term policy. When he took office the club owed the bank £14,000, and had made a loss for the 1926-27 season of £1500 with first team receipts totalling £15,000. By 1935-36, the club had made a

---

[8] Tony Collins, 'Amateurism and the Rise of Managerialism: The Case of Rugby Union, 1871-1995', *Sport in History* 30, no. 1 (2010): 112.

[9] *Express and Star*, June 28, 1927, 7.

[10] Wolverhampton Wanderers FC Minutes, 23 August 1933, 29 August 1933, 3 October 1933.

[11] *Athletic News*, May 2, 1927, 19.

profit of £17,000, were in credit with the bank to £4000 and gate receipts had increased to £32,000.[12] Football managers were often compared to 'horse traders', because they bought and sold players and Buckley built himself a reputation for 'wheeling and dealing' in the transfer market, and, importantly, finding new talent. Between 1935 and 1938 the club's income from transferred players was £110,658, an overall profit of £68,000.[13] At the centre of this turnaround was the Wolves' scouting system and Buckley's ability to sell on players for large profits. In 1938, for example, Wolves sold Bryn Jones to Arsenal for a record £14,000.

To compliment this overall strategy, under Buckley Wolves developed a youth system. This was arguably his most important legacy and was to be the forerunner for clubs such as Manchester United in the 1950s. The Wolves 'nursery system' recruited boys of 15 and 16 following trials for over 100 during a season. There were several channels for hearing about players in addition to the club's scouts.[14] These included former Wolves player, Mark Crook. He established a nursery club in Yorkshire for Wolves, Wath Wanderers, which produced the likes Roy Swinbourne and Ron Flowers when Stan Cullis was manager in the post-war period.[15]

However, it was also a ruthless business and Wolves were as quick to turn down as sign up players. Peter Doherty's younger brother, Kevin, was rejected by Buckley. Wolves had signed Kevin, aged 15½, on amateur forms to play for a local works team. He had also been given a job on the ground. However, after only two months he was sent back to Coleraine. Peter Doherty, a leading football trade unionist, had argued with Buckley over his treatment of Kevin, stating that his 'indiscriminate "sacking" of youngsters who didn't make the grade in a very short time was unfair and did a great deal of harm'.[16]

Managerial Style

It is perhaps unsurprising that Buckley, given his background, developed a reputation as an authoritarian figure. He was the

---

[12] *Guide and Ideas*, May 1, 1937, 3.

[13] P.M. Young, *Centenary Wolves* (Wolverhampton: Wolverhampton Wanderers FC, 1976) 109; Stanley Cullis, *All for the Wolves* (London: Rupert Hart-Davies, 1960), 94.

[14] *Guide and Ideas*, May 15, 1937, 4; June 5, 1937, 8.

[15] Young, *Centenary Wolves*, 128; Ron Flowers, *For Wolves and England* (London: Stanley Paul, 1962), 19; Cullis, *All For The Wolves*, 45.

[16] Peter Doherty, *Spotlight on Football* (London: Art and Educational Publishers, 1947), 17-19.

embodiment of the military model of management who projected a military-like persona when handling players. Billy Walker, probably looking back nostalgically to the 1930s, remarked that Buckley belonged to a group of managers who had an 'absolute sense of authority'.[17] This is perhaps unsurprising as the football world that Buckley inhabited was a highly masculine one that placed an emphasis on the attributes of hardness, courage and loyalty.[18] Not dissimilar to modern managers, he also had an obsessive streak. His office at Molineux, for example, was situated in the foyer of the main stand so everyone who went in had to go past it.[19]

An early practitioner of the hair-dryer treatment, Buckley employed a form of verbal authoritarianism; the word 'martinet' was never far away when people described his managerial style. When he was at Blackpool, the supporters' club had complained that the players had lost their enjoyment of the game because of his authoritarian manner and that this was the reason for the team's lack of success.[20] Don Bilton, who joined Wolves just before the outbreak of the Second World War, said that Buckley ruled by fear and that 'If you had a rotten game you'd hardly dare go in at half-time, you were going to get the biggest bawling at ... cursed and swore at you. So from that point of view he was a terrible chap.'[21] Jackie Sewell described him as 'a very frightening man', when he was his manager at Notts. County, who could 'make grown men have tears in their eyes.'[22]

Buckley probably had a preference for managing young players as it allowed him to impose his own style on them more easily than those who were both older and more worldly wise. Because of the club's recruitment policy, young players predominated and at one point, in 1937, Wolves did not have one married man amongst the forty players on their books. It was also claimed that Buckley wanted to know when and who a player was going to marry.[23]

---

[17] Billy Walker, *Soccer in the Blood* (London: The Soccer Book Club, 1960), 107.
[18] Neil Carter, *The Football Manager: A History* (London: Routledge, 2006), 3-10.
[19] Interview with Don Bilton, February 26, 1999.
[20] R. Calley, *Blackpool: A Complete Record, 1887-1992* (Derby: Breedon Books, 1992), 60.
[21] Interview with Don Bilton, February 26, 1999.
[22] Rogan Taylor and Andrew Ward, *Kicking and Screaming: An Oral History of Football in England* (London: Robson Books, 1996), 34
[23] *Albion News*, January 16, 1937, 195. Evidence of the club's long-term policy of developing young players came in 1932 when it paid out a record six benefits. Young, *Centenary Wolves*, 106, 114

Nevertheless, Buckley mixed his autocratic tendencies with acts of paternalism, especially towards young players, but the underlying message was that he was in charge – always. He felt that a 'manager must be prepared and qualified to act as a "father" to … young boys'. He impressed upon them the importance of saving money and to send money home to their parents each week.[24] On occasions, he supplied young players from poor backgrounds with new clothes. In 1938, the club purchased a hostel for them. It was fitted with recreational and educational facilities, a small medical room and a garden.[25] However, there was also an ulterior motive: to keep the players under the one roof, making their supervision easier.[26] Buckley also drew up a list of strict rules for the players, which, for example, banned dancing after Wednesday night. In addition, he had a network of spies throughout Wolverhampton's pubs and clubs to observe whether the players were behaving themselves and not breaking any curfews.[27]

Coaching Innovations

Buckley was particularly noted for his innovations in the training and preparation of players, which singled him out from most of his contemporaries. Up to 1939, there was little coaching in English football. There were no FA coaching courses until the late 1930s while training was generally a combination of lapping, head tennis and sometimes 5-a-side. By the inter-war years, trainers were generally ex-professionals who had little knowledge themselves of coaching, apart from the experience gained during their playing days and the main part of their job was to treat players' injuries.[28] During the week players could be denied any training with the ball because it was believed that they would be hungrier for it on a Saturday. And of course, when they did get the ball many didn't know what to do with it. Ironically, by the inter-war period, European footballers were benefitting from the instruction of British coaches.

Buckley, like Chapman, was one of the few managers who had recognized the benefits of coaching much earlier, and had an obsession with physical as well as mental fitness.[29] During the inter-war period,

---

[24] *Guide and Ideas*, May 8, 1937, 5.

[25] Young, *Centenary Wolves*, 114.

[26] *Express and Star*, December 23, 1964, 8.

[27] Interview with Don Bilton, February 26, 1999.

[28] See Neil Carter, 'The Rise and Fall of the Magic Sponge: Medicine and the Transformation of the Football Trainer', *Social History of Medicine* 23, no. 2 (August 2010): 261-79.

[29] *The Times*, December 24, 1964, 11; Peter Morris, *The Team Makers* (London: Pelham, 1971), 39.

there was an acceptance of the need for better coaching and training within sport more generally.[30] In athletics, for example, there was a substantial increase in the publication of technical manuals and the emergence of scientifically minded coaches such as F.A.M. Webster.[31] Soon after Buckley's appointment at Blackpool in 1923, it was reported that a 'pleasing feature of the training ... is that the manager dons the jersey and joins the boys giving them advice and practical demonstration of what to do and how to do it'. Buckley also held practice games on Friday afternoons aimed at developing a better understanding between the players.[32] At Wolves, Buckley introduced mechanical innovations to supplement training sessions. A rowing machine was an early example. He also had a machine purpose-built that fired out footballs at different angles for players to control. A room under a stand was fitted with rubber walls at which players kicked a ball that would then return at unpredictable angles again with the aim of improving their ball control.[33] One of Buckley's most peculiar practices was to encourage players to go ballroom dancing. This, he believed, would improve their balance and movement. On occasions, he would insist on players dancing with each other in training.[34] Buckley was very keen that all players, including goalkeepers, should be able to kick proficiently with both feet. In practice matches, for example, right-wingers would play on the left wing for this purpose. He wanted his players to be versatile and would play them in a number of different positions.[35]

Moreover, during the inter-war years, more managers began to make themselves responsible for tactics, where previously the players, especially the captain, had taken on this role. With the change of the offside law in 1925, football speeded up. There was a greater emphasis on athleticism as the game became more stretched. Arsenal had been one of the first clubs to successfully adapt to the new rule, adopting a more defensive and counter-attacking style. Under Buckley Wolves's

---

[30] For a wider discussion of coaching in this period, see Neil Carter, ed. *Coaching Cultures* (London: Routledge, 2011).

[31] Neil Carter, 'From Knox to Dyson: Coaching, Amateurism and British Athletics, 1912-1947', *Sport in History* 30, no. 1 (2010): 68-72.

[32] *Blackpool Times*, July 31, 12; August 7, 1923, 5.

[33] *Express and Star*, August 3, 1927; Interview with Don Bilton, February 26, 1999.

[34] Interview with Don Bilton, February 26, 1999; Taylor and Ward, *Kicking and Screaming*, 34-5

[35] Interview with Don Bilton, February 26, 1999; Cullis, *Wolves*, 13.

play became more direct and eschewed a close inter-passing game.[36] The traditional slow build-up of attacks in English football had seen the full-back pass to the half-backs who would pass the ball amongst themselves before playing the ball forward. Stan Cullis, the centre-half, was instructed to move the ball quickly to Bryn Jones, the inside-left. It was his job then to play it into a shooting position for a colleague as quickly as possible. Moreover, Buckley was not overly concerned with using wingers. Instead, the plan was to attack through the middle.[37] Critics termed this style 'long ball' or 'kick and rush'. However, it worked.[38] In addition, because of Buckley's training methods, his teams were also renowned for their high levels of fitness. To take advantage of their stamina, Buckley regularly flooded the pitch before every home game. He claimed later that a softer pitch would lead to fewer injuries.[39]

Another major characteristic of the Wolves style under Buckley was its emphasis on the physical. 'It's easier to play against nine or ten than eleven', was Buckley's philosophy it was claimed.[40] Wolves's physical approach though fell foul of the authorities' attempts to clean up the game.[41] In 1936-37 the club was given seventeen cautions, more than any other, and as a punishment the FA Council vetoed its proposed European tour.[42]

Buckley was also unafraid to experiment with emerging scientific ideas in the quest to find a competitive edge. In the 1930s, football clubs had begun to try psychology, and at one time Wolves players attended regular sessions at a local psychologist in an attempt to build

---

[36] Taylor and Ward, *Kicking and Screaming*, 31-2; Morris, *Team Makers*, 33

[37] Cullis, *All For the Wolves*, 42-3.

[38] In 1927, when Buckley was appointed, Wolves were in the second division. They gained promotion in 1932 as Division 2 champions, and remained in the first division throughout the 1930s, steadily improving their position. Their league positions were: 1933 – 20; 1934 – 15; 1935 – 17; 1936 – 15; 1937 – 5; 1938 – 2; 1939 – 2.

[39] Taylor and Ward, *Kicking and Screaming*, 33; Young, *Centenary Wolves*, 115.

[40] Jimmy Guthrie, *Soccer Rebel: The evolution of the professional footballer* (Newton Abbot: Readers Union, 1976), 17.

[41] Nicholas Fishwick, *English Football and Society* (Manchester: Manchester University Press, 1989), 83-85

[42] Football Association Council Minutes, April 30, 1937; Football Association Disciplinary Committee Minutes January 18-June 26, 1937. Buckley did not help Wolves' cause by a curt letter he sent on the matter to Stanley Rous, the FA secretary.

up their confidence. However, it may just have been a form of cod-psychology that was popular during this period.[43]

During the inter-war years coaching had been stimulated by significant developments in ideas of the athletic body.[44] Beamish and Ritchie have argued that during the inter-war years a 'paradigm shift' took place in the scientific understanding of the training of athletes and the discipline of exercise physiology was pioneered in both America and Germany. The work of the British scientist, Archibald Vivian Hill on physiological responses to exercise also led to a greater understanding of the capacity of athletes' bodies to more systematic training regimes.[45] The use of ergogenic aids was also becoming increasingly common in other sports. Aids included the use of ultra-violet light rays to speed up recovery from injuries. Sports such as cycling were also not averse to providing chemical stimulants for their athletes, and football was no different. At Blackpool, Buckley himself had handed out pep pills to players before a cup-tie in the mid-1920s.[46] Leslie Knighton also gave pep pills to Arsenal players before a cup-tie with West Ham in 1925.[47]

Buckley, however, was perhaps best known for the so-called Monkey Gland Affair in which he was accused of injecting Wolves players with a form of gland treatment in order to improve their performance. The whole episode though caused a major stir in the football world with some claiming it was immoral and a form of doping. One famous player was quoted as saying, 'We're not blooming guinea pigs.'[48] The implantation of 'Monkey glands' had been popularised by the Russian Serge Voronoff in the 1920s who claimed that the injection of testicular

---

[43] Cullis, *All For The Wolves*, 16; Morris, *Team Makers*, 39; Tony Pawson, *The Football Managers* (Newton Abbot: Readers Union, 1973), 34.

[44] Neil Carter, 'From Knox to Dyson': 67.

[45] Rob Beamish and Ian Ritchie, 'From Fixed Capacities to Performance-Enhancement: The Paradigm Shift in the Science of 'Training' and the Use of Performance-Enhancing Substances', *Sport in History* 25, no. 3 (2005): 418; Bassett, David R., 'Scientific contributions of A.V. Hill: exercise physiology pioneer', *Journal of Applied Physiology* 93 (2002): 1573-8.

[46] Ray Daniels, *Blackpool Football: The Official Club History* (London: Robert Hale, 1972), 36.

[47] Bernard Joy, *Forward Arsenal* (London: Phoenix, 1952), 32-3

[48] For a wider discussion on this point see Paul Dimeo, *A History of Drug Use in Sport 1876-1976: Beyond Good and Evil* (London: Routledge, 2007), 44-46.

implants would rejuvenate the patient.[49] It was essentially an example of alternative medicine, which operated in a medical marketplace that was open to fads. In 1937, Buckley had been approached by Menzies Sharp, possibly more of a businessman than a scientist, who persuaded Buckley of the benefits of this treatment for footballers. The players were given a course of treatment over a six week period during which they received an injection every three or four days, and this was to last them over the whole season. The main idea behind their use, it was said, was to prevent staleness within players – a perennial fear amongst coaches of athletes – as well as improve their mental speed, stamina, physical fitness and resistance to illness.[50]

However, because of the improved form of Wolves, other clubs also began to experiment with gland treatment, including Portsmouth and Tottenham. Ironically, the 1939 FA Cup Final was contested by both Wolves and Portsmouth and has since been known as the 'Monkey Gland Final', which Portsmouth won 4-1. The treatment was not regarded as successful at other clubs. In February 1939, twelve players from relegation bound Chelsea volunteered to undergo 'gland treatment'. However, following their demotion to division two they discontinued the treatment. The Football Association later held a conference on the matter and decreed that while the treatment was permissible, individual players had the right to refuse it.[51] With the onset of war, the matter faded out of the public consciousness.

The Myth (Making) of Frank Buckley
Finally, perhaps it would be beneficial to reflect on how the life of Frank Buckley has been constructed and to what extent this has been due to perceptions based on the sources available. There has been much recent debate over the writing of life stories of athletes.[52] John Bale, for example, has argued that there are several layers of truth in writing a biography and that in his study of Ernst Jokl, the so-called 'father of sports science', the edges of truth and fiction became

---

[49] Deborah Brunton, 'The Rise of Laboratory Medicine', in *Medicine Transformed: Health, Disease and Society in Europe, 1800-1930*, ed., D. Brunton (Manchester: Manchester University Press, 2004), 101-02.

[50] *News of the World*, April 3, 1938, 19; *Express and Star* (Wolverhampton), March 29, 1939, 12.

[51] Bob Ferrier, *Soccer Partnership: Billy Wright and Walter Winterbottom* (London: Heinemann, 1960), 88-9.

[52] See John Bale, Mette K. Christensen and Gertrud Pfister, eds, *Writing Lives in Sport: Biographies, Life-histories and Methods*, (Aarhus, DK: Aarhus University Press, 2004).

blurred. [53] The questions Bale raises have mirrored wider methodological debates over how historians approach sources. As Martin Johnes has pointed out, many of these anxieties have revolved around a false dichotomy between postmodernism and empiricism. Most empirically-based historians though – or at least good ones – are critical in their approach to sources. They treat them with caution and don't regard them as 'simple repositories from where truths can be simply retrieved'. [54] Writing history, therefore, in the pursuit of knowledge, is a balancing act in which the evidence needs to be interpreted rather than taken literally.

Some of the sources used in this essay have been the staple for the history of sport: newspapers, both local and national, and autobiographies.[55] The use of newspaper sources reminds us how the experience of sport has been derived essentially from the meanings communicated through the media. In Britain, until the 1960s, the newspaper was the primary means by which people 'knew' sport; how to understand, interpret and make sense of it. However, newspapers were also businesses and had their own agendas; they constructed their own stories around real events to appeal to a particular audience. As Hill has argued, 'Themes of community, locality, "our town" provided the main tropes of local newspaper reportage. The voice assumed by the local press was the voice of 'us', the locality; the local spoke, or was felt to speak, for the people of the community it served'.[56] By contrast, the national tabloids, especially from the 1930s, developed a more populist and sensationalist tone due to a circulation war. There was a greater emphasis on personalities and human-interest stories.

Football and the press established a symbiotic relationship at an early stage. First secretaries then mangers were the first point of contact for reporters. Managers, therefore, became the de facto public face of a

---

[53] John Bale, 'The Mysterious Professor Jokl' in *Writing Lives in Sport: Biographies, Life-histories and Methods*, eds, John Bale, Mette K. Christensen and Gertrud Pfister, (Aarhus, DK: Aarhus University Press, 2004), 25-39.

[54] Martin Johnes, 'Archives, Truths and the Historian at Work: A Reply to Douglas Booth's "Refiguring the Archive"', *Sport in History* 27, no.1 (March 2007): 127-35.

[55] Buckley's had an autobiographical account of his life and career serialised in *Guide and Ideas*, May-June 1937.

[56] Jeffrey Hill, 'Anecdotal Evidence: Sport, the Newspaper Press and History' in *Deconstructing History: A Postmodern Analysis*, ed., Murray G. Phillips, (Albany, NY: State University of New York, 2006), 121.

football club. During the 1930s, a proficiency in public relations, with the aim of drumming up publicity by keeping the club's name in the papers, was becoming part of a manager's job. It was also an important aspect of twentieth century modernity. When he was at Blackpool, Buckley changed the colour of the club's shirts to tangerine to this effect.[57] Herbert Chapman had certainly recognized this and even more so his successor at Arsenal, George Allison, who was the BBC's first football commentator. In addition, as the papers increasingly reported on the actions of clubs in terms of managerial activity, football managers were becoming 'the story'. Because Buckley was at its centre, the coverage of the Monkey Gland Affair demonstrated, how significant a figure a manager had become by 1939. However, the press tended to construct reality as well as reflect it, and the powers that managers actually held did not always reflect the media's perception of these powers. Instead, managers fulfilled a particular role for the media, but in the context of the aims of the local or national press.

Managers were not passive agents in this relationship with the media. Buckley was more aware than most of its power and used the media to create a certain amount of myth-making about himself. He cultivated his own mythology and an aura of an all-powerful figure. His autobiography, 'Football is My Life Story', was serialized in the little known paper, *Guide and Ideas*, in May and June 1937. It was a tabloid in its appearance as the paper mixed short paragraphs, large headlines with pictures and an aggressive, sensationalist tone. It can be argued that these articles contain a number of statements in which the edges between truth and fiction may have become blurred. When he took over at Wolves in 1927, for example, he claimed that he 'decided on a five year plan and though advancement was slow, it was nevertheless steady and in the right direction'.[58] This statement suggests more than a sense of history with hindsight; that Wolves's success – and admittedly, the club was relatively successful under him – had all been carefully planned from the beginning to an inevitable conclusion with Buckley in control at the helm. However, it fails to acknowledge any sense of the anxieties and uncertainties of the moment in which the future is difficult to predict in football management or any other activity. Moreover, as has been mentioned above, it was only six years after he took over that Buckley was given sole power over picking the team, and there is unsurprisingly no reference of this as it would dent his all-powerful image.

---

[57] Quirke, *The Major*, 61.
[58] *Guide and Ideas*, May 1, 1937, 3.

Newspapers though also gave managers a forum to pontificate their opinions on a wide range of footballing matters. Herbert Chapman, for example, had a regular column in the *Sunday Express*. Buckley used his autobiography to express his views on the future of football. In it he stated 'I foresee the game being played indoors on rubber pitches illuminated by powerful floodlighting.' Other predictions were equally prophetic and included 'the formation of [a] super international league embracing all the leading European clubs. Every club will own its own twenty-two seater air-liner.' He warned that football in England must be ready for 'progressive reforms'.[59]

Conclusion

Of course, just by having this platform, it both reinforced and reflected the notion that the football manager was now an important and central figure within the football world, and that Buckley was one of the most prominent practitioners. Along with Herbert Chapman, he had helped to modernise the role. Not only with respect to the skills required in becoming a manager but also in elevating the public perception of the job through the media. This image was further enhanced when in 1939 Buckley led out his team (along with Portsmouth's Jack Tinn) at the FA Cup Final.[60] Yet Buckley was also a man of his time. He left Wolves in 1944 for Notts. County for a then huge salary of £4,500, making him the highest paid manager in the country. However, he failed to replicate his success at Wolves at his next four clubs. His abrasive and authoritarian manner had become outdated with players who like in other areas of post-war Britain society were becoming increasingly less deferential. Nevertheless, through the reputation he established at Wolves ensured that his story, whether truth or fiction, would continue to be part of football's history.

---

[59] *Guide and Ideas*, June 19, 1937, 8.
[60] This was possibly the first time this had happened.

7

Alec Nelson: Professional Runner, Athletics Coach and 'Entrepreneur-Client'[1]

Ian Stone

Introduction

This chapter considers the sporting life of Alec Nelson (1871-1944), first, as an athlete, and then as a professional coach. It sets his career in its wider social and sporting context, arguing that he was a significant contributor to British athletics in the decades up to World War II. A crucial part in the story is played by a prominent social and political figure, whose ambition to bring about change in British athletics brought him into an ongoing alliance with Alec Nelson, the gifted coach of his era. Surviving records and correspondence suggests that a patron-client relationship existed between the two men. Such a model is useful in seeking to understand Nelson's life and career – allowing for the fact that the relationship was conditioned by the patron's distinctive outlook on life and by his client's entrepreneurialism.

The study arises out of my interest in family history. Alec Nelson was my great-great uncle. Received information from family about his life was confined to some simple facts: he worked as a coach at Cambridge University and, as a conscientious objector, serving in the ambulance service during the Great War. My image of him was based on a photograph (c1915), inscribed 'Alec Nelson' on the reverse. It shows a man, clearly well-to-do, taking a salute from uniformed Red Cross ambulance men. Everything in the photograph reinforced the impression of 'Uncle Alec' conveyed by my (aspirant middle-class) grandmother and her sister. A few clicks on Google, however, revealed that Nelson was not the principal subject of the photograph; rather, he

---

[1] I am grateful to Dr David Day for certain factual material on Alec Nelson, and advice regarding its interpretation, and to Margaret Roberts, for her invaluable family history support, including resolving census cul-de-sacs. Librarians and archivists at Churchill College Archives, Cambridge University, Cambridge County Archives, The Cambridge Collection, and the Religious Society of Friends in Britain have been especially helpful in tracking manuscripts and illustrations.

was one of the men *giving* the salute.[2] Moreover, those clicks also suggested that there was more to Alec Nelson than I had imagined, and that his was indeed a sporting life worthy of further investigation.

Family background
Nelson's father, it is virtually certain, was Robert Nelson (1820-85), an agricultural labourer from Fife, Scotland, who, with his wife, Margaret, relocated to Hayes in the mid-1850s. He and other male family members worked as farm and garden labourers; females found positions as domestic servants[3]. Alec's mother was Elizabeth Reeves (b. 1837), whose family moved from Wiltshire to Orpington, Kent in the mid-1800s; her father was an 'own account' carpenter. Alec, along with twin sister Beatrice and older brother William, were all products of a relationship between Robert and Elizabeth. Born in 1871, he was registered 'Leopold Reeves', with no father's name appearing on the birth certificate. He later took the name 'Alec Nelson' - Alexander being a common name on his father's side. Although Robert and Elizabeth never married, Alec's mother consistently recorded her name as 'Nelson' in censuses, and her status as 'widow', even prior to Robert's death. Census records show that she and her children lived first in the crowded household of brother Stephen Reeves, and subsequently with one or other of her own children, contributing to the family budget by working as a dressmaker and confectioner.

In the early 1890s, Nelson was living with his sister Beatrice and her husband Jack Levy; working with him in the local paper mill. On 20 January 1897, he married Catherine Smith, of Sawston, Cambridgeshire, in a ceremony at St George the Martyr Anglican Church, Southwark. His profession, according to the marriage certificate was 'clerk'. The couple had four children, of whom three

---

[2] Indeed, in addition to photographic evidence regarding the identity of people in the family photograph, a Pathé News clip was quickly revealed, featuring the December 1934 Varsity Relay Races at Fenners. Proceeds from the meeting went to Nelson's benefit appeal, and the clip features part of an interview with him. www.britishpathe.com/results.php?search=alec+nelson. The Pathé film archives contain many clips of inter-war Varsity sporting events, including some of Cambridge-Oxford versus Harvard-Yale, and afford an opportunity to observe the setting for the events, including the old Queens club ground, as well as the style and techniques of the athletes themselves, frequently shown in slow motion.

[3] On his marriage certificate, Nelson entered his (deceased) father's occupation as 'farm bailiff', but there is no evidence to confirm that he actually achieved this occupational level.

survived early childhood: Stanley (b. 1902), Winifred (1893) and Millicent (1900).

Athletics career

Little is known about Nelson's childhood, but, athletically, he appears to have been naturally gifted. Indeed, his fleetness of foot as a boy led to his losing a delivery job for an Orpington butcher: As he later recalled, his boss considered he had been impossibly quick in delivering some kidneys and dismissed him on the spot. He became a member of Cambridge Harriers, moving in 1895 to Goldsmith's Athletic Club, for which he competed in handicap races from 100 yards to 2 miles; in 1899, he switched to Brighton & County Harriers. Presumably, the successive moves were precipitated by job changes.

Lacking in height, but powerfully built and possessing an electrifying burst of speed, Nelson was a proficient performer on the amateur national circuit. In the 1986 amateur championships at Northampton[4], and again in 1901 at Huddersfield, he came 3rd in the half-mile. At Reading on 26 August 1898, in 'a race of exceptionally interesting character' he broke (or possibly set) the ¾ mile (1320 yards) British amateur record, beating his great rival Joe Binks in a time of 3m 11 and 4/5 secs.[5] Shortly afterwards, on 17 September 1898 in the 1,000 yards Invitation Scratch race at the Kennington Oval, he broke the grass record for the event: 'some good running was shown by A. Nelson of the Goldsmiths' Institute, winning by ten yards in front of J. Binks in 2 min 15 secs.[6] Against the same opponent and at the same venue on 9 September 1899, he achieved a victory by six yards in the half-mile in a fast time of 1 min 58 and 2/5 secs.[7]

Betting odds and lack of place affiliation in newspaper reports suggest that he was competing as a professional pedestrian in the early 1900s. While for A.R. Downer and Alfred Shrubb, who both received AAA bans for taking money, there are clear dates for their transition to the professional ranks, it is hard to be definite with regard to Alec Nelson. Place affiliation for professionals changed according to whim - and possibly to confuse the bookies. Thus, in 1905 A. Nelson (Dundee) contested the 300 yards £100 event at the New Year Powderhall handicaps, in front of a 16,000 crowd – 'the biggest ever seen at a

---

[4] *Yorkshire Herald, and The York Herald*, July 1, 1896, 6; *Observer*, July 5, 1896, 3; *Reynolds's Newspaper*, July 5, 1896; *Morning Post*, July 6, 1896, 3.

[5] *Pall Mall Gazette*, August 23, 1900

[6] *Observer*, September 8, 1898, 3; *The Times*, September 19, 1898, 10.

[7] *Morning Post*, September 11, 1899, 2; *The Times*, September 11, 1899, 9.

pedestrian meeting in Edinburgh'.[8] Nelson won the qualifying heat in 'a good race' in 31 and 4/5 secs, equal fastest of the eight heats, but Lockhart (Glasgow, at bookies' odds of 2 to 1) won 'with a bit to spare' from Waddell (Linlithgow) and Nelson (3-1 against) in a time of 31 and 4/5 secs.

Figure 1. Nelson (left) *vs* Joe Binks, scratch ¾ mile limit race, Reading 26 August 1899 (courtesy of Cambridgeshire Archives)

Later the same year, on 17 June 1905, in 'one of the most interesting contests held in Britain for some time', Nelson (Blackpool) took on George Tincler (Inverness) in a half-mile race at Rochdale. The 37 year-old Tincler apparently came out of retirement to contest for a stake of £50 against Nelson.[9] In drizzly conditions, 500 spectators watched Tincler lead from the start, and seem the likely winner until, reaching the home straight, Nelson passed him 'in electrifying fashion' to win by two yards in 2 min 1 and 2/5 secs. Whether this was *the* 1905 race that decided the professional half-mile championship, referred to on the frontispiece of Nelson's book and elsewhere, is unclear. Certainly, the American H. Stomberg, 'the crack runner', let it be known that 'he would like to meet Alec Nelson in a half-mile professional race'[10] - at the time when Nelson was described as 'the

---

[8] 'The Powderhall New Year Handicaps', Pedestrianism, *The Scotsman*, January 4, 1905, 3.

[9] *Star*, August 11, 1905, 1.

[10] Challenges, *The Police Gazette*, New York City 1905, 3.

latest star in the athletic world.' [11] In truth, worthy pedestrian opponents were scarce and contests few and far between. To challenge Alfred Shrubb in 1906,[12] Nelson had to agree to race over 3 miles, even though – according to 'Expert' in *Sporting Life* - he no longer had 'pretensions to be regarded as a distance champion, a mile being almost his limit as a class man.' With Tincler and Sid Thomas both well past their prime, Alec Nelson ('of London') took on opponents such as Liverpool footballer Jack Cox, over 300 yards.[13]

What prompted Nelson to turn professional, when to accept money for racing likely resulted in a ban? The decision may have been induced by the fact that he was in his thirties, and his best days as an amateur were behind him. Another possibility is the need to earn some money. His younger daughter Millicent suffered from Congential Talipes (club foot). Somehow, Nelson had managed to secure funds for her to have specialist surgery, and a 23-day stay, in Great St Ormond's Children's Hospital. The operation, performed in 1907 by (later Sir) H.A.T. Fairburn, a leading authority in the field, was said to have 'greatly relieved' the condition.[14]

Professional coach (1908-14)

After hanging up his spikes, Nelson was appointed coach for Cambridge University Athletics Club (CUAC) in 1908. It is unclear how this came about, or, indeed, on what basis in terms of requisite skills etc. - although he did have a geographical connection, through his Cambridge-born wife. All we know, from a BBC wireless broadcast he made, after the Varsity Sports at White City on 20 July 1935, is that he 'met a prominent official of the CUAC at the London Athletic Club in 1907' and that this led eventually to his being 'invited to take up the position'. In practice, the appointment was for a limited number of weeks annually – mainly the term leading up to 'the Sports' (Cambridge *vs* Oxford, held just prior to Easter at Queen's Club, London). Outside the weeks taken with this engagement, he appears to have also secured a position organising sports activities for the 2,000 employees of JS White & Co., a warship-building firm on the Isle of Wight. His coaching talents must have been relatively quickly revealed, since he was appointed professional track and field coach for the British team at the 1912 Olympics held in Stockholm.

---

[11] *Star*, August 11, 1905, 1.

[12] *Penny Illustrated Paper and Illustrated Times*, February 17, 1906, 102.

[13] *Kalgoorlie Western Argus*, January 22, 1907, 39.

[14] S.T. Buxton, 'Sir Thomas Fairbank, An Appreciation', *Journal of Bone* Surgery, 38B:1 (1956)

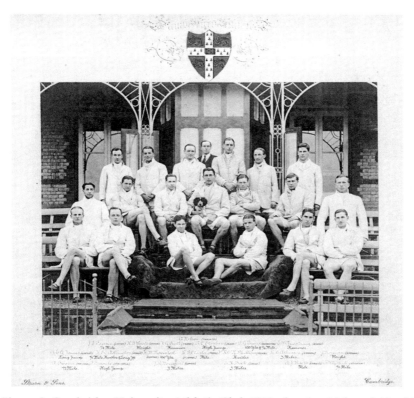

Figure 2. Cambridge University Athletic Club 1913, showing Nelson (at back) and R.S. Woods (back row, 2nd from left) (courtesy of Cambridgeshire Archives)

In March 1913, when plans were being made for the Oxbridge vs Yale-Harvard track and field meet in America, it was noted in the US press that Alec Nelson, was expected to accompany the combined team.[15] This not only suggests an extension to his coaching work at Cambridge, but is also consistent with a 1932 report that his approach to training had benefited from studying the methods practised in different countries he had visited, including America, France and Germany.[16]

---

[15] *New York Times*, March 25, 1913.
[16] 'Alex Nelson Coming to Cavan', cutting, unidentified Irish newspaper, Churchil College Archives, Cambridge University, Philip Noel-Baker papers, NBKR 6/14 (hereafter cited as NBKR papers, file no.). Philip Noel-Baker is hereafter referred to in these notes as PNB, and Alec Nelson as AN.

The outbreak of war, however, soon interrupted his coaching career. Athletics at Cambridge was suspended as his present and former undergraduate athletes went off to serve in the trenches.

Friends' ambulance service (1914-18)

In World War I, Alec served in France and Italy with the Friends' Ambulance Unit (FAU), organised by the Quakers.[17] He appears to have undergone the necessary training, alongside Quaker volunteers, at the Buckinghamshire village of Jordans.[18] The FAU was initially an unofficial body, under the direction of the British military authorities,[19] established in response to deficient arrangements for dealing with the many casualties in the battle zone. Nelson arrived in Dunkirk in October 1914 as one of the initial 43 (out of an eventual 120) FAU personnel at the Malo-les-Bains HQ. Their work at the Front was 'almost exclusively [dressing and] transportation of wounded' Eighth Army soldiers from stations around Ypres to hospital ships and the *hôpital d'evacuation*.[20] The focus of fighting subsequently moved away from Ypres,[21] precipitating the Unit's shift to the Italian front.

Figure 3. Postcard photograph of Nelson in FAU uniform, 1915

[17] A. Tegla Davies, *Friends Ambulance Unit, The Story Of The F.A.U. in The Second World War 1939-1946*, Council of the Friends Ambulance Unit (London: George Allen & Unwin, 1947)

[18] Nelson later claimed to have taken a medical course that helped his coaching work; it is likely that this was a reference to his training at Jordans. A postcard of the Friends meeting house, in the Stone family archives, suggests he participated in this training.

[19] M. Tatham and J.E. Miles, eds, *The Friends Ambulance Unit, 1914-19: A Record* (London: Adam Matthew Publications, 1920)

[20] 'Report of FAU of the British Red Cross Society, from October 31 1914 to January 27 1915', NBKR Papers, 11/3

[21] Speech by PNB (CO at Malo HQ), dated May 17, 1915, NBKR 11/7/1

A censored postcard to his twin-sister, Beatrice, shows that, on 17 March 1915, Nelson was in Dunkirk, where the FAU first operated. From around August 1915 he served at the front against Austria-Hungary in north-eastern Italy, and appears to have remained there until 1918. From his base in Udine came a cheery postcard to his mother, dated 5 September 1915: 'Just going up near firing line. Going on splendid. Happy to help the Italians all we know, they are giving us a Royal Welcome and all so good to us. Love to you and all. Affectionate Son. Alec.'

But how did he come to be there? Although not a Quaker himself, Alec was known to be a conscientious objector. Nelson's family – the Reeves side, at least - was fiercely patriotic, so enrolling for ambulance duty meant he could serve the country in an honourable, yet non-combatant, capacity. Indeed, initially, it seemed that FAU service might have been chosen in the face of conscription, since Nelson was not in a reserved occupation, and would have had no employment as a coach in wartime. In fact, his involvement appears to have been purely voluntary, since it was not until April 1916 that conscription for married men was introduced, and when he joined the FAU he was already *above* the maximum age (40) that was to be set for conscription.

Nelson is referred to in a December 1914 report on FAU's Dunkirk operations: 'the establishment of the Unit is now complete and that from the commanding officer, Baker, down, each man has his daily duties. They have their own cook and the "butler" is a well-known English athletic trainer and celebrated starter, and what a character he is, too!'[22] Nelson's medal record, under the British Expeditionary Force,[23] records his 'rank' as 'chauffeur'. There is strong suggestion from these sources that Alec Nelson was Baker's orderly or batman. The discovery of this connection to Philip Noel-Baker proved to be the key to unlocking our understanding of Nelson's career and contribution as an athletics coach - at least from around 1910.

---

[22] Report, 16 December 1914, Malo-les-Bains, quoted in *Canadian Medical Association Journal* 5:2 (1915): 156-57
[23] Roll 31, October 1914

Philip Noel-Baker (1889-1982)[24]

Philip Baker was from a Quaker industrial family producing baking equipment in Brent (Joseph Baker & Sons Ltd).[25] The business was strongly ethical in the mould of Quaker concerns, showing rare respect for its workers. Baker[26] was educated at Quaker institutions (Bootham School, York, and Haverford College, Penn. US). At Cambridge, he

was president of both Cambridge Union (1912) and CUAC (1910-12), and a 1500m finalist at the 1912 Stockholm Olympics. The Baker family organised the Friends' ambulance service at Ypres in 1914, and Philip was active on the ground. In 1915 he moved on, as Adjutant to the FAU, to lead operations in Italy, where was awarded the Mons star and silver medal for valour (1917) and *croce di guerra* (1918).

Following the war, he resumed his athletic career, gaining silver at the Antwerp Olympics in 1920, while also becoming increasingly engaged in the administration and development of the sport. He was the leading figure in the formation

Figure 4. Philip Baker, ID photo, Friends' Ambulance Unit, 1914-18 (by permission of the Religious Society of Friends in Britain)

of the Achilles Club in 1919, which arranged matches and tours for Oxford and Cambridge athletes, undertook athletics development in public schools, etc. Noel-Baker was also largely responsible for instituting the Oxford-Cambridge Relay races in 1920. He was appointed Professor of International Relations at London University (1924-29), where, inevitably, he also pursued projects to develop athletics facilities and support for London students. At a national level, in the early 1920s, he was captain of the British Olympic team, a member of the British Olympic Council and British delegate to Olympic Conference. His service to sport continued throughout his

---

[24] The *Oxford Dictionary of National Biography* is a key source for this section; See also: D. Whittaker, Fighter for Peace: Philip Noel-Baker, 1889-1982, (York: Sessions, 1989).

[25] Later involved in a merger and thence called Baker-Perkins Ltd.

[26] Philip Baker adopted his wife's family name, Noel, as an additional surname after their marriage in 1915.

life: he was British Olympic team Commandant in 1952, and President of UNESCO's International Council of Sport & Physical Recreation in the 1960s.

Alongside his academic and sporting activities, Noel-Baker somehow found the time – to the evident frustration of his wife - to develop a full career in international affairs and politics. His wartime experiences made him committed to the cause of international cooperation and disarmament. He was a member of the British delegation at the Paris Peace Conference, and was involved during 1921-24 in the League of Nations, including as secretary to the British delegation. From the late 1920s he was a labour politician, first as MP for Coventry (1929-31) and then Derby (Derby South) (1936-70). After the war he became Secretary of State for the Commonwealth, before being moved to the Ministry of Fuel & Power. He published a number of books on international affairs, notably *The Arms Race: A Programme for World Disarmament*, 1958, which contributed to his winning the Nobel Peace prize in 1959. Noel-Baker's papers are voluminous, covering as they do his many activities within and outside the world of sport. Virginia Woolf reflected this in her diary: 'Phil Baker should try to do half what he does, and should drink wine'.[27]

Professional coach (1919-39)

On his return from Italy, Nelson went back to Cowes, resuming his post at J&S White & Co. His mentor, Noel-Baker, meanwhile, worked assiduously to set up conditions for his return to his old position as CUAC coach. This involved constructing a package of activities – 'engagements' – that would provide an adequate income. Noel-Baker arranged with CUAC officials for him to be offered a fee of £5 per week for a short-term appointment and also tried to set up similar work at the new Achilles Club for the seasonal lull over the summer.[28] Notice terms of just a single week did not deter Nelson, since post-war lay-offs in shipbuilding rendered insecure his contract at Whites. 'Whatever you say, Mr Philip, I'm doing' he wrote trustingly to his patron in December 1919.[29]

---

[27] *Oxford Dictionary of National Biography* – PNB entry
[28] CUAC Hon Treasurer, Canon Joey H Gray, refused to sanction a fee above the level (£2.10s) paid to the incumbent trainer, but Club President A.C. Telfer agreed to take on Nelson at £5 per week and to 'risk making it up from the members', reasoning that, 'Webster is coming over once a week and, with Alec, Fenner's ought to be worth joining.' (Correspondence between A.C. Telfer and PNB in early 1920, NBKR papers 9/38/5)
[29] AN to PNB, December 15, 1919, NBKR papers 9/38/5

Figure 5. CUAC team, 1924, showing coach Alec Nelson, son Stanley (front 2nd from left) and DGA Lowe (second row, 3rd from left) (courtesy of Cambridgeshire Archives)

He returned to Cambridge in January 1920. His coaching contract then, and perennially, was confined to the Michaelmas and Lent terms (ending respectively with 'the Sports' in March and Relay Races in December). This was fewer than 18 weeks in the year, even allowing for additional work with the Hare & Hounds Club, which organised cross-country events against Oxford.

At the Achilles Club, as well as coaching members, his duties included giving advice on, and supervising, the conversion of the old '3 lap' track at Queen's Club to one of 4 laps.[30] He coached for Achilles until 1928, when the club's loss of the Queen's ground made this untenable. In 1920, he was once again invited to be the British Olympic track coach for the Antwerp Games. This appointment, it turns out, was principally Baker's doing - through his position both as team captain and member of the British Olympic Council. The BOC readily endorsed the appointment after Noel-Baker proposed that the Achilles Club would cover the costs.

---

[30] Queens Club was important to both Cambridge and Oxford graduate athletes, many of whom – such as Guy Butler - lived in London and wanted good facilities for training.

His growing reputation in the immediate post-war period, led to his engagement also as coach by the Army Council. The army's interest was sparked by the realisation that many competitors at the Bisley Rifle Championships 'were entirely ignorant of the basic principles of running'. In attack shooting, soldiers were becoming out of breath and unable to fire straight. As his training regimes produced improved performances,[31] army engagements became a regular part of Nelson's summer calendar for the next 10-15 years, with typically two weeks stints at Lydd in Kent, Catterick, Colchester and the Tank Corps camp in Bovington, Dorset.

Noel-Baker's professorship at London led to him developing schemes that gave rise to new opportunities for his loyal servant. From 1928 Alec Nelson thus worked as a coach on behalf of the University of London Athletic Union, as well as advising on, and supervising, development of the track facilities and buildings.

The other major known coaching engagement took him to Ireland, and an appointment as national coach. The 14-week contract was followed, in 1932, by an engagement for 20 weeks. He visited athletics centres, including schools and colleges, gave lectures and demonstrations, and also helped leading athletes prepare for the Los Angeles Olympics – notably Bob Tisdall (formerly of CUAC) who won the gold medal in the 400m hurdles.

Advocates of change in British athletics

The 1920s saw frequent expressions of concern over how British athletics was managed, and the implications for its international competitiveness, especially relative to the USA. Nelson's emergence as a leading professional coach was bound up with the challenge mounted, by men such as Philip Noel-Baker, to what David Day terms 'the grip of amateur officials upon athletics' and cult of 'effortless superiority'. Noel-Baker and his associates argued the need to improve international performance via competent scientific athletics instructors.[32]

---

[31] Within months, advances in performance were apparent, leading to acknowledgement by the Army Council that the decision to appoint Nelson was entirely justified, and that it was possible that the times allowable per hundred yards in attack shooting could be reduced without diminishing the scores. 'Bisley Begins, Bisley Camp, July 10', *The Times,* July 11, 1922, 7.

[32] David Day, 'London Swimming Professors: Victorian Craftsmen and Aquatic Entrepreneurs', *Sport in History*, 30:1 (2010): 32-54.

Lt-Colonel A.N.S. Strode Jackson, 1500 metres gold medallist at Stockholm,[33] gave voice to this view in *The Times* in 1919, arguing that, for future success, the lessons of the 'Swedish model' needed to be learned - specifically, central coordination of effort, a national stadium and the availability of a considerable fund for building athletic strength.[34] Such a fund would allow the appointment of 'supervising trainers' such as Alec Nelson for athletics who could then devote 'their whole time to this work' in order to produce a systematic approach to producing talent to compete in the Olympic competitions.[35]

Noel-Baker worked to bring about change at an operational level. He sought to develop the athletics infrastructure (physical and organisational), improve the quality of coaching, increase opportunities for (largely Oxbridge) graduate athletes to engage in international competition; and widen participation in the sport – especially at university level (notably London), but also within public schools.

Consistent with, and parallel to, Noel-Baker's efforts relating to the civilian world, it seems likely that his friend, Arnold Strode Jackson, was behind the Army Athletic Association's move to overhaul its athletics structure and adopt professional coaching methods. Nelson's job, as the new Army Head Athletic Coach, was to develop, through courses, a corps of qualified training personnel, and to supervise their activities at unit level. This, combined with new training facilities at Aldershot, was seen as the way to increased British military representation at 1924 Olympics.[36]

---

[33] Arnold Strode Jackson (1891-72) was, like his friend PNB, a private entrant to the 1912 Olympics, having failed to gain official selection. Both men competed in the 1500 metres at Stockholm, and Strode Jackson remains the youngest ever winner of the event (at age 21). His concern over the growth of USA athletic strength may have been influenced by his experience in this race, in which seven of the competitors were from the US and three deliberately ran abreast in an attempt to obstruct other runners. He later cooperated with PNB in both founding the Achilles club and developing facilities at Queens Club for former Oxbridge athletes.

[34] A. Strode-Jackson, 'The Olympic Games', *The Times*, September 29, 1919, 4.

[35] Strode Jackson's own preparation for winning gold at the 1912 Games hardly conformed to the more 'systematic approaches he was later to advocate: according to Wikipedia, he cut short his holiday in Norway to compete and his training thus consisted of 'massage, golf and walking'.

[36] 'Important Army appointment', *Observer*, May 14, 1922, 20.

Nelson as a coach

Reasoned assessment indicates that Alec Nelson was an outstanding coach of his time. This is indicated by the relative performance of his athletes and teams. The dominance that CUAC established in competitions against its Varsity rival, Oxford, was apparent from the start: 1908-14 was 'predominantly a Cambridge era.'[37] Throughout his almost 25 years as CUAC coach, he won three out of every four of the contests against Oxford, and 14 out of 18 between 1921-37.[38] Starting from a balance of wins in 1908 slightly favouring Oxford, by 1937 Cambridge led 36-27. This superior performance was recorded in the face of Oxford's advantage from having Rhodes Scholarships, which enabled it to recruit the best athletes from overseas, while Cambridge relied upon developing the talents of young men from public schools.[39]

Cambridge's 8-3 victory over Oxford in 1931, in front of 9,000 spectators at Stamford Bridge, was its sixth in succession. Harold Abrahams, in *The Times*, observed that 'Cambridge not only won eight events, they also had seven second and seven third places'.[40] Victories over Oxford became so routine – and emphatic[41] - that Noel-Baker, after narrow defeat in 1933 to an Oxford team strongly bolstered by overseas talent, consoled Nelson by saying 'You can't win every year, Alec!'[42]

---

[37] Achilles Club history (www.x.achilles.org)

[38] The results presented relate to the years up to 1937, after which the scoring system was radically changed in favour of an experimental points system. The proportion of wins was similar in the annual Varsity Relays Competition, inaugurated in 1920: his CUAC team was successful in 11 of the 14 events for which results were available to this research (i.e. up to 1935).

[39] Referring to March 1914, R.S. Woods wrote in his autobiography 'Five of us won the Sports for Cambridge against an Oxford team in which 9 of their 10 first strings were Rhodes Scholars – hand-picked athletes from all over the world – and the tenth no less a person than A.N.S. Jackson, who had already won the Olympic 1500m for Britain in Stockholm in 1912.' R. S. Woods, *Cambridge Doctor* (London: Trinity Press, 1962). See also, discussion of this issue in 1927: 'Oxford's Lost Laurels', *Observer*, April 3, 1927, 29.

[40] NBKR papers 6/2, sports cuttings (n.d.)

[41] The margin of victory was also 8-3 in 1926, 1928 and 1936; it was 9-1 in 1922 and 9-2 in 1927.

[42] PNB to AN, 3 March 1933, NBKR papers 6/54. Oxford followed up this rare victory with another the following year. Again, Baker was philosophical in corresponding with Nelson: 'The truth is that we had too many people with Olympic experience against us' (PNB to AN, 16 March 1934, NBKR papers 6/54). Oxford's team included triple winner C.F. Stanwood and N. Hallowell (both from the USA) and New Zealand distance runner J.E Lovelock.

Nelson coached many prominent athletes - Noel-Baker, Harold Abrahams, Douglas Lowe, Henry Stallard, Lord Burghley, Guy Butler, and Robert Tisdall - leading R.S. Woods to argue that: 'During the reign of Alec Nelson... the CUAC almost certainly gained more Olympic medals than any other club in the world, besides contributing a high proportion of the members of successful British Olympics, British Empire and English International teams'.[43]

Another indication of Nelson's standing is found in the reaction to Austrian Franz Stampfl's appointment as southern region AAA coach in 1938. Stampfl, an international athlete, was considered fully able to lecture and demonstrate – practically and theoretically – track and field events. Senior figures of the National Fitness Council, main funders of the appointment, voiced concern that the position should go to someone from overseas. Neil Carter notes that AAA secretary E.J. Holt 'doubted if any Englishman was up to the same standard as Stampfl... the only possible candidate was the Cambridge University coach Alec Nelson, who was then seventy'.[44]

An article in *The Observer* put Cambridge's dominance over Oxford, Rhodes scholars and all, down to the teaching 'British Public School boys' received at Fenners from 'that doyen of English athletic coaches, Alec Nelson'. It deduced that there was no shortage of English talent; the important thing was to move beyond the limit of a individual's natural capacity for improvement through proper coaching: 'the well-taught athlete is continually learning something new and does not mind the time or exertion involved in building up his physique to stand the strain of intensive training and competition.'[45] Nelson's value as a coach derived principally from his ability to identify and then develop an individual's motivation and talent through all stages to his competitive performance. This approach is apparent from his book, *Practical Athletics*,[46] and from his letters to Noel-Baker reporting on promising freshmen, their progress, and preparation of the team

---

[43] Woods, *Cambridge Doctor*. Woods listed others that might be added to this list: H.M. Macintosh, J. Ainsworth-Davis, G.C. Weightman-Smith, J. Rinkel and A.G.K. Brown. It is possible that, over time, aspiring school athletes were attracted to study at Cambridge, as awareness developed of the coaching support provided to them at Fenner's. This may have contributed to a better pool of English talent being available to CUAC.

[44] Neil Carter, 'From Knox to Dyson: Coaching, Amateurism and British Athletics, 1912-47', *Sport in History,* 30 No.1 (2010): 55-81.

[45] 'Oxford's Lost Laurels', *Observer*, April 3, 1927, 29.

[46] London: C Arthur Pearson Ltd, 1924

and individuals for events.[47] In common with most published work on training prior to the era of scientific testing, the ideas in Nelson's book are based on his intuition and personal observations. Their credibility depended upon the competitive performance of his athletes.[48]

Nelson devoted great attention to detail, leaving nothing to chance. A development programme was devised specifically for each individual athlete, with staged preparation to reach peak condition on race day. Thus, in late January 1935, he was 'giving them long, slow steady work and holding them back for speed, as the Sports are much later this time'.[49] He carefully observed each athlete, and experimented, before selecting their best event; then worked on developing their strengths and eradicating weaknesses, both the physical and psychological aspects – including strategies for dealing with those with a tendency to 'get the wind up', and for achieving the electric finish for which he was renowned as an athlete.[50] There is evidence of strong motivational skills, both individually and collectively: his teams were noted for their *esprit de corp*.[51] He looked to achieve balance within the team, exploit opportunities for teamwork, and adopt effective race tactics - all informed by intelligence carefully gathered on the opposing team -

[47] Noel-Baker showed continuing interest in activities at Fenner's. Typical of Nelson's reports was one sent on 27 November 1934 (NBKR papers 6/54): 'I strode my Half Milers over 600 yards today, without gutting them in 1.16. I sent my milers over 1,200 yds doing 2min 50 1/5. Mr Stothard beat my find Mr Gunn by 12 yds, Emery another 6 yds back – very satisfactory. My four sprinters are top hole, doing 39½ for the 4x100. My 4 quarter-milers are showing 50 to 51 sec – Good. My hurdlers are pretty feeble.'
[48] Another measure of a coach's effectiveness is the period over which their ideas continue to have currency. Nelson was not the only practitioner to stress the role of 'long, strong walks' in building up the body and stamina – Alf Shrubb and James Sullivan, among others, argued something similar – but he is the one whose training programmes for long distance running (notably a 16-week one for the marathon) are still recognised today. See Tim Noakes, 'Step 5: Learn the 15 Laws of Training', www.coachr.org/learn_the_15_laws_of_training. Indeed, 'The Nelson Programme' is a generic term used to denote training based on a mixture of walking and running. I discovered this, coincidentally, when meeting distant family relatives, Heather and Tracy Stone, who use the Nelson programme in their women's gym in Simcoe, Ontario.
[49] AN to PNB January 25, 1935, NBKR papers 6/54
[50] DGA Lowe, in the 1924 Varsity mile race, produced 'that electrifying burst of speed for which Cambridge men have become so justly famous, since Alec Nelson took them in hand'. 'Oxford and Cambridge Tie, The King Present', *Observer*, March 23, 1924.
[51] Woods, *Cambridge Doctor*.

their form, tactics etc. - and invariably set down in matrix form. Coaching also required management skills, and Nelson developed effective methods for organising the coaching of a diverse range of events, while also ensuring he could attend to more strategic considerations. He instituted systematic delegation of tasks within CUAC. He was especially interested in the running events, and, particularly as the range of events widened, 'it became the tradition for outstanding Blues to hold regular classes in their own events, giving him more time to keep an eye on the Club as a whole and, especially, fire the imagination and ambition of the freshmen'.[52]

While he coached many athletes whose outlook was mature and motivation unquestionable, often he worked with individuals who were somewhat less focused. Patience, courtesy and tact were plainly at a premium in dealing with privileged undergraduate athletes.[53] A remarkable letter detailed the challenges he faced in preparing his 'overconfident' team for the 1935 Sports.[54] He describes how the CUAC Committee chose to prepare in Brighton (against his own preference for the more mundane Hunstanton); how student athletes with their own cars chose to train at different places (apart from those who did not train at all – either because of a 'stomach upset' or through having forgotten training pumps – though both had 'dates' in the evening and returned late, 'with me on the doorstep'); and how the shot-putter had packed a shot of incorrect weight, etc. On top of that, his 1st string long jumper only informed him at the last minute that he was not fit to jump (after pulling a muscle through not preparing properly); and arrangements still had to be made for the team's heavy luggage to be transported from rail station to the hotel (to conserve the athletes' energy and avoid strains).[55]

---

[52] Ibid.

[53] Consistent with the formalities of the day, he always referred to his undergraduate athletes by surname with the prefix 'Mr'.

[54] In his words: 'what a horrible nerve racking (sic) job a Coach is in England', AN to PNB April 3, 1935, NBKR papers 6/54.

[55] AN concluded: 'Coach Alec has to do a lot of silly kidding to get an English Varsity team to do what is right and good for them. Don't please think that I am slating the whole team. The majority was as good as gold... but I know you will understand what little things mean in youth and buoyed up energy. Fancy after 25 years I should have allowed all this... Leave off Alec. Yours ever, Love Alec'. AN to PNB, April 3, 1935, NBKR papers 6/54.

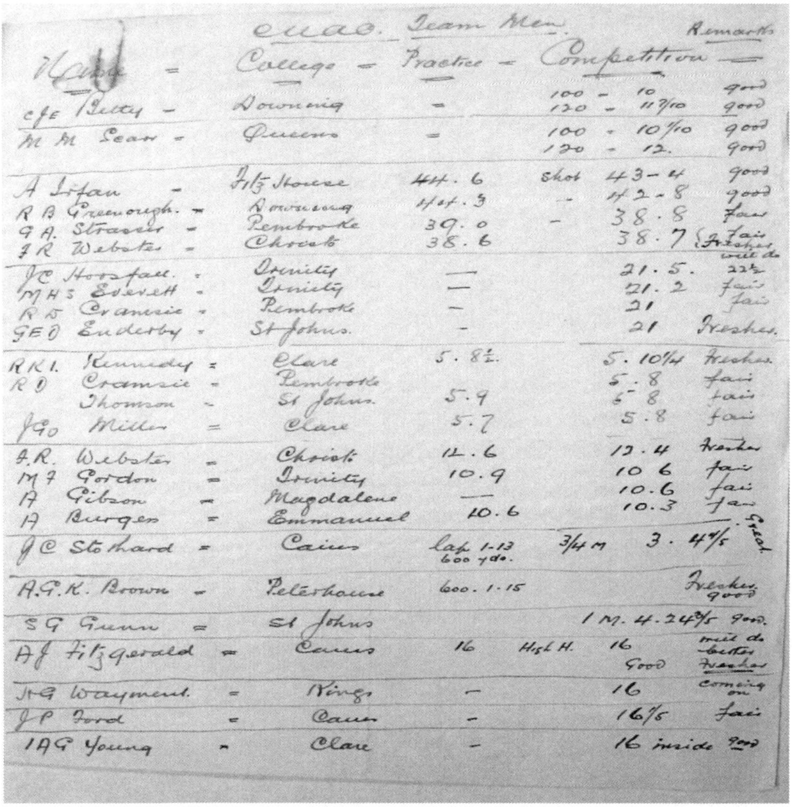

C.U.A.C. Team Men.

Name	College	Practice		Competition	Remarks
C F E Petty	Downing	=	100 –	10	good
			120 –	11 7/10	good
M M Sear	Queens	=	100 –	10 1/10	good
			120 –	12.	good
A Lifan	Fitz House	44.6	Shot	43–4	good
R B Greenough	Downing	44.3	–	42–8	good
G A Strasser	Pembroke	39.0	–	38.8	fair
J R Webster	Christs	38.6		38.7	fair Fresher
J C Horsfall	Trinity	—		21.5.	will do 22½
M H S Everett	Trinity	—		21.2	fair
R D Cramsie	Pembroke	—		21	fair
G E D Enderby	St Johns.	–		21	Fresher.
R K I Kennedy	Clare	5.8½.		5.10¼	Fresher
R D Cramsie	Pembroke			5.8	fair
Thomson	St Johns.	5.9		5 8	fair
J G O Miller	Clare	5.7		5.8	fair
J R Webster	Christs	12.6		12.4	Fresher
M F Gordon	Trinity	10.9		10 6	fair
A Gibson	Magdalene	—		10.6	fair
A Burgess	Emmanuel	10.6		10.3	fair
J C Stothard	Caius	lap 1-13 600 yds.	3/4 M	3. 4 4/5	Great.
A G K Brown	Peterhouse	600. 1-15			Fresher good
S G Gunn	St Johns			1 M. 4.24 4/5	good.
A J Fitzgerald	Caius	16	High H.	16 Good	will do better Fresher
J G Wayment	Kings	–		16	coming on
J P Ford	Caius	–		16 1/5	fair
I A G Young	Clare	–		16 inside	good

Figure 6. Letter from Nelson to Noel-Baker, 4 March 1935; detailed assessment of CUAC team's progress (courtesy of Noel-Baker papers, Churchill College Archives, Cambridge)

Though from a pronouncedly different background to that of his student athletes, Alec Nelson successfully bridged the class divide and was very popular with the undergraduates (whom he fondly called 'my Blues'), often keeping in touch with them (and their training) in off-season.[56] His famous sense of humour helped him form a bond with the young men. Denys Williamson recalled the high jump advice Nelson had given him in 1939: 'Mr Williamson, throw your leg over the bar... and follow it as soon as possible'.[57]

---

[56] Woods, *Cambridge Doctor.* Guy Butler, Cambridge and Olympic athlete, illustrates this sentiment in a comment he made to PNB in 1920, 'I'm glad you have got Alec involved with the Queens track. He is such a treasure.'
[57] Incident recalled in Nelson's Obituary: 'Death of Alec Nelson', *The Times*, January 12, 1944, 6.

Patron-client relationship

It was suggested above that the patron-client model helps explain the relationship between the two men and, indeed, Nelson's career as a professional coach. [58] Much about that relationship is revealed in correspondence between them. Theirs was a close and enduring relationship, with a high degree of mutual trust and responsibility toward the other.[59] Over a period of 30 years, Noel-Baker acted as mentor, adviser and 'fixer' for Nelson, who reciprocated with great loyalty and respect. The nature of the relationship partly derived from Noel-Baker's innate decency and distinct family background that gave him an ability to relate to people of a different class; but it was undoubtedly strengthened by benefits each gained from their association. Noel-Baker - the person, according to R.S. Woods, who 'discovered him' - recognised that Nelson's skills, energy and inventiveness made him a most valuable asset, and it was this realisation that was central to a most fruitful sporting partnership[60].

Nelson's letters contain a mix of the loyal retainer's care for a patron's welfare and the concern that would be shown by a true friend. He often expressed his hopes that Noel-Baker's talents on the international stage would be better recognised. He was well aware of his patron's tendency to take on too much: 'I am deeply sorry to hear that you have been ill', he wrote in early 1935. 'I am afraid you work too hard and get terribly run down. Go steady now and thoroughly build yourself up.'[61] On another occasion, he expressed his caring sentiments more bluntly: 'I am informed that Mrs Baker is looking remarkably

---

[58] The Patron-Client model had particular currency among anthropologists, sociologists and social geographers in the 1970s and 80s, especially in relation to peasant societies, or socially/economically dualistic contexts. See for example, L. Graziano, 'Patron-client relationships in southern Italy', *European Journal of Political Research*, 1:1 (1974): 3-34. Originating in Roman times, where it was typically formally structured, the concept refers to a mutually obligatory arrangement between an individual (the patron) possessing authority, status and resources and another individual (the client) who benefits from the former's support and influence. The concept is flexible, but typically the patron is the client's guardian and protector both in his private and public interest. Commonly, both parties regard the link between them as a personal attachment, similar to the bond of affection holding members of a family or kin group together.

[59] The level of trust is shown in PNB sending, in November 1934, a blank cheque for Nelson to complete in payment of expenditures for seat tickets at White City and running shoes for his son; AN insisted upon 'holding your cheque until I see you'. AN to PNB November 27, 1934, NBKR papers 6/15.

[60] Woods, *Cambridge Doctor*.

[61] AN to PNB December 3, 1933, NBKR papers 6/14/4

well, which is a great pleasure. On the other hand, I learn that you are looking very seedy. May I suggest one good cure, 24 hours fasting together with 24 hours in bed.'[62] Nelson also regularly undertook various tasks on behalf of Baker - keeping him informed about athletics at Cambridge, procuring tickets for varsity events and ordering items of running equipment for 'Master Francis' Baker.

Noel-Baker's support for his client was genuine, consistent and wide-ranging in nature. In putting together an income package to enable Alec Nelson to return as CUAC coach in 1919, he paid Winnie, Nelson's daughter, for typing his letters (even helping her to acquire a typewriter). Mrs Nelson, who fabricated silk shorts for the CUAC team, also received similar commissions from Baker himself. Noel-Baker sent a regular Christmas cheque to Nelson, used his contacts to arrange for him to do a BBC wireless broadcast in 1933 - for which Alec received a fee - and acted similarly with respect to a series of newspaper articles in the *News Chronicle*. He also initiated, and was heavily involved in, Nelson's Benefit Appeal.[63]

Through Noel-Baker, his patron's network, and contacts with the sporting offspring of elite families, Nelson indeed had friends in high places. One, Strode Jackson, probably played a role in his being offered the army coaching position. Another came to his aid in 1937, when he appeared at Cambridge Court on a drink driving charge.[64] The police surgeon testified that Nelson's breath suggested he had been drinking, and that he was argumentative, garrulous and 'at one time had wanted to fight me while being examined'. The defence contended his condition and behaviour were explained by his having tripped and fallen when getting out of his car. Vital supporting evidence came from witness, Dr R. Salisbury Woods, a respected local GP who had subsequently examined the accused. He noticed no smell

---

[62] AN to PNB, January 25, 1935, NBKR papers 6/54

[63] For example Nelson wrote to PNB on February 28, 1935 (NBKR papers 6/54): 'I thank you for speaking kindly about me in the News Chronicle and you know I will never let you down'. One other area in which PNB may have used his influence to support Nelson was with regard to his son, Stanley. No letters have been found that relate to this period, but it is intriguing that the son of a University servant had the opportunity, first, to attend Perse School, a public school in Cambridge, and, second, to study for a degree at Cambridge (in engineering). Stanley, incidentally, became a Cambridge Blue (vs Oxford, 1924; see CUAC official photograph for that year), and went on to become a professional engineer.

[64] *Manchester Guardian*, March 31, 1937.

of alcohol, and 'found it extraordinarily difficult to determine whether Nelson's dazed condition was due to slight concussion through his fall, or by reason of having had too much to drink'. The case was dismissed. Reports of the proceedings do not mention the fact that the witness was the same 'Dr R.S. Woods' who was Hon Treasurer of CUAC and indeed recent organiser of the Nelson Appeal.[65]

The term 'entrepreneur-client' was used above to indicate that Alec Nelson did not passively await engagements facilitated by his patron. He was active in using his network to help boost his income. 'Mr Philip' was very much at the heart of that network: 'You have been such a tower of help to me always and you have always been a great Organiser that perhaps you would tell me how to bring my experience to fruition'.[66] The *News Chronicle* articles of athletics were, in fact, Alec Nelson's own idea. Others business ideas included: a Correspondence School of Athletics; authorship – not only *Practical Athletics*, but a further book, in the early 1930s, of his experiences and those of the various athletes with whom he had worked;[67] supporting Oxford & Cambridge Achilles athletes on their visits to public schools ('providing ocular demonstrations, answering questions, etc'); and lecture programmes for the armed forces and public schools on athletic technique, psychology and coaching.

He also had ideas for the development of athletics in *all* schools, not just public schools.[68] He was confident enough to use contacts his

---

[65] The case was dismissed, but Nelson had nonetheless already been chastised by his (presumably teetotal) mentor: 'I remember very well giving you a lecture more than 20 years ago about the dangers of a trainer's life... You are getting some of your biggest triumphs now, ...you must be very careful to do nothing to spoil your position' (PNB to AN, June 22, 1935 NBKR papers 6/54). Nelson tried to defend himself by saying that 'even great men have kinks, even Oscar Wilde' and suggested the occasional transgression should be forgiven. However, he was quick to say that Baker was 'the last person in the world I should want to upset' (AN to PNB, July 3, 1935 NBKR papers 6/54). In his typical humorous manner, he added that, since he was away in Hampshire on an army engagement, 'Mrs Nelson opens all my letters and sends them on to me and I got a good lecture from her'.

[66] AN to PNB (n.d. August? 1935), NBKR papers 6/54.

[67] Only one section of the book has been located – a hand-written piece sent to Noel-Baker for comment, and contained within the NBKR papers (6/15). PNB's views are not known, but no published book appears to have resulted, and the quality of the excerpt suggests that, unlike *Practical Athletics*, the extent of its appeal to the market might have been limited.

[68] 'I really think I could help every games master in every school.' (AN to PNB (n.d. August?) 1935 NBKR papers 6/54.

coaching role gave him within the Establishment.[69] On hearing about a Prince of Wales Fund for an A1 Nation, he sketched some ideas for certificated coaching courses specifically targeted upon schools, which he asked one of his CUAC athletes to give to his father, a member of one of the relevant committees. His letter was subsequently forwarded, via Herbert Morrison, to Lord Astor[70] 'There are hundreds of school masters', he later explained to Noel-Baker, 'who sadly want such teaching. I find the same in the Services Clubs and other places where boys have recreative games'.[71]

In a similar vein, he set out ideas for developing a system of 'measurable athletics standards' to guide improvement within schools – an attempt at 'benchmarking' that has a decidedly modern ring. His ideas for extending athletic and fitness development activities beyond the realm of the public schools – albeit still confined to boys and young men - represented an ambition to involve a broader cross-section of the community. While the scope of this particular initiative was perhaps somewhat beyond Noel-Baker's agendas, for the most part, Alec Nelson's entrepreneurial instincts ensured that his schemes would find favour with his patron.

Never enough 'engagements'

In spite of his resourcefulness, and generous help from his mentor, and others, Alec Nelson was always short of the number of engagements that would yield an income sufficient for a comfortable lifestyle. In 1920s Cambridge, his CUAC fee was £5 per week, plus end of term tips from individual athletes (later converted to a pool). He supplemented his Cambridge earnings by fees from other coaching, plus payments for helping individual Achilles members, fees for lectures, newspaper articles, book royalties, etc. For all his successes as a self-employed portfolio worker, the problem of intermittent work,

---

[69] Alec Nelson certainly encountered members of the social elite. At the Sports, he reported to his mentor on March 14, 1934 (NBKR papers 6/14): 'Lord Burghley ran up to me and we had a little chat about the meeting, followed by Mr Baldwin. Lord Desborough also came and spoke to me.' He wrote to both Lord Aberdare and Lord Astor in connection with his ideas for the 'A1 Nation', the concept of which much appealed to him.

[70] AN to PNB, October 3, 1935 NBKR papers 6/15. In response, Baker tried to restrain Nelson's enthusiasm, on the grounds that the Central Council of Recreative Physical Training was only just beginning its work. 'I am sure to meet Lord Astor casually somewhere, and I therefore think it is better not to write to him specially about it, but to wait until I can first have a talk' (PNB to AN October 4, 1935)

[71] AN to PNB June 17, 1937 NBKR papers 6/14

and thus uncertainty of income, was ever-present. He described his predicament to Noel-Baker in the mid-1930s: 'I cannot claim out of work dole, although engagements are scarce from March to October each year; I've no employment card, nor any health insurance, and no old age pension';[72] 'I'm forced to seek diligently for jobs each summer and travel all over England, devoid of many comforts.'[73]

Recognising this, and in light of his loyal service over the years, his supportive network rallied present and former athletes in a benefit appeal, launched in 1934. Indeed, the notice that appeared in the *Times*, and was posted out to current and former members of CUAC and Achilles, was signed by the big names in athletics.[74] While it was Noel-Baker's idea, the Appeal was organised by Dr Rex Salisbury Woods, CUAC Hon. Treasurer, who, with 'Mrs Rex', addressed 2000-odd envelopes. Total donations, including receipts from the 1934 Relay races, raised £462 16s 1d – worth roughly £75,000 today.[75]

The purpose was to provide Alec Nelson with a house. The family had always lived in rented property: in Cambridge, the basement of 4 All Saints Passage, next to the Hawks Club and Mrs McKenzie's Goldfish Café. Much was made in the Appeal of Mrs Nelson's failing health and her need to live in a more comfortable home without stairs.[76] Providing the Nelsons with a home of their own was not straightforward, since the sum raised fell some way short of prevailing house prices. 'I've £400 to make up over house and land' wrote

---

[73] AN to PNB, October 2, 1933 NBKR papers 6/14

[73] AN to PNB July 3, 1935 NBKR papers 6/54

[74] 'The Alec Nelson Appeal', *The Times*, October 24, 1934, 5. Through PNB's press contacts, such as Guy Butler, it appeared in a number of dailies, including the *Morning Post* and *News Chronicle*. Signatories were: A.E.D. Anderson, J. Noel Baker, R. Salisbury Woods, Guy M. Butler, W.R. Seagrove, Harold M. Abrahams, Henry B. Stallard, Wilfred G. Tatham, D.G.A. Lowe, Burghley, J.W.J Rinkel, M.H.C. Gutteridge, and CUAC President E.I. Davis.

[75] PNB personally sent a cheque to Rex Woods for the Appeal: Five guineas from him, four guineas from his wife and one guinea from well-known Cambridge economist, Professor A.C. Pigou. PNB's former teacher (PNB to Rex Woods July 24, 1936, NBKR papers 6/14). Today's equivalent sum is based upon wage inflation indices; the amount was considerably less in terms of retail inflation – below £25,000.

[76] This was probably an exaggeration for the sake of marketing, since, in the event, Elizabeth outlived her husband by seven years, and even then did not succumb to the her heart ailment, but to complications of influenza.

Nelson, 'So Mr Philip, anything you can do to helping in A Fit Nation, or any engagement, I shall appreciate ever so much.'[77]

He eventually had constructed a simple bungalow in Barton village, three miles from Cambridge.[78] The proud owner of the 'really dinky house' delighted in inviting people to visit, but its cost, and distance from Fenners, worried him. 'I should be able to carry on at CUAC', he wrote to his mentor, but if 'illness or anything happen, I dread to think of the larder. Perhaps CUAC would still help for any unlooked for eventuality.' In 1940, with 'every Commodity going up, up, up', he contemplated renting out the house, going back to All Saints Passage, to derive income from the net difference in rents.[79]

Conclusion

Alec Nelson was an outstanding coach of his time. He learned his trade by drawing from his own experience as an athlete, combined with years of observation, experimentation, and identification of 'what worked'. His personal attributes - creativity, enthusiasm, humour, patience, etc. - were vital to his success, as was his instinct for engaging young people whose life experience and social background invariably differed from his own. His talents vitally underpinned the inter-war mission of a small elite group to develop Britain's capacity in athletics via professionalising coaching, widening the base of participation in the sport, developing its infrastructure and increasing competitive opportunities. With the help of a circle of friends and associates, a unique individual, Philip Noel-Baker, ensured Nelson gained full public recognition for his contribution. However, this support could not overcome the perennial problem of restricted opportunities for professional coaches in an inter-war Britain where amateur values and organisational forms still prevailed. The talents of this gifted, hard-working and innovative individual were thus consistently both under-exploited and under-rewarded.

---

[77] AN to PNB, March 22, 1937, NBKR 6/14
[78] Named 'Leobeth', based on their given names.
[79] The address used on letters in 1939-40 suggests that he indeed did rent out the house, on a short-term basis.

8

Joey Nuttall: The 'Lightening Merman' of Stalybridge

Keith Myerscough

Introduction

It was against a background of great social and economic upheaval that Joey Nuttall found a means of earning a living outside his family home in the Lancashire mill-town of Stalybridge. As industrial migrants, the Nuttall family had moved some six miles (10km) from Hulme, in Manchester to Stalybridge in 1870. At this time Joey was only a year old but the new public baths was to provide the family with a means for 'rational recreation' and an opportunity to bathe their bodies and wash their cloths in purpose-built facilities.[1] Joey and his siblings were to grow up in an environment where the baths became a central focus of their early lives. Having outgrown the 'novelty' of swimming in the local Huddersfield Narrow Canal and washing in the River Tame, the Nuttall family were to make full use of the local 'penny scrub'. By 1884, at the age of fourteen, Joey was earning a living as a coal hawker during the day and entering swimming events in his leisure time; his destiny to be determined through his exploits as a 'speed' swimmer.

Throughout the 1870s the Stalybridge Baths Committee controlled all aspects of the facilities provision, enthusiastically promoting swimming as a means of generating extra income. The baths not only encouraged the take-up of recreational swimming by the local community in large numbers but also served to promote the use of the baths as a very profitable venue for swimming galas. In the first week of the baths operation over two thousand visits had been made, with the *Ashton Reporter* suggesting that, 'With the cleanliness, privacy, and completeness of the arrangements of the new baths we are in strong hopes that during the summer months our canals will be denuded of bathers, even of the poorer classes.'[2]

---

[1] Bishop Bloomfield spoke of the bath-house as a form of 'social salvation' in the House of Lords (1846), quoted in Peter Bailey, 'Leisure and Class in Victorian England: Rational Recreation and the Contest for Control, 1830-1885', (London: Methuen & Co. Ltd., 1987), 63.

[2] *Ashton Reporter*, 'Opening of the New Baths at Stalybridge', May 14, 1870, 4.

The growth of the swimming gala as a form of recreational entertainment was dependent upon the rate at which local councils adopted the principle of providing public bathing facilities. The *Baths and Washhouses Acts of 1846 and 1847* had helped to establish the principle of promoting public hygiene and the ideological pursuit of physical culture as a responsibility for local authority governance. The reluctance of local council's to make provision for swimming was based upon a Victorian doctrine that celebrated fiscal prudence whilst promoting the notion of self-improvement. It was left to the local entrepreneur to make provision for indoor bathing facilities based upon growing public proclamations of its benefits to the development of both body and soul. It was not until the 1870s that local authorities within the industrial heartland of Britain reluctantly began to provide publicly owned baths and wash-houses for their communities. This provision was haphazard throughout the rest of the nineteenth-century and was initially dependent upon local businessmen with a philanthropic predilection towards their local communities.[3]

The need for sound fiscal management of swimming baths had driven the sport into the hands of the new leisure entrepreneur in the late-Victorian period. Joey Nuttall benefited from the status of swimming in the 1880s and 1890s when he became the focal point for the split of the Professional Swimming Association (PSA) from the Amateur Swimming Association (ASA). Nuttall was seen by the new leisure elite as a participant who represented the worst excesses of the professionalization of swimming.[4] The draw of large crowds to witness swimming challenges and the large sums of money being gambled on the outcome attracted the attention of the 'wrong sort' as far as the swimming authorities were concerned. The entertainment value of swimming exhibitions of scientific natation was considerable and drew large audiences. By the 1880s many 'champion swimmers' viewed the swimming gala circuit as a logical career move in becoming a professional natationist. It was the domain of the swimming instructor or 'professor', and quite often their families, as it provided them with a means of earning a good living to supplement their teaching. The promotion of aquatic exhibitions not only became an integral component in the staging of swimming galas but it also enabled its practitioners to earn a more reliable living on the 'bread

---

[3] Christopher Love, 'A Social History of Swimming in England, 1800-1918, Splashing in the Serpentine', (London: Routledge, 2008), 53
[4] Claire Parker, 'The Rise of Competitive Swimming 1840 to 1878', *Sport in History*, 21 No.2 (2001): 54-67.

and butter' variety theatre circuit. [5] From the 1890s to 1914 an exhibition of natation often appeared on the schedule at many of the variety theatres throughout the UK.[6] Indeed, many of the theatres that were built during the late-Victorian and Edwardian periods had a water tank constructed under the stage.[7]

Amateur Champion, 1881-1888

Nuttall's home-base at Stalybridge Public Baths served him well in his formative years; it was not through expert tuition that he honed his skills but rather through regular competition at local swimming galas throughout the region. As his fame spread he was invited to swim both in 'open-' and 'still-water' races throughout the UK. Joey's exploits as an amateur swimmer began in 1881when he became 'boy champion' at the age of twelve and concludes at Lambeth Baths, London by winning the 220 yards Championship of the World for the second time in 1888. His dominance of swimming was such that:

> He has met and defeated every Amateur of the day, and travelled over 6000 miles, competing for Championship Honours winning 18 Championship Races in succession out of 20, and over 150 prizes, including 25 guinea and 15 guinea Cups, 25 guinea Watch, 20 guinea Diamond Medal, 15 guinea Silver Fruit Vase, 10 guinea Medal, and holder of [*the Ulph Challenge Trophy*] 100 guinea Cup.[8]

On October 06, 1886 Joey had claimed his first world title at the age of seventeen when he became the 500 yards Champion of the World at Lambeth Baths in London. In 1887 Joey was the amateur world champion at five distances: the mile (in open water), half-mile, 500yds, 220yds and 100yds. From 1886-1888 Joey had won the 500yds amateur world championship for three consecutive years; he had won the Ulph Cup in two consecutive years, 1887 and 1888; he was the 100yds amateur world champion for three consecutive years, 1886-1888; and he was the 220yds amateur world champion for two consecutive years, 1887 and 1888. [9]

---

[5] William Broadhead owned sixteen variety halls often referred to as the 'Broadhead Circuit' where he provided aquatic acts. He also owned and ran the Prince of Wales Baths, Blackpool.

[6] The Bristol Hippodrome (1912) had two tanks holding 100,000 gallons.

[7] There is still a water tank under the circus stage at Blackpool Tower, built in 1894.

[8] A Sidebottom, 'Joey Nuttall', 1888. See also, Coggan's Tailoring, 'Records and Championships of Joey Nuttall, Champion Swimmer of the World', 1890.

[9] Coggan's Tailoring, 1890.

Alas, Nuttall was not without his detractors for when he was defeated in the mile and half-mile open water championship races at Welsh Harp, Hendon in July, 1888 some of the press reports were very critical of his efforts. It was suggested that this was the end of Nuttall's dominance of the swimming scene in Britain, some newspapers were questioning his preparation for both events and that he now considered himself unbeatable. The *Stalybridge Reporter* came to his defence by offering an insight into his life-style as a prominent amateur swimmer:

> ... tobacco and alcohol were avoided, early to bed and early to rise was the rule, and good long walks, with plenty of swimming, were indulged in every day. This, with good food, carefully prepared by his mater, brought him in good enough condition ...[10]

The most bizarre event in the history of the ASA and of Nuttall's amateur career was to occur at the 220 Yards Amateur Championship race at Lambeth Baths on Monday, October 08, 1888. Nuttall had won the event the previous year but due to the entrenched stance being taken by the ASA on the eligibility of competitor's and the value of the prizes awarded, the top amateur swimmers in the country had taken a collective decision not to race. Many newspapers reported the race entries to be the 'worst ever received' and that the actions of the Association had raised the issue of reform.[11] It would appear that many of the country's elite swimmers had long considered the actions of the ASA to be an 'interference with the rights and privileges of swimmers'.[12] The threat was that undisclosed parties would set up their own rival amateur swimming association which would result in 'a rapid transformation of amateurs into professionals'.[13] The swimmers and their financial backers wanted a definition of an amateur that would permit:

> The two sections [*amateur and professional*] ... to test their relative merits for prizes other than money. But now an amateur must not swim an exhibition race with a professional swimmer, but the same amateur is allowed to compete in many other branches

---

[10] *Stalybridge Reporter*, 'Joey Nuttall's Defeat, To the Editor of the Reporter', August 4, 1888, 5.

[11] *Stalybridge Reporter*, 'The 220 Yards Swimming Championship', October 13, 1888, 5.

[12] Ibid, October 13, 1888.

[13] Ibid.

of sport with professionals at meetings where filthy lucre is charged for admission. And yet a professional at one sport is a professional at all.[14]

Comment was made in the local and national sporting newspapers that 'the 220yds championship of 1888 is not likely to be forgotten by swimmers for some time to come, as it has led to several protests, objections, &c.' Commentary on the situation by Jim Hardman of the *Stalybridge Reporter*, who wrote under the pseudonym 'Cork Belt' added to the speculation that Nuttall was being led in his actions by others behind the scenes with a vested interest in competitive swimmers being financially recompensed for their efforts. A witness to the events at Lambeth Baths was Mr Edmund J. Wakeling who was president of the Pacific Swimming Club, and commented thus:

> The 220 yards championship has evidently been boycotted, and the question is for what reason and by whom. Is it Nuttall? Oh, no. Nuttall swims although it is only a medal. I excuse Nuttall for not sending in his entry, because I do not believe he knows anything at all about what he is doing, but is being advised by one of our biggest 'pot hunters'. What man with any sense would advise the association to give a challenge cup without first knowing where the money comes from. If our big 'pot hunter' has such a great desire to see a challenge cup why does he not either give a cup or else advise someone else to do it, for he (the pot hunter) has not done so badly out of swimming?[15]

This statement provides further evidence that Nuttall was being manipulated by powerful forces that clearly had a vested interest in attracting the best swimmers to compete for prizes worthy of their efforts.

The 220 yards National Championship was to prove to be a defining moment in the relationship between the ASA and club swimmers. Many of the best swimmers in the land had excluded themselves from the 220 yards championship race because of the stance the ASA was taking on the question of professionalism in swimming. The countries top amateur swimmers viewed the stance taken by the ASA in defining the term 'amateur' as being unfair to those dedicated club swimmers who simply wished to compete in exhibition races against professional swimmers. The position adopted by the ASA was seen to

---

14 Ibid.
15 *Stalybridge Reporter*, 'Swimming Notes', October 13, 1888, 5.

'severely strain' the definition of the term 'amateur'. The consensus of opinion amongst the club swimmers was that the amateur and professional swimmer should be 'permitted to test their relative merits for prizes other than money.'[16] The inconsistency of approach appears to be the main concern rather than issues of professionalism.

The events of that night were described as being 'more a burlesque than a reality.'[17] One of the four entrants, Walter Brickett declined to start the race and formally 'lodged a protest against the illegal resolution of the Amateur Swimming Association.'[18] This act left a field of three competitors, but unknown to them Joey Nuttall had arrived in secret with the intention of swimming should the ASA force the issue. The situation was then inflamed by Messer's Smith, Welch and Jorneaux who insisted upon being given the opportunity to challenge for the championship title. Nuttall appears to have reacted forcefully to this affront by concocting and executing a plan of action designed to cause maximum embarrassment to the ASA. It is questionable as to whether Nuttall had the wherewithal to plot and carry out the protest on his own cognisance. He was a shy and poorly educated man who could not have expressed himself in the written word as displayed in 'his' letter of protest. He disliked the attention heaped upon him because of his phenomenal swimming exploits and would certainly not have welcomed the attention his actions that night in the pool inevitably brought him.

The remaining three challengers were determined to swim so Nuttall appeared bath-side ready to race. A letter explaining his actions was given to a journalist from the *Sporting Life* at bath-side for publication:

> Sir, - I should be thankful if you will kindly do me the favour of inserting the following letter:- In consequence of the action of the A.S.A in withdrawing the challenge cup, which was put up according to rule, and giving a medal in its place, and having signed the petition, which was published in your issue of Wednesday last. I had intended not to help the association to break its own rules by not swimming for the prizes put up. But, to my surprise, I found that a few second-class men thought fit,

---

16 *Stalybridge Reporter*, 'The 220 Yards Swimming Championship', October 13, 1888, 5.

17 *Stalybridge Reporter*, 'The 220 Yards Swimming Championship, Easy Victory for Nuttall', October 13, 1888, 3.

18 *Stalybridge Reporter*, 'The 220 Yards Swimming Championship', October 13, 1888, 5.

under the circumstances, to start for the medals; hence my starting as a protest against these would-be champions. In conclusion, I fail to understand what logical objection the A.S.A can have to giving as a cup the price of three separate wins.

P.S - I, Joseph Nuttall, beg to state that I start protesting against the race being swum, as it is held contrary to Rule 70, and in consequence of not being cognisant of the rule on previous occasions, I took no action.[19]

During the race Nuttall poured further scorn on the Association by waiting at each turn for his opponents to catch up with him. He eventually won by four yards to 'a burst of laughter and ironic cheers' in the slowest time ever recorded for this championship race of 3 mins 15 and 3/5 secs.[20] Nuttall turned professional some ten days later on Thursday, October 18, 1888 at the Lambeth Baths, the very scene of his protest against the prejudice being displayed by the ASA.

Professional Champion and Aquatic Entertainer, 1888-1907

The PSA held its annual 1,000 yards Topping Challenge Cup race at Lambeth Baths ten days after the ASA had held its 220 yards amateur championship race. The main attraction was the appearance of Joey Nuttall in what was to be his inaugural race as a professional swimmer. The public's interest in the race was said to be 'widespread' as the fame of Nuttall as an amateur had not gone unnoticed within the 'sporting classes'.[21] It must have been a promoters dream, having the world amateur champion now competing against the pick of the countries professionals. The ASA had gifted the professional circuit their best swimmer and crowd-puller in their decision to ignore article 70 of their Association rules with Nuttall having 'decided to shake off the thrall of amateurism, and make his plunge into the professional ranks'.[22]

The week before the race considerable interest had been generated by various newspaper articles that speculated as to the wisdom of Nuttall's decision. The task before him was considerable as he would be swimming against 'such famous professors of the art of natation' as: James Finney (the holder of the Topping trophy), J.J. Collier (the ex-

---

[19] Ibid, October 13, 1888.

[20] Ibid.

[21] *The Stalybridge Reporter*, 'The Thousand Yards Swimming Championship, Joey Nuttall Turns Professional and Beats the Record', October 20, 1888, 8.

[22] Ibid, October 20, 1888.

champion from Salford), Charles Beckwith (son of the famous Professor Beckwith), and G. Kistler (from Penzance).[23] The race had attracted so much interest that there was standing room only at the time of the race. There were a number of well-known 'racing men' in attendance and betting was said to be brisk. The betting odds at the start of the race were: Evans-Nuttall, 2-to-1 against Finney, 4-to-1 Collier, and 10-to-1 Kistler. After the first length of the race it was clear that Nuttall would triumph as he totally dominated the race. Collier finished in second place, some 20 yards behind Nuttall who claimed a new record time of 14 mins 17 and ½ seconds.[24] Nuttall proved to be a success from the outset of his professional career both with the swimming and gambling fraternities. The dominance of Nuttall's performance and the ease with which he dispensed with the 'cream of the professionals' certainly encouraged a healthy interest in the world of professional swimming and in particular, the career of Joey Nuttall.

By 1890 Nuttall's dominance was such that despite large crowds at the PSA Championships at Lambeth Baths little interest was being shown in betting on the 1,000 yards challenge cup race. The event was one of the 'chief races of the professional season'. However, the result was considered to be a foregone conclusion such was the dominance of Nuttall.[25] Some of the best professional swimmers in Britain were to challenge for the cup, more in hope than expectation, such was the dominance of Joey at this time. Nuttall had won the event the previous two years and there was little to suggest that any one of the 'five well-known professors' (J.F. Standing, R. Foster, J.J. Collier, Reddish and J.H. Taylor), would be able to take his title away from him.[26] Indeed, odds of 20-1 were offered against his closest rivals, J.F. Standing of Manchester and R. Foster of Salford. The dominance of Nuttall could not have pleased the book-makers but at least he had the ability to attract large crowds of spectators to aquatic events in the 1890s. Nuttall won the race by 108 yards in a new record time of 13 mins and 55 secs, lapping his opponents in the process several times. His dominance was further underlined with the Topping Cup being presented to him in perpetuity as it was Nuttall's third consecutive victory.

In December, 1890 Nuttall, Standing and Taylor were appearing at the Royal London Aquarium in six nights of swimming handicap races

---

[23] Ibid.

[24] Ibid.

[25] *Daily News*, 'Sporting Intelligence, Swimming, The 1,000 Yards Professional Championship', October 17, 1890.

[26] Ibid, October 17, 1890.

with prize money of £120 on offer.[27] The entrance fee for spectators was one shilling or two shillings for a reserved seat. The aquatic entertainment was organised and paid for by the famous Beckwith Family. The father, Professor Beckwith was an ex-champion swimmer and manager to his famous daughter Agnes Beckwith. The financial rewards for professional swimmers were considerable if they toured the country appearing in swimming club galas. The professional races attracted 'professors' of swimming to challenge for either expensive gift's that could be sold on and/or for prize money. In August 1892, Nuttall appeared at the Exeter Swimming Club annual gala where he won thirty shillings for the 100 yards race and £6 for the half-mile Grand Challenge Race.[28] In total, the swimming club provided £100 in prizes for fourteen events, which included a water polo match. Whilst this gala followed a now tried and tested formula it was unusual in that the events took place not in a swimming baths but in the local canal at 'the Turf'. In the August of 1893 Nuttall took part in an International Swimming Championship contest for prize money of £500 and a championship cup. The challenge came from American swimmer, J.L. McCusker and took place at Hollingworth Lake near Rochdale in water described as being of a 'comfortable temperature' on 'open still water'.[29] Nuttall beat McCusker comfortably by over 200 yards in a time of 26 mins and 8 secs, beating the old record set by J.J. Collier in 1884 by two minutes.[30]

Nuttall's services were very much in demand by 1893 as his presence would certainly attract large paying crowds to swimming events. In September 1893 he was hired by Captain Boyton's World's Water Show at West Brompton, in order to compete in a proposed swim off with the American champion, J.L. McCusker and ex-amateur English champion S.W. Greasley of Leicester; McCusker did not enter the race and Greasley came a disappointing second by 25 yards to Nuttall.[31] Nuttall collected a gold medal to the value of twenty guineas and prize money of ten guineas.

[27] *Pall Mall Gazette*, 'Advertisements and Notices, Royal Aquarium – Six Great Nights' Swimming Handicap', December 3, 1890.

[28] *Plymouth and Cornish Advertiser*, 'Exeter Swimming Club, Annual Matches at Turf', August 13, 1892.

[29] *Glasgow Herald*, 'Special Notes on Sports', August 21, 1893.

[30] Ibid, August 21, 1893.

[31] *Plymouth and Cornish Advertiser*, 'Swimming, The Half-Mile at Boyton's, Nuttall Wins', September 2, 1893.

In 1894 Nuttall embarked upon a new phase in his swimming career by appearing in the aquatic entertainment show at the newly opened Blackpool Tower Aquatic and Variety Circus.[32] This was a seasonal commitment from April until the end of August, appearing three times a day in the aquatic show. His exhibition of speed swimming was but one part of an extensive show performed by a whole host of professional swimmers earning a living by displaying 'the art of natation'.[33] Each season for the rest of the decade brought a cast of some of the most famous swimmers in Britain to the Tower Circus. Although Nuttall appeared on the programme he was never given the title of 'professor'. This may well be because he had never earned a living as a teacher or instructor and he certainly never performed anything other than his exhibition of 'fast swimming'. He was either unwilling or unable to perform the vaudevillian feats labelled as being 'scientific exhibitions' of ornamental swimming which were so desired by audiences who simply wanted to be entertained in their newfound leisure time.

By the summer of 1897 Nuttall was establishing his international reputation by challenging the Australian professional swimmer, British émigré Ernie Cavill, to a race at Roundhay Park, Leeds. Nuttall declared that he needed two months in order to meet any 'stake suitable to the Australian.'[34] The 'Great National Swimming Race' took place on Wednesday, September 08, 1897 in order to take advantage of the sporting crowds that were in town for the St. Leger horse race.[35] Nuttall started as the favourite for the £200 prize money, with odds of 7-1 against Cavill which accurately reflected the gap in abilities between the two swimmers. Nuttall completed the 500 yards in a time of 6 mins 50 and 1/4 secs; Cavill left the water on the eleventh length of the pool as he was a full length behind Nuttall.[36] Nuttall was now considered to be invincible with many prospective opponents withdrawing from challenging him. In October 1897 he was competing at the Edinburgh Baths in Scotland as a guest at the Rosebery Swimming Club Gala in the 220 yards race; Nuttall having set the record some two years earlier at 2 mins and 37 secs. The club had organised international competition for Nuttall in the shape of three Australians, Cavill, Hellings and Lindley only for all three of them to

[32] Blackpool Tower, 'The Tower, Blackpool Programme', August 19, 1895, 3.

[33] *Era*, 'Amusements in Blackpool, Tower Circus', June 8, 1895.

[34] *Plymouth and Cornish Advertiser*, 'Swimming Notes', July 6, 1897.

[35] *Liverpool Mercury*, 'Swimming and Water Polo', August 16, 1897.

[36] *Freeman's Journal and Daily Commercial Advertiser*, 'Swimming, The Great National Swimming Race', September 9, 1897.

withdraw at the last minute.[37] On October 29, Nuttall had moved down to Sunderland in order to swim in the Sunderland Swimming Club Annual Gala where he was to attempt to break his own world record over 200 yards.[38] Despite suffering from an abscess under his arm Nuttall did reduce the record to 2 mins 23 and 1/5 secs on that occasion.

In September, 1898 Nuttall's dominance of the professional indoor circuit at the mid-distances had led one backer to issue a challenge to any swimmer other than Nuttall. The barring of Nuttall from the £200 a-side wager served to announce the beginning-of-the-end for Joey, ironically not because of his declining abilities but because he was no longer a man who attracted wagers. J.H. Tyers and E. Cavill were invited to take up the challenge. Nuttall continued to tour the various local galas offering his name as a draw for paying spectators. Many of Nuttall's races were now being described as swimming exhibitions; Nuttall and Tyers raced each other over four lengths (156 yards) of the Osborne Street Baths, Manchester in October, 1898. The outcome was a dead-heat in a time of 1 min and 57 secs.[39] The dead-heat was repeated by the duo at the Leeds Swimming Club gala in the January of 1899 when they conspired to achieve the same outcome over 250 yards. The *Leeds Mercury* commented that both swimmers 'seemed to cover twice the distance of the average amateur with half the effort.'[40] The success of their exhibition races encouraged further ventures in 1900 when Nuttall and Tyers appeared at Lambeth Baths to swim in aid of the Music Hall Home fund, sponsored by the *Sporting Life*.[41]

By 1902 it would appear that Nuttall's superiority in speed swimming was ebbing. At Hampstead Baths in July, 1902 he failed to beat his own record time for the 500 yards by a full 13 seconds at 6 mins 37 and 1/5 secs. He had only set the current world record a year before in Leicester.[42] In September 1904 *The New York Times* reported that Nuttall had won first prize in a race around the inner harbour of Newport, Rhode Island. The course was three miles in length with Nuttall winning in a time of 1 hour 35 mins 30 and 2/5 secs. His opponents were: Percy Cavill of Australia, who finished second, and in third place was John McCusker of Boston USA. For his efforts that day

---

[37] *Pall Mall Gazette*, 'Sporting Notes and News, Swimming', October 23, 1897.

[38] *Northern Echo*, 'North Country News, Swimming Record', October 29, 1897.

[39] *Pall Mall Gazette*, 'Sporting Notes & News, Swimming', October 15, 1898.

[40] *Leeds Mercury*, 'Swimming, World Champions in Leeds', January 4, 1899.

[41] *Era*, 'Advertisements and Notices, Swimming Carnival', June 2, 1900.

[42] *Penny Illustrated Paper and Illustrated Times*, 'Swimming', July 26, 1902, 54.

Nuttall won a gold medal and $450, second place got $150 and third place won $75. Nuttall was to face the two main protagonists repeatedly throughout his professional career almost exclusively in the UK.[43] In September, 1905 it was reported that Nuttall had competed in an inaugural competition to swim in the River Seine, France. There were over 800 entrants with about 100,000 spectators along the seven-and-a-half-mile course to witness Nuttall fail to complete the distance due to cramp.[44] By 1907 Nuttall had retired from competitive swimming and opened a public house in his home town of Stalybridge.[45] He was landlord of the Greyhound Inn from 1907-1910 when the beer-house closed down; it would appear that Nuttall was in considerable debt to the brewery who claimed most of his trophies in part payment for his debts. Sometime after 1911 Joey left his hometown of Stalybridge in order to take up residence in Blackpool, where he had been fêted as a natationist and entertainer.

Conclusion

Joey Nuttall is a significant figure in the world of Victorian natation not only because of his dominance of 'speed swimming' but also because of the stance he took against a leisure elite who attempted to limit his earning potential as a swimmer. His 'sporting life' exemplifies the veracity of the late-Victorian puritanical mind-set towards the professionalization of sport and the pursuit of respectable forms of recreation.[46]

The 'ownership' of competitive swimming was essentially dominated regionally by local swimming clubs who saw the imposition of draconian codes of conduct by those in governance as a means of restricting their income. The conundrum faced by talented working-class swimmers was not so much how to earn a living as a swimmer but rather, how to supplement a 'respectable' living with the pecuniary rewards associated with success on the swimming gala

---

[43] *New York Times*, 'Nuttall First in Swim', September 4, 1904.

[44] *Penny Illustrated Paper and Illustrated Times*, 'Swimming', September 16, 1905, 166.

[45] Robert Magee, 'Stalybridge Pubs 1750-1990', (Neil Richardson Publishers, 1991).

[46] Peter Bailey, 'Leisure and Class in Victorian England: Rational Recreation and the Contest for Control, 1830-1885'; G Cross and J Walton, 'The Playful Crowd: Pleasure Places in the Twentieth Century', *Journal of Social History*, (Spring 2007): 754-6.

circuit. [47] The value of a trophy and the payment of legitimate travelling expenses appear to have been clouded by the sports inextricable links with gambling and the new phenomenon of the leisure entrepreneur. It was against this backdrop that Joey performed as an 'amateur' swimmer from 1881-1888 and then as a 'professional' swimmer from 1888-c1907.

Although Joey continued to perform at the highest levels as a professional swimmer, post-1888 he was forced to supplement his income from competitive racing by performing as an aquatic entertainer in leisure destinations such as Blackpool.[48] From exhibiting his talents within the comfort of local swimming galas he was now reluctantly entertaining the masses at sea-side resorts and open-water shows. The trend for the working-classes to escape the confines of their industrial environment for that of leisure destinations was fully exploited by the new leisure entrepreneurs and provided the opportunity for Joey to earn a living as an aquatic entertainer. A 'profession' that provided inclusive employment for both male and female natationists. The dominance of those earning a living in employment associated with swimming (baths attendants, coaches/instructors and, increasingly aquatic entertainers) merely served to stiffen the resolve of the sports administrators to limit their influence. The stance being taken by both sides finally came to a head at the *National Swimming Championships* in October, 1888; a defining moment in the history of swimming in the UK. The ASA, who had been established in 1886, eventually gained exclusive control of swimming with the demise of the PSA in 1891 and the subsequent decline in popularity of aquatic entertainments by 1914.

Joey was not only a real champion of natation but an iconic figure to the inhabitants of Stalybridge in that he espoused the benefits of a work ethic that had provided him with a means of self-improvement and self-reliance, which made him a productive member of Victorian and Edwardian society. Research to date indicates that Joey may well have involved himself in coaching J.A. Jarvis to some degree but further investigation is necessary in this respect. The success of Jarvis appears to be as a result of the development of the 'Jarvis-Nuttall Kick'

---

[47] Christopher Love, 'Social Class and the Swimming World: Amateurs and Professionals', *International Journal of the History of Sport,* 24 No.:5 (2007): 603-619.

[48] Keith Myerscough, 'Blackpool's Triplets: Health, Pleasure and Recreation, 1875-1904', (Masters Dissertation, De Montfort University, 2009), 41-3.

which brought Jarvis international success at the 1900 Olympiad in Paris and the 1906 Intercalated games in Athens.

The personal sacrifices Nuttall made in achieving sporting excellence came at a price; Joey married in 1906 at the age of 37 and he died in 1942 at the age of 72, being buried in an unmarked grave, his occupation declared him to be a 'general labourer, retired'. How different it may have been if Joseph Nuttall, *Champion Swimmer of the World*, and holder of 14 world titles could have plied his trade in this modern era of the iconic professional sports superstar.

9

John Hulley – An Olympic Innovator

Ray Hulley

Many of us will have enjoyed watching the events of the Beijing Olympics in 2008 and look forward to the London Olympic Games in 2012. I will be particularly keen because I have discovered my own Olympic hero during my family history researches in the past 4 years. I am a member of the Guild of One-Name Studies, the Manchester and Lancashire Family History Society and the North Cheshire Family History Society and have been researching my surname since 1980. In November 2006 I came across an article about a John Hulley of Liverpool in the Winter 2001 edition of the *Journal of Olympic History*. The title included a representation of the 5 Olympic rings and the mystery was because he had been the forgotten man of British Olympic history and all trace of him after 1868 had been lost. Never shirking a challenge of this nature, I decided to follow up this lead to try to solve the mystery. I discovered that Hulley had been born in Liverpool in 1832 and was a descendant of a Hulley family from Frodsham and previously Macclesfield. I have researched this family back to 1488 so he is well founded. His father, 2 uncles, a grandfather and great grandfather had been surgeons or physicians and another uncle had been a chemist and druggist. The Family Tree on the following page shows four generations of ancestors of John Hulley.

My next step was to find out more about John and his family in Liverpool and I discovered him in 1841 living at Gloucester Street Liverpool with his mother.[1] He had had a keen interest in physical activities, education and fitness and it was reported that in his early years he had been taught by Louis Huguenin, the famous French gymnast who had settled in Liverpool in 1844 as a teacher of Gymnastics. John attended Huguenin's school in a court at the top of Lord Street for several years before matriculating from the Collegiate Institute, Shaw Street, Liverpool in 1850.[2] In 1851 John was a visitor to his Uncle Hugh Speed's Brookhouse Farm at Huyton where no doubt

---

[1] 1841 census The National Archives (TNA) reference HO 107/558/8 folio 21 reverse.

[2] Some Old Liverpudlians [By One Of Them] - No. 11 - John Hulley, Gymnasiarch *Liverpool Citizen*, February 25 1888, 7.

he enjoyed the fresh air and farmyard activities.[3] John Hulley was again living at a farm in Huyton in 1861, but this time he was a visitor to his uncle Edward Speed at Woolfall Hall where there were 90 acres of farmland.[4]

Jasper Hulley
Born 1697 Macclesfield
died 1778 Macclesfield

|

James Hulley (+ 8 others)
born 1750 Macclesfield
died 1799 Frodsham
Surgeon

|

Thomas Boydell Hulley (+3 others)
born 1784 Frodsham
died 1839 Lymm
Surgeon

John Nevitt Hulley	**Robert Churchman Hulley**	**James Ridley Hulley**	**Thomas Hulley**
b. 1803 Frodsham	b. 1809 Frodsham	b. 1818 Frodsham	b. 1820 Liverpool
d.1840 Manchester	d. 1862 Australia	d. 1837 Lymm ?	d. 1857 Prescot
Surgeon	*Surgeon/Physician*	*Chemist & Druggist*	*Surgeon Apprentice*

|

JOHN HULLEY
b. 1832 Liverpool
d. 1875 Liverpool
Gymnasiarch

The Role of Physical Education

John Hulley's first public presentation was given on 25 April 1861 at the Theatre Royal Liverpool, and was part of a display by members of the 79th Lancashire Volunteer Rifles, (composed predominantly of the middle class) entitled "A Grand Assault of Arms." By the kindness of Colonel M. Martyn, of the 2nd Life Guards, several of the picked swordsmen of that regiment were permitted to take part in the contests.

John Hulley who was a member of the 79th, opened the proceedings by delivering an address on "Physical Education" in which he said –

> There is scarcely one of us whose physical state is what it ought to be. Poor, weak, pale, dyspeptic beings we are, unworthy of the name of a man, whatever learning or mental attainments we

[3] 1851 census TNA reference HO 107/2193 folio 296 reverse.
[4] 1861 census TNA reference RG 9/2741 folio 45.

may possess. We may dazzle our fellow men by these one-sided accomplishments, we may win their short-sighted praise, but we shall not cheat nature, nor reap ought but her punishment to us and our children. When our day of physical affliction comes, as come it certainly will, to everyone who neglects his body, when the retribution head is laid heavily on ourselves and on our children, then shall we feel the vanity and delusiveness of our preference for one set of our faculties above the other.

A man who cultivates his personal appearance and takes a pride in his handsome and athletic figure is called a coxcomb, while the puny delicate man of letters, who exalts in his mental superiority, and who boasts of the triumph of mind over matter, is thought to have a noble and excusable pride. The attention and reverence for physical beauty is one of the best safeguards for health and manly vigour. Beauty of face and figure is only to be maintained and perpetuated to coming generations by exercise of our body powers and is one of the best signs of a well-spent life. In truth the great want of physical beauty and manly strength and elegance of frame, which is so widespread among us, is as distressing and as deeply to be deplored, as the prevalence of moral evil, of which, in fact, it is the outward and visible type. No qualities of mind can make up for this sinful and miserable neglect of the body. The moral virtues themselves are to be promoted at present through the physical ones, for in the present state of physical degradation, in which we live, it is a vanity to imagine that high moral excellence can prevail. Therefore the earnest culture of the bodily powers by every one of us is the surest means to elevate mankind.

We should not be contented with a low standard of physical elevation. We should make it our religious aim, that every one of us, man, woman, and child, should possess a large, powerful frame, whose blooming health shall set consumption and other diseases of debility, at deliverance. Each man and woman should take as much pride, in the cultivation of the bodily as of the mental faculties, feeling deeply that the grand truth, that the interests of our race are just as much bound up in the right development of the ones as of the other. We should not be content until the thews and sinews, the powerful bodied and manly minds of our ancestors become prevalent among us and are blended with the advantage of our advanced civilisation, with our greater enlightment and refinement, and a longer average of life, we should cultivate all those sports and manly exercises which promote bodily health and vigour, just as sedulously as we cultivate any other branch of education, for no amount of mental cultivation, intellect, or wealth will ever make up to a community for the lack of manly mode ability and pluck.

History is full of examples of intellectually developed nations, but intellectual only, falling a prey to others of inferior mental calibre, but of daring and overwhelming physique. Therefore we should have an equal honour to physical as to mental excellence. Whenever we see it, we should learn to take an equal pleasure in it, and to have an equal reverence for the physical and the mental sciences and to attain to a well valued grandeur a like of the material and of the moral universe.[5]

Another "Assault at Arms" organised by John Hulley was again held at the Theatre Royal on 5 December 1861, with Hulley repeating the address given at the same place in April.[6]

The First Liverpool Olympic Festival
In June 1862 John Hulley initiated the first Grand Olympic Festival at the Mount Vernon Parade Ground in Liverpool, which was a forerunner of several of these competitions with a physical prowess flavour. In the advertisement for the Festival it was stated that no effort would be spared by the Committee not only to render the Festival worthy of its immortal title, but also to make it the means of drawing more public attention to the important subject of physical education.[7]

Gold, silver and bronze medals were awarded in these 3 competitions: 1100 yards Steeplechase; 1½ mile Race; 4 mile Walking Race.

Silver and bronze medals were awarded in the following competitions: Fencing; Vaulting; ½-mile Race for LAC members; Broadsword; Boxing; Throwing the Disc; Sabre v. Bayonet; 120 yards Race; Throwing the Cricket Ball; Jumping; 300 yards Race; Indian Club Exercises; Leaping; ½-mile Race for Youths; Dumb-bell Exercises.

A gold medal or ten guineas was also awarded for the best essay on Physical Education.

---

[5] *Liverpool Mercury*, April 25, 1861, 3.
[6] *Liverpool Mercury*, December 5, 1861, 7.
[7] Ibid June 2, 1862, 1.

Figure 1. Charles Pierre Melly

The Festival was a success and Mr Melly, President of the Liverpool Athletic Club said that before they left the ground he thought it was his duty to tell them through whose exertions that delightful afternoon's amusement had been afforded to them. They were indebted for it to Mr John Hulley, the excellent honorary secretary of the club, and it was entirely owing to his indefatigable and praiseworthy exertions that the festival had been brought to such a successful and highly satisfactory issue. Mr Melly then called for three cheers for Mr Hulley, which were given right heartedly, with "one cheer more." The report ended with wholesome praise for John Hulley. "It is due to Mr. Hulley that the whole direction and management of the festival devolved upon him. He was unremitting in his exertions throughout the day, and there is no doubt that to his courtesy and zeal that the successful issue of the undertaking was mainly attributable.[8]

Establishment of the Rotunda Gymnasium, Bold Street Liverpool
Later in 1862 the Rotunda Gymnasium was established in Bold Street, Liverpool by a partnership between John Hulley who looked after the Gymnasium side of the business, and Samuel W. Ackerley, who raised the capital for a mortgage deposit on the premises. It was clearly understood between them that Hulley's practical experience was to be considered as of equal value with his capital. Ackerley was to look out for premises and both took steps to secure the Rotunda in joint names. The actual purchase, however, was made in Mr. Ackerley's sole name, but with a clear understanding that if in future the property was sold the profit should be equally divided between them. The President of the Gymnasium was Charles Pierre Melly, great grandfather of the late George Melly, musician and entertainer, and Andre Melly, film actress. Charles Melly was a Liverpool philanthropist born in 1829. He was famous for providing 43 public drinking fountains around Liverpool in the mid-19th c, as well as being instrumental in the founding of the Gymnasium.

[8] Ibid June 16, 1862, 5.

The reputation of John Hulley in the sphere of physical education increased dramatically over the next year or so. The good example set by him at Liverpool was replicated at Manchester, where newly established Athletic Club held an Assault-at-Arms in the Free Trade Hall. Several of the pioneers of the physical education movement had been invited to attend and take part in the proceedings, including John Hulley. A correspondent to the Liverpool Mercury reflected the mood of the time regarding physical education in Liverpool, writing,

> "Gentlemen, I think there could not be a better time than the present, now that such a deal is being made, said and written on the important subject of physical education, to express my opinion with regard to a testimonial being presented to Mr John Hulley, honorary secretary of the Athletic Club. I think no one man in Liverpool has done more for his fellow-townsmen than Mr Hulley. He, in a great measure, may be called the pioneer of the great movement in this town.[9]

Even the landed gentry were aware of the undoubted progress made with physical education and the leading part played in its promotion by John Hulley. Sir Edmund Lachmere, 2nd Baronet of Hanley Castle, and High Sheriff of Worcestershire wrote to him requesting a copy of the rules and other particulars of the Liverpool Athletic Club. Sir Edmund was very desirous to encourage athletic sports and a competition for prizes in the pleasure grounds at Worcester, and he wished to procure all the information he can as to the establishment of athletic games in other places.

The second annual great Olympic Festival (now entitled 'International') in connection with the Liverpool Athletic Club took place at the Mount Vernon Parade Ground Liverpool on Mr. Hulley, the indefatigable honorary secretary, and the committee, had used every excursion to render the affair a complete success, and the thousands who were present on Saturday, must admit that this second Olympic Festival was highly successful in every respect.[10]

The public pressure for the importance and advantages of physical education reached the edges of the Lake District with the small town of Ulverston inviting John Hulley and 12 of his Liverpool Athletic Society colleagues to the town in October 1863. Gymnastic

---

[9] Ibid June 16, 1862, 5.
[10] Ibid June 15, 1863, 3.

illustrations were a novelty in Ulverston, and the meeting attracted one of the largest and most intelligent audiences ever assembled within the Concert-hall. John Hulley was warmly welcomed by the audience who listened attentively to what he had to say about his favourite topic – Physical Education.[11]

Another Grand Assault-at-Arms was held at a crowded Theatre-Royal in December 1863 by members of the Liverpool Athletic Society and organised by John Hulley. But the year closed with a shock announcement by Samuel Ackerley, the co-partner of Hulley in the Bold Street Gymnasium that Hulley will cease to have any share in the Direction of the Establishment from 31 December 1863. This came as a complete surprise to John Hulley, who explained his side of the case very clearly and in great detail in the local newspapers. Ackerley had reneged on an agreement and simply dissolved the partnership.[1213]

Establishment of the New Liverpool Gymnasium

This setback was only a temporary one for within 3 months a new company had been formed with the Mayor as President, Charles Melly as Chairman and John Hulley as Manager. The prime object of the company is to "erect in a suitable place a gymnasium, such as shall fairly express the devotion to physical education, which has happily become so common in Liverpool, chiefly through the exertions of its most eminent and spirited apostle, Mr John Hulley, and such as to spread widely around the conviction of the necessity and the appreciation of its enjoyments."[14]

On the 6th July Charles Melly and John Hulley attended the Crystal Palace in London as part of the Gymnasium Festival organised by Herr Ravenstein of the Turnverein, or German Gymnastic Society. The Liverpool Mercury reported the visit as a "distinguished triumph" for John Hulley and continued:

> We trust we may deem it as an omen of the good fortune
> that awaits him on Saturday. The German Turners of London,
> under the presidency of Herr Ravenstein, met on that day at the
> Crystal Palace, and a vast and brilliant throng attended to
> witness their feats. Among the candidates were three Liverpool

---

[11] *Cheshire Observer and Chester, Birkenhead, Crewe and North Wales Times,* October 24, 1863, 6.
[12] *Liverpool Mercury,* January 1, 1864, 1.
[13] Ibid January 4, 1864, 7.
[14] Ibid March 19, 1864, 6.

men, and each carried off a prize, although the contests were particularly exacting The London press unanimously award high praise to the Liverpool men, and also mention in terms of honour Mr. Melly and Mr. Hulley as the principal supporters of the athletic movement in Liverpool. We may add that the plans of the new gymnasium about to be erected in Liverpool were exhibited, and the proposed working of the institution by the gymnasiarch, Mr. Hulley, explained.   Both received warm encomiums.[15]

Figure 2. Front View of Gymnasium

The newly formed gymnasium was eventually relocated in Myrtle Street opposite the Philharmonic Hall. The Foundation Stone was laid by the Mayor on July 22 1864. The site of the building occupied 1450 square yards. On the principal floor, on the level of the ground, were the entrance hall, 12 feet wide, gentlemen's rooms, committee room, ladies' room, bathrooms for ladies, bathrooms for gentlemen, lavatories, storeroom, professor's room, office, and the gymnasium proper – 105 feet long, 75 feet wide and 45 feet high. The building was one-third larger than the one recently commenced at King's-cross, London, and as far as was known, the largest of its kind in the world.[16]

[15] Ibid July 8, 1864, 6.
[16] Ibid July 19, 1864, 6.

Figures 3 and 4. Inside the Gymnasium

Olympic Festival at Llandudno

The 3rd Olympic Festival took place at the Zoological Gardens Liverpool on 9 July 1864 after being postponed from 2 July due to unfavourable weather conditions. John Hulley, Vice-President of the Athletic Society, was the Director of Festival. The 4th Olympic Festival was held on the 22nd July at the Croquet Grounds, Llandudno instead of in Liverpool. Hulley had a passion about bathing and bathing dress for both males and females and had written at length to The Times and The Liverpool Mercury on the subject in June 1864. He had advocated a new style of dress suitable for both men and women and this had been adopted by the authorities in Llandudno to boost tourism to that seaside resort. The Festival was a great success but a Grand Procession of Illuminated Boats on the Bay, together with a Grand Swimming Race of 100 yards had to be called off due to dispute with the Llandudno boatmen. Seven boats had been engaged by Mr Hulley, coloured lanterns provided for them, and music prepared. It was proposed to have the swimming-match, and that over a procession of boats, with the coloured lights and music on board. The boatmen, however, after having hired themselves to Mr Hulley, again let their boats for a higher sum, so that when that gentleman appeared, he was unable to fulfil his programme, and the swimming had to be adjourned to the following Monday.

In spite of this set-back, the local press were most enthusiastic for a repeat performance. The North Wales Chronicle said that the athletic meeting was still a favourite topic of conversation in Llandudno and its neighbourhood, and was still remembered with pleasure. Associated with this pleasant recollection were the names of Colonel McCorquodale, Mr. Hulley, and Colonel Walmsley. It went on to suggest that could not these gentlemen, assisted by any of the visitors or residents now at Llandudno, organise one more such a gathering.

They would be doing a kindness to the town, and would give great gratification to both residents and visitors. The former gathering was a numerous one, but a second one would be far more so. They hoped that Mr Hulley would answer to their appeal.[17]

Figure 5. Grand Procession of illuminated boats at Llandudno

Hulley responded positively and organised a novel Water Fete two weeks later on Saturday evening, 19th August 1865. The whole of the houses facing the sea were lit up, and numbers of boat elegantly decorated, and filled with ladies bearing coloured lampions formed a procession and sailed round the bay. The rocks surrounding the town were brilliantly illuminated, and a carnival was held on the sands by thousands of visitors carrying variegated lanterns of every possible hue. [18] In recognition of Hulley's to publicise Llandudno, a beautifully illuminated address on vellum, signed by all classes of the inhabitants was forwarded "to the celebrated Gymnasiarch of Liverpool, to whom Llandudno owes so much."[19]

Opening of the Myrtle Street Gymnasium
Although there was pressure from various quarters to have the gymnasium formally opened, John Hulley delayed this auspicious occasion until a suitable person was available. It had been jokingly

---

[17] *North Wales Chronicle*, Llandudno, Wales, August 5, 1865, 3.
[18] *Morning Post*, August 22, 1865, 3.
[19] *Wrexham Advertiser, Denbighshire, Flintshire, Shropshire, Cheshire & North Wales Register*, Wrexham, Wales, January 6, 1866, 6.

reported that the delay was caused by the determination of the directors to wait till the Prince of Wales visits Liverpool, when he can formally open the Gymnasium and that the Queen herself would be coming down to preside at the opening, and inaugurate the proceedings by having a bout at single-stick with the great Gymnasiarch himself. Eventually Lord Derby formally opened it on Tuesday 6 November 1865 and in his speech said that he congratulated the managers upon having in Mr Hulley, a director, who was working, not merely for the salary which he earns, and which they will be the first to admit is a very inadequate recompense for his labour, but who was working out a very real and enthusiastic interest in the business which he was employed to do.[20]

Formation of the National Olympian Association

John Hulley always had a clear view of what constituted an Olympic Education. In 1864 he expressed this in a lecture at the Theatre-Royal Liverpool in which he said "The need for athletic institutes for public gymnastic exercises...for both sexes…in all our towns and cities for 'the free use of the people,…an agreeable resort for the aged and a pastime for the young.'

On 7 November 1865 The Liverpool Mercury reported the formation of the National Olympian Association (NOA) with its inaugural meeting held at the Liverpool Gymnasium, Myrtle Street with the following persons present:

Mr. John Hulley of Liverpool; Chairman;
Dr. Brookes, Much Wenlock;
Mr. E.G. Ravenstein, president of the German Gymnastic Society, London;
Mr. William Mitchell, Fearness Hall, near Manchester;
Mr. Keeling, Liverpool;
Mr. Murray, London;
Mr. Phillips, Shrewsbury;
and Mr Ambrose Lee, Manchester.
There was also a M. Durbec of Paris listed. [21]

This meeting was the forerunner of the modern British Olympic Association and was formed mainly through the efforts of John Hulley, Dr. Brookes and Mr Ravenstein – the triumvirate of the 19th century Olympic movement.

---

[20] *The Times*, November 7, 1865, 5.
[21] *Liverpool Mercury*, November 7, 1865, 7.

The link between physical education and the Olympic idea was expressed nicely by John Hulley in 1867. He said 'What I desire to impress upon you is that Olympic Festivals are not the end of physical education. Physical Education, or rather its dissemination, is the end. Olympian festivals are a means of securing that end.'

The NOA lasted until 1883 and its Olympian Games "were open to all comers". The NOA and its motto were inherited by the National Physical Recreation Society (NPRS) in 1885/1886 and the NPRS was a founder body of the British Olympic Association in 1905. Indeed the President and the Treasurer of the NPRS were members of Coubertin's "Comite Brittanique" in 1902. So there is a direct link between Hulley's views and aspirations in 1864 and the modern British Olympic movement.

Hulley was certainly a tour de force. He began to define Olympism long before the formation of the International Olympic Committee. Like Brookes and Ravenstein he influenced the thinking of the young Coubertin.

Further Olympic Festivals and Displays at Liverpool and Llandudno
Following further Assaults-at Arms at the Gymnasium in December 1865 and March 1866, The Weekly journal "Porcupine" heaped lavish praise on Hulley's gymnastic and physical education organisational abilities. "To Mr Hulley belongs the honour of establishing the physical culture as a pursuit in the north of England, if not throughout the country, and the success he has achieved has exceeded the utmost anticipations of the few who believed in him, and placed in the most ridiculous light those who ridiculed his endeavours. All that can be done by unfaltering example and by contagious enthusiasm has been done by Mr Hulley, and, beyond this, his direction of the movement has been as wise as it was energetic. He has made himself an authority on his favourite topic; his gymnasium is a model with which athletic students all over the country are eager to compare their institutions; and it only remained for him to develop a system by which it would be possible to constitute the judgements of the gymnasium, as recognized acknowledgements of physical prowess and skill.[22]

Another Athletic Festival was held over a 3 –day period at Llandudno in May, 1866, under John Hulley's direction but his role of chairman of the National Olympian Association (NOA) seems to have ended by

---

[22] *The Porcupine*, March 24, 1866, 507.

June 1866. It was reported that the NOA had been organised into 3 areas – the Metropolitan and southern counties under Mr. Ravenstein of London, the midland counties under Dr. Brookes of Wenlock, and the northern counties under Mr. Mitchell of Rossendale. John Hulley made an appearance at the First National Olympic Festival held at the River Thames at Teddington for aquatic events and at the Crystal Palace cricket ground for other events. He was dressed in the garb of a Turk was supposed to represent the East – hardly an appropriate display for the first chairman of the NOA, but that was typical of the publicity seeker! [23]

Further gymnastic displays were held at the Gym throughout 1867 and the famous public school at Rugby contacted Hulley for advice on physical education for its pupils. The highlight of the year was the Grand Olympic Festival held at the Gymnasium and the Sheil Park Athletic Grounds in Liverpool on the 28th and 29th of June. There were competitors from Paris, Marseilles, London, a large contingent from Manchester, and most of the Northern counties were represented. It was, in fact, quite a national competition. John Hulley, as President of the Athletic Association, made a speech about the importance of physical education in which he said " What I desire to impress upon you is that Olympic festivals are not the end of physical education. Physical education, or rather its dissemination, is the end. Olympic festivals are the means of securing that end."[24]

It appears that John Hulley took a back seat in the organisation of this event because the report of this event which read: "And the programme was got through very shortly after the appointed time, and this act of itself testifies to the completeness of the arrangements. A better managed Olympic festival has not been held in Liverpool; and this is in great measure due to the exertions of Messrs J.B. Lee and W. D. Hogarth, who, after winning many laurels in the ranks as competitors, this year appeared in the character of joint honorary secretaries."[25]

The financial position of the Liverpool Gymnasium gave cause for concern at the Annual General Meeting held in November 1868. Receipts had dropped by 27% and a loss of £114 had been incurred. John Hulley was not present at the AGM nor at the annual grand athletic fete held in December of that year, but he was back to his

---

[23] *The Penny Illustrated Paper*, August 11, 1866, 84 by Our Gossiper.
[24] *Liverpool Mercury*, June 29, 1867, 6.
[25] Ibid July 1, 1867, 9.

normal exuberant self in the early months of 1869 when he was the leading light in bringing the new-fangled invention of the velocipede to Liverpool. The Gymnasium was the centre of this very popular attraction and the Liverpool Velocipede Club was formed there. Events, including a tournament, riding displays and races all helped to publicise the new craze and Hulley was at the centre of most of them. Public races were held at Chester, Rock Ferry and Hoylake where over 1000 spectators witnessed three events.[26]

John Hulley's marriage

On 16 July 1869 at the Ancient Unitarian Chapel, Toxteth Park John Hulley married Georgiana Bolton, only daughter of Mr. Robert Lewin Bolton, merchant of Liverpool and grand-daughter of the late Mr. Thomas Bolton who was Mayor of Liverpool in 1840. The marriage was an explosive affair with her parents locking her in her room to prevent the ceremony from going ahead. However, love prevailed in the face of adversity and the happy couple tied the knot a day later. This attracted widespread press coverage throughout the country and several reports of the on-off-on marriage filled the columns of the Bradford Observer, Dundee Courier & Argus, Glasgow Herald, Leeds Mercury, Liverpool Courier and Liverpool Mercury for several days after the event.[27]

His later years and early death

John Hulley's position in the administration of the Liverpool Gymnasium declined in the following months and years. He addressed a crowded gymnasium at the winter re-opening in October 1869, but he was succeeded as manager by Mr. Phillip Shrapnell in September 1870. There were later reports of him visiting North America and roaming through the backwoods, teaching his "noble art" in every village and settlement through which he passed, and driving a whole tribe of Red Indians into the forest by a mere flourish of the huge Indian clubs, which he handled like bulrushes. He was also an avid European traveller and often visited the south of France and Biarritz, especially in the cold English winters.

His death announcement at the early age of 42 came as a shock to many Liverpudlians and the local press paid tribute to him as a well-known and most enthusiastic teacher of gymnastic exercises, and by his advocacy of the importance and value of physical training.[28] A

[26] Ibid May 24, 1869, 5.
[27] Ibid July 17, 1869, 5.
[28] Ibid January 8, 1875, 6.

tribute paid to him 13 years after his death said "John Hulley, professor of gymnastics and Gymnasiarch, is still a pleasant memory in this native city. Hulley was born with a mission, which he fulfilled; and, take him for all and all, we may never see his like again".[29]

His death marked the end of a unique Liverpudlian but the start of a quest by myself to discover more about John Hulley. My first task was to track down the location of Hulley's grave. I was assisted by the report of his funeral In the local paper dated 12 January 1875. This read *inter alia* "The funeral of the late Mr. John Hulley, the "gymnasiarch," took place yesterday morning at the Smithdown-lane cemetery, the body being conveyed in a hearse drawn by four horses, and followed by two mourning coaches and the private carriage of Mr. Aaron Brown." Liverpool Record Office was very helpful in locating the grave reference and on one of my trips to Lancashire I decided to look for the actual grave in Smithdown Lane (now Road) cemetery. Thanks to a large plan at the entrance it was a simple task to find the grave – number G493.[30] Unfortunately it had been badly damaged in that the headstone had been removed from the main covering stone and the grave was in a very bad condition from 130 years of atmospheric pollution.

The John Hulley Memorial Fund
I contacted Don Anthony, the author of the 2001 article about John Hulley, and Ray Physick of Liverpool, an author of sports books who had expressed an interest in the John Hulley story, and we decided to set up a Memorial Fund through a website to raise money for the restoration of Hulley's grave; to increase awareness of his part in the founding of the British Olympic movement and to revive the interest in him as one of England's finest and forward-looking men. This took several months but thanks to generous donations from the International Olympic Committee, the British Olympic Association, and members of the public, sufficient funds were raised to engage a stonemason. We obtained quotations from several Liverpool stonemasons, one of whom gave us a surprise. We were informed that Hulley's grave consisted of two separate sections – the vertical headstone which had been laid down and the 'covers' of the actual grave next to it. Because the latter had no identifying marks on it, I

---

[29] Some Old Liverpudlians [By One Of Them] - No. 11 - John Hulley, Gymnasiarch *Liverpool Citizen,* February 25, 1888, 7.
[30] *Liverpool Mercury,* January 12, 1875, 6.

had not realised that it was part of the grave. The stonemason was quite adamant that it could be brought back to its original condition.

Restoration and Rededication of John Hulley's grave

Figure 6. The Grave after Restoration

He was right! This was taken after the Rededication ceremony in June 2009. Left to right - Don Anthony, Rev. Graham Murphy, Ray Physick and myself. The Olympic flag had been borrowed from the IOC. Let the words of the Revd Graham Murphy B.A. Dip.Post.Theol., Minister of Toxteth Unitarian Chapel Liverpool spoken at the rededication ceremony on Sunday 14 June 2009 under a bright sunny sky, be a fitting conclusion to this story.

> "Perceptive men and women of Hulley's time recognized the boundless vitality, enthusiasm and daring of a true pioneer of sports science. It was easy to ridicule him, and there was no shortage of armchair critics to do just that, not realising how Hulley was simply ever-reinventing himself to ensure his cause was never out of public view. If the advancement of athletics and physical education required him to be a showman, that he would be; he was nothing if not brave and indomitable. Until now, Hulley has suffered from obscurity, following his early death. Let the restoration of his grave be an end to that. It is with great pleasure that I declare this restoration to be the granting to John Hulley of a place in history, which he undoubtedly deserves."

10

George Martin, 'Wizard of Pedestrianism' and Manchester's Sporting Entrepreneur

Samantha-Jayne Oldfield

The public house during the nineteenth century was at the heart of the Victorian community; flower shows, fruit and vegetable shows, glee clubs, amateur and professional dramatics, bowling, quoits, pugilism, foot-racing, and society meetings were provided within their grounds.[1] Although appearing to help rationalise recreation time, the innkeepers were 'fully aware of the profit-making potential of such an enterprise', and pioneering publicans used entertainments to attract audiences with some establishments forming allegiances with specific ventures in order to gain higher proceeds.[2] Sport essentially became property of the drinks trade and it was these entrepreneurial landlords who were fundamental to the survival of sport in industrial cities, however, 'sufficient credit has never been given to the nineteenth century managers and professional running grounds for laying the foundations of the modern athletic meet', a topic in need of further exploration.[3] This paper provides a biographical study of one of these individuals, the innovative George Martin (1827-1865), one of Manchester's athletic sporting entrepreneurs.

---

[1] Peter Bailey, *Leisure and Class in Victorian England: Rational Recreation and the Contest for Control 1830-1885* (London: Redwood Burn, 1978), 166; Tony Collins and Wray Vamplew, 'The Pub, The Drinks Trade and the Early Years of Modern Football', *The Sports Historian*, 20, no.1 (2000): 2-3; Warren Roe, 'The Athletic Capital of England: The White Lion Hackney Wick 1857-1875', *BSSH Bulletin*, no. 17 (2003): 39-40.

[2] *Manchester Guardian*, October 11, 1845, 12; Dennis Brailsford, *British Sport: a Social History* (Cambridge: The Lutterworth Press, 1997), 68; Emma Lile, 'Professional Pedestrianism in South Wales during the Nineteenth Century', *The Sports Historian*, 20, no.2 (2000): 58; Mike Huggins, *The Victorians and Sport* (London: Hambledon and London, 2004), 47.

[3] Peter Lovesey, *The Official Centenary of the AAA* (London: Guiness Superlatives Ltd., 1979), 15; Stephen Hardy, 'Entrepreneurs, Organizations, and the Sport Marketplace: Subjects in Search of Historians', *Journal of Sport History*, no. 13 (1986): 23; Geoffrey T. Vincent, '"Stupid, Uninteresting and Inhuman" Pedestrianism in Canterbury 1860-1885', *Sporting Traditions*, 18, no.1 (2001): 47.

Figure 1. George Martin.
© Deserts Island Books

George Martin was born in 1826 in Blackwater, Hampshire, son of Prudence and James Martin, a local shoemaker. [4] From a working class background, Martin entered into the family trade in his adolescence, a common practice in nineteenth century Britain; entrusting kin with skills for employment, or providing funds to apprentice them in an appropriate trade was imperative to the father-son relationship as this provided independence and status for the family, and 'property in skill' which secured the future. [5] Residing with his grandparents, John and Martha Yeoman, in Frimley, Surrey, by 1841 Martin was practising as a journeyman shoemaker. [6] However, at the age of 18, Martin turned to sport for his fortune and moved to

---

[4] *Parish registers for Frimley, 1590-1914* (0804127), George Martin baptised on September 24, 1826 in Frimley, Surrey to James Martin and Pandora (sic); *Census Returns*, George Martin 1841 (HO107/1074/1); (HO 107/2227); *Bell's Life in London and Sporting Chronicle* (Hereinafter called *Bell's Life*), 24 December 1848, 7; *Marriage Certificate*, George Martin and Alice Holden 1851 (MXE 606479).

[5] *Penny Illustrated Paper*, January 17, 1863, 43; Andrea Colli, *The History of Family Business, 1850-2000* (Cambridge: Cambridge University Press, 2003), 29; David Vincent, *Bread, Knowledge and Freedom: A Study of Nineteenth-Century Working Class Autobiography* (Cambridge: Cambridge University Press, 1982), 74; Sonya O. Rose, *Limited Livelihoods: Gender and Class in Nineteenth-Century England* (London: Routledge, 1992), 140; Rob Hadgraft, *Deerfoot: Athletics' Noble Savage: from Indian Reservation to Champion of the World* (London: Desert Island Books, 2007), 58.

[6] *Census Returns*, 1841 (HO 107/1074/1), Hamlet of Frimley, George Martin, 15, 'Shoe m j'; 1841 (HO 107/684/12), St Pancras, Marylebone, Clarence Gardens, James Martin, 45, Prudence Martin, 40, Mary Martin, 15, Maria Martin, 12, Henry Martin, 8, all noted as occupation 'Shoe m'; 1851 (HO 107/1493), St Pancras, Marylebone, London, 47 Clarence Gardens, James Martin, 56, 'Shoemaker'; Prudence Martin, 53; Henry Martin, 18, 'Shoemaker'.

London to pursue a career in pedestrianism under the care of 28-year-old Edward "Ned" Smith, the 'West-End Runner'.[7] Throughout his career he continued to practise as a shoemaker and boot closer, which affected his attendance at some events, causing him to forfeit matches, and led to insolvency claims.[8]

Martin followed traditional practices, as illustrated in *The Training Instructor*;

> ...as soon as a man determines to go into training, it is, of course, advisable that he go into training quarters. These, if they can be obtained in another town to that in which he lives, will be all the better from the fact that they are situated some distance from the pedestrian's old haunts...and if he lodged in a public house it would not matter. [9]

He resided at the White Hart, Drury Lane, with mine host, Ned Smith, and proprietor, John "the Regent Street Pet" Smith, who provided facilities for several athletes.[10] Both men were well established peds, 'celebrated trainers', and athletic backers, Ned a hurdling champion and John a sprinter, originally trained by brother, Ned, with his preferred distance being a quarter of a mile.[11] The Smith brothers used their expertise to train novices and create first-rate pedestrians; the most successful graduates being Patterson, alias 'Pet', 'Blower Brown', Spooner, and Martin himself, nom de plume being 'Ned Smith's Novice'.[12]

Pedestrianism, or foot-racing, provided the majority of entertainment during the mid-century, a well-established amusement in which large numbers of people took part.[13] Sprinting (from 110 to 880 yards) and

---

[7] *Bell's Life*, August 19, 1841, 7; September 21, 1845, 7; October 19, 1845, 7.

[8] *Bell's Life*, May 17, 1846, 6; February 21, 1847, 7; *Manchester Guardian*, May 27, 1858, 2.

[9] Sportsman, *The Training Instructor* (London: Sportsman Offices, 1885), 50-51.

[10] *Bell's Life*, January 4, 1846, 7; November 1, 1846, 7; November 15, 1846, 7.

[11] *Bell's Life*, January 7, 1844, 7; March 16, 1845, 7; January 11, 1846, 6; December 30, 1860, 7; September 22, 1861, 7; John Dugdale Astley, *Fifty Years of my Life in the World of Sport at Home and Abroad* (London: Hurst and Blackett, 1895), 282.

[12] *Bell's Life*, January 11, 1846, 6; February 8, 1846, 6-7; March 15, 1846, 7; John Dugdale Astley, *Fifty Years of my Life in the World of Sport at Home and Abroad* (London: Hurst and Blackett, 1895), 282.

[13] George M. Young, *Early Victorian England 1830-1865* (Oxford: Oxford University Press, 1951).

the "Miler" were the events of choice for most athletes and spectators alike, due to their fast paced nature, although, by the 1840s, hurdling also became as popular, with men jumping over obstacles of all shapes and sizes.[14] Such events attracted large crowds, regularly in their thousands, with the publican reaping the rewards through drink proceeds, betting commission, and eventually gate fees when these ground became 'enclosed for a specific sporting purpose'.[15]

At 8st 6lb Martin was conditioned as a 120 yard sprinter and short distance hurdler, making his first appearance in 1845, at the age of 18.[16] After a successful start to his athletic career, support and admiration for Martin was apparent, resulting in backer, Smith, to challenge any young pedestrian in England to beat his man, which was quickly accepted by Birmingham based ped Joseph Messenger, and provided Martin with his first race outside the metropolis.[17] The competition was reported in *Bell's Life*, detailing the expense to which the grounds proprietor, Mrs Emerson, had gone to accommodate both youths, and although Martin lost he was highly praised, with reports stating 'two smarter fellows could not be picked in England, but Martin looked in the best condition, although he had but a week's training'.[18] On his return to London, Martin appeared in hurdling events at the Beehive Cricket Ground, Walworth, where his previous failures were eclipsed by his successes with prizes which included a silver snuff-box, a silver watch, and a silver cup for a '300 yards, and to leap 15 hurdles' event.[19] Again, Martin and his trainer were praised, with reports stating 'the pedestrian school that he [Martin] was brought up in must be a first-rate one, in producing so good a runner, who will, no doubt, with care, prove something extraordinary'.[20]

---

[14] Sportsman, *The Training Instructor* (London: Sportsman Offices, 1885), 75; Peter Lovesey, *The Official Centenary of the AAA* (London: Guiness Superlatives Ltd., 1979), 15.

[15] John Lowerson, *Sport and the English Middle Classes* (Manchester: Manchester University Press, 1995), 89; Dennis Brailsford, *Sport: a Social History* (Cambridge: The Lutterworth Press, 1997), 68; Tony Collins and Wray Vamplew, *Mud, Sweat and Beers: A Cultural History of Sport and Alcohol* (Oxford: Berg Publishing, 2002).

[16] *Bell's Life*, September 21, 1845, 6; January 4, 1846, 7.

[17] *Bell's Life*, January 4, 1846, 7.

[18] *Bell's Life*, January 25, 1846, 6.

[19] *Bell's Life*, February 22, 1846, 7; March 15, 1846, 7; April 12, 1846, 7; June 21, 1846, 7; July 5, 1846, 7.

[20] *Bell's Life*, March 15, 1846, 7.

Towards the end of 1846, Martin was unbeatable and started to gain negative press for illegally entering competitions.[21] Soon afterwards, Martin filed for bankruptcy and was remanded for two months and, after a quiet year, moved out of London only to re-emerge in the pedestrian community as 'George Martin of Sunderland' in 1848.[22] Residing at 'sporting victualler' Mr Harrison's, Golden Lion, Sunderland, Martin challenged men in the North East to sprinting and hurdling events, many of which he won with ease.[23] Not content with human competition, Martin tested his talent against horses and his events became the main attraction at Sunderland's running grounds luring spectators in their thousands, although betting was minimal.[24] However, his previous reputation had followed him and it was not long before controversy surrounded the ped, with many supporters of the sport concerned about Martin's hoaxing of the public, with *Bell's Life* announcing, 'Martin frequently offers to make matches, but as frequently disappoints parties. Let us have a little more work, and not so much talk'.[25] Nonetheless he continued to race as many spectators, and sporting papers, still supported the infamous hurdler and his indiscretions became secondary to his skill. This was not the first and last time Martin's reputation was threatened as towards the end of his career allegations of match-fixing, violence and fraud were widely reported; a common component of professional foot-racing, especially towards the 1860s and 1870s.[26]

In 1849, Martin, a 'pedestrian of celebrity', ventured towards Manchester where he trained and conditioned himself for athletic competition. His physique was marvelled, 'being well built about the chest and thighs, with a waist as fine as a lady', and his dominance in the sprinting world was greatly admired.[27] Regularly spotted at the White Lion, Long Millgate, Martin formed a friendship with James Holden, the 'great stakeholder of Lancashire pedestrianism' and proprietor of aforesaid public house.[28] Holden's inn was well

[21] *Bell's Life*, July 5, 1846, 7.

[22] *Bell's Life*, January 9, 1848, 7; *Era*, January 30, 1848, 6.

[23] *Bell's Life*, March 19, 1848, 7; April 9, 1848, 6; April 16, 1848, 6.

[24] *Era*, January 2, 1848, 5; *Bell's Life*, January 2, 1848, 7.

[25] *Bell's Life*, June 25, 1848, 7; October 22, 1848, 6; *Era*, March 11, 1849, 6.

[26] Don Watson, 'Popular Athletics on Victorian Tyneside', *The International Journal of the History of Sport*, 11, no. 3 (1994): 485-494; Emma Lile, 'Professional Pedestrianism in South Wales during the Nineteenth Century', *The Sports Historian*, 20, no.2 (2000): 58.

[27] *Bell's Life*, April 1, 1849, 6.

[28] *Era*, January 8, 1843, 10; *Bell's Life*, August 20, 1848, 7; November 4, 1849, 7; November 25, 1849, 7.

renowned for holding monies for most of Manchester's events ranging from the average pedestrian feat, rabbit course and quoits fixture to the more obscure bell ringing challenges, and the 1846 'match for a Yorkshireman to fight a main of cocks'.[29] Stakes, deposits and articles of agreement were regularly produced and held at the White Lion, and professional athletes would use this establishment as a meeting place where contests could be arranged, financed and promoted.[30] *Bell's Life* and *The Era* would regularly print Holden's name and public house within their pedestrian sections showcasing their gratitude for the 'respectable stakeholder, James Holden'.[31]

A small group of pedestrians which included Martin, Henry Reed of London, Edward "Welshman/Ruthin Stag" Roberts, Henry Molyneux of Halifax, John "Regent Street Pet" Smith, Charles Westhall, and George "the American Wonder" Seward, regularly competed against each other in hurdling and sprinting events at different venues throughout England.[32] In July 1849, Seward recognised the potential for an exhibition demonstrating athletic prowess and the "Seward Benefit", which saw himself and Reed 'tour through the towns that he has visited' throughout his time in England, was established in July 1849.[33] 5ft 7, 11st American, Seward, was born in Newhaven, Connecticut on 16 October, 1817, beginning a triumphant athletic career in October 1840. In 1843 he travelled to England searching for new athletic competition, working and living in Durham, and befriending Martin in the process. British pedestrians 'succumbed to his truly astonishing powers' and he was named 'Champion of England and America', although the term "Champion" was rather 'loosely employed' and given to athletes by pedestrian promoters as a means of generating public patronage.[34] Nonetheless, his pedestrian feats attracted thousands of spectators, but by 1849 his audience had dwindled. The American secured funding for a 'monster pavilion (capable of holding 10,000 persons)' which was to travel around the

---

[29] *Bell's Life*, December 3, 1843, 8; January 25, 1846, 6.

[30] *Bell's Life*, January 26, 1840, 7; May 16, 1841, 7; August 7, 1842, 6; November 12, 1843, 7; August 4, 1844, 7; November 16 1845, 7; March 22, 1846, 7; July 4, 1847, 7; February 27, 1848, 7; *Era*, March 11, 1849, 11.

[31] *Bell's Life*, October 2, 1842, 7.

[32] *Bell's Life*, July 1, 1849, 7; July 9, 1849, 6.

[33] *Bell's Life*, July 15, 1849, 3.

[34] *Bell's Life*, July 1, 1849, 7; David A. Jamieson, *Powderhall and Pedestrianism* (London: W. & A.K. Johnston Ltd, 1943), 35; Rob Hadgraft, *Deerfoot: Athletics' Noble Savage: from Indian Reservation to Champion of the World* (London: Desert Island Books, 2007), 129.

United Kingdom performing 'old English sports and pastimes…which many "first-raters" have entered', one of which was 22-year-old Martin. This short-lived amusement, aptly named 'The Great American Arena', was to commence at Peel Park Tavern, Pendleton, on 24 September, 1849, but was postponed until 1 October since the canvas could not be constructed in time.[35] On its grand opening, in the presence of approximately 2,000 people, George Martin defeated Roberts, Flockton and Smith in a 300 yard hurdle race to win a silver snuffbox before Seward conquered "Black Bess", Mr Harwood's mare, in a 100 yard event.[36] The circus soon ended when it became impossible to dismantle, transport, and erect the tent effectively, with the final performance being held in Rochdale on October 8, 1849.[37]

Martin, for many, was a pedestrian sensation, his 'condition, style, and manner, became the theme of admiration', and, although short in stature;

> Martin's skin was clear, step elastic, eye…bright as a diamond, and as full of confidence as man could possibly be…Martin is as smart a pedestrian as can be met…and, when he chooses, can run both beautifully and excellently, in fact he is a little model.[38]

Martin's association with the Holden family, and his growing relationship with daughter Alice Holden, encouraged the ped to frequent Manchester more regularly and eventually led to his relocation to the city in 1851.[39] On January 14, 1851, 'the smart and dapper George Martin…led the good tempered Miss Alice Holden, eldest daughter of the great pedestrian banker, to the alter', at St John's Church, Manchester, and two month later took proprietorship of the Plasterer's Arms, 29 Gregson Street, Deansgate, Manchester.[40] The role

---

[35] *Bell's Life*, September 23, 1849, 7; September 24, 1849, 7; September 30, 1849, 7.

[36] *Bell's Life*, October 7, 1849, 7.

[37] Rob Hadgraft, *Deerfoot: Athletics' Noble Savage: from Indian Reservation to Champion of the World* (London: Desert Island Books, 2007), 129.

[38] *Bell's Life*, September 17, 1848, 7; *Era*, August 11, 1850, 9.

[39] *Bell's Life*, November 4, 1849, 7; *Census Returns*, George Martin 1851 (HO 107/2227).

[40] *Marriage Certificate*, George Martin and Alice Holden 1851 (MXE 606479) *Era*, 26 January 1851, 5; *Manchester Guardian*, 26 March 1851, 5; *Census Returns*, George Martin and Alice Holden 1851 (HO 107/2227); W. Whellan & Co., *A New General Directory of Manchester and Salford, Together with the Principle Villages and Hamlets in the District* (Manchester: Booth and Milthorp, 1852), 216.

of licensed victualler became a popular business venture for many professional sportsmen; in London in the 1840s, prizefighter Young Dutch Sam gave lessons at The Black Lion, which was 'patronized by the friends of boxing and athletic sports in general' while Frank Redmond, at The Swiss Cottage, entertained all the 'celebrated pedestrians'. [41]   Professional swimmer Frederick Beckwith was, variously, landlord of The Leander, The Good Intent and The Kings Head, all in Lambeth, between 1850 and 1877, while The Feathers in Wandsworth, run by rower John H. Clasper, was popular with both scullers and swimmers. [42]   Outside of London, peds owned and frequented specific pubs. In 1855, pedestrian trainer James Greaves took over the Ring of Bells where anyone attending foot races in Sheffield area would 'meet with every accommodation'. [43]   The professional mile record, set in a dead-heat at Manchester in August 1865, was established by William "Crowcatcher" Lang, host of the Navigation Inn, Ancoats Street, Manchester, and William "The Welshman" Richards, landlord of the White Horse, Tollawain.[44]

> Through their social functions, pubs had a long and important history in shaping loyalties to locality. They were places where fields were provided, sport sponsored, pedestrian challenges agreed, bets were laid and teams changed. Frequenters of "sporting houses" often had their own allegiances, and lent general support to a particular, rower, pugilist or pedestrian before a match.[45]

Martin continued the trade of father-in-law James Holden, and his pub became a pedestrian base where stakes and deposits could be paid. His old sporting friends lodged at his hostelry and he continued to race himself within the Manchester area.[46] Due to his expertise in the

---

[41] Frank Lewis Dowling, *Fistiana: or, the Oracle of the Ring* (London: Bell's Life in London, 1841), 271-272.

[42] *Bell's Life*, 3 August 1878, 8; Dave Day, 'London Swimming Professors: Victorian Craftsmen and Aquatic Entrepreneurs', *Sport in History*, 30, no.1 (2010): 35.

[43] *Bell's Life*, March 18, 1855, 6.

[44] *Bell's Life*, July 30, 1864, 7; December 22, 1866, 7; Rob Hadgraft, *Beer and Brine: the Making of Walter George, Athletics' First Superstar* (London: Desert Island Books).

[45] Mike Huggins, *The Victorians and Sport* (London: Hambledon and London, 2004), 195.

[46] *Bell's Life*, July 6, 1851, 7; August 31, 1851, 7; January 18, 1852, 6; February 4, 1852, 7; February 8, 1852, 6.

sport, Martin also became a trainer for many young sprinting peds; a preferred distance for many as training was not laborious.[47] His protégés included William Neil of Stockport, his old rival Edward "Ruthin Stag" Roberts, and an amateur Grenadier Guard, Sergeant Newton.[48] Martin regularly requested matches for himself and his athletes in the pages of *Bell's Life*, as well as informing the athletic community of his booths where pedestrians could view his athletes before entering into articles of agreement.[49] His travelling huts, '25 yards by 10, and canvas top. The fittings consist of a counter, seats, spirit kegs, pots, &c.', provided alcohol at race meetings in and around Manchester, where, besides flat-racing, pedestrian, gymnastics and horse riding events were showcased; a demonstration of Martin's early entrepreneurial vision.[50] The sporting publican as early as the 1840s extensively endorsed pedestrian races, and the sport 'which had its own heading in *Bell's Life* in 1838', gained popularity, peaking in the 1860s, by which time the organisation of amateur sport by middle class society lead to a decline in professional activities.[51]

In 1852, Martin's family expanded with the arrival of son James, his first of six children, and soon afterwards Martin left The Plasterer's Arms, transferring the license to ex-professional rower, and brother-in-law, George Piers in 1853, and returned to London with his family and athletes, and resurrected his shoemaking business in the capital.[52] Ex-

---

47 Sportsman, *The Training Instructor* (London: Sportsman Offices, 1885), 71; John Henry Walsh, *British Rural Sports; Comprising Shooting, Hunting, Coursing, Fishing, Hawking, Racing, Boating, and Pedestrianism, With All Rural Games and Amusements* (London: Frederick Warne & Co., 1886), 615.

48 *Bell's Life*, February 11, 1849, 6.

49 *Bell's Life*, June 8, 1851, 7; August 22, 1851, 7.

50 *Manchester Guardian*, March 5, 1853, 3; *Scotsman*, April 13, 1870, 7.

51 George M. Young, *Early Victorian England 1830-1865* (Oxford: Oxford University Press, 1951), 272; Peter Bailey, *Leisure and Class in Victorian England: Rational Recreation and the Contest for Control 1830-1885* (London: Redwood Burn, 1978), 84; William J. Baker, 'The State of British Sport History', *Journal of Sport History*, 10, no.1 (1983): 59; Peter G. Mewett, 'History in the Making and the Making of History: Stories and the Social Construction of a Sport', *Sporting Traditions*, 17, no.1 (2000): 2-3; Geoffrey T. Vincent, '"Stupid, Uninteresting and Inhuman" Pedestrianism in Canterbury 1860-1885', *Sporting Traditions*, 18, no.1 (2001): 47.

52 *Manchester Guardian*, February 23, 1853, 5; *Census Returns*, 1861 (RG 9/2923), St Bartholomew, Salford, 14 Walter Street, George Martin, Head, 34, 'trainer of pedestrians', b. Surrey, York House; Alice Martin, Wife, 32, b. Lancashire, Manchester; James Martin, Son, 9, b. Lancaster, Manchester; George Martin, Son, 7, b. Middlesex, London; Thomas Martin, Son, 5, b. Middlesex, London; Elizabeth Martin, Daughter, 3, b. Lancaster, Salford; Harry Martin, Son, 1, b.

professional rower, and brother-in-law, Piers, patron of the Manchester Arms, Long Millgate, married Sarah Holden at Manchester Cathedral in 1852.[53] Traditionally a printer, Piers had been inaugurated into the pedestrian faction through his wife Sarah, who was apprenticed in the drinks trade by her father, James Holden.[54] In Holden's absence, Piers would often be present as starter, referee and timekeeper for local athletic and shooting events, eventually acquiring The Royal Hunt, Bury Street, Salford, where he became involved in rabbit coursing.[55]

Suffering from mental illness and unable to cope, Martin's father, James, in 1854, murdered wife Prudence and then committed suicide at their home at Clarence Gardens, St Pancras.[56] As the eldest son, Martin returned to the capital to organise funeral arrangements, comfort his siblings and to manage the family shoe-making business.[57] He continued to be active within the pedestrian community by coaching army athletes and training professional pedestrians whilst competing locally and arranging events from his new residence at 7 Little Windmill Street, Golden Square, Westminster.[58]

In May 1858, Martin again filed for bankruptcy and soon after, at the age of 30, he announced his retirement from the sport of pedestrianism

---

Lancaster, Manchester; 1871 (RG 10/4054), St Michael, Manchester, 11 Brass Street, Alice Martin, Head, Widowed, 43, 'Dress Maker', b. Lancashire, Manchester; Alice Holden, Daughter, 9, b. Surrey, Handsworth.

[53] *Bell's Life*, February 21, 1847, 5; *Marriage Certificate*, George Piers and Sarah Holden 1852 (MXF 084965); *Manchester Guardian*, October 9, 1852, 10.

[54] *Census Returns*, 1861 (RG 9/2950), Cathedral Church, Manchester, 4 Long Millgate 'White Lion', James Holden, Head, 62, 'public house keeper'; Elizabeth Holden, Daughter, 20; George Pearse, Son-in-Law, 30, 'letter-press printer'; Sarah Pearse, Daughter, 27; Sarah A. Pearse, Grand-child, 7; Elizabeth Pearse, Grand-child, 4; Isaac Slater, *Slater's Directory of Manchester* (Manchester: Isaac Slater, 1855), 725; *Will and Probate*, James Holden, 16 August 1865 (G 3000 6/63).

[55] *Era*, June 7, 1857, 8; October 10, 1858, 10; October 17, 1858, 10; April 14, 1861, 10; *Bell's Life*, August 27, 1864, 7; *Manchester Guardian*, October 28, 1861, 4.

[56] *Essex Standard*, March 31, 1854, 1; *Daily News*, 31 March 1854, 6; *Examiner*, April 1, 1854, 6; *Hampshire Advertiser & Salisbury Guardian*, April 1, 1854, 3; *Era*, April 2, 1854, 13; *Derby Mercury*, April 5, 1854, 7.

[57] *Saint Pancras Parish Church, Register of Burials, Including Burials at Kentish Town Chapel, Dec 1854* (p90/pan1/191), 74.

[58] *Bell's Life*, January 8, 1854, 6; August 20, 1854, 6; February 17, 1856, 6; October 26, 1856, 7; November 30, 1856, 7; December 14, 1856, 7; December 21, 1856, 7.

stating that he wished to pursue training full-time, housing athletes in his home at 14 Walter Street, Regent Road, Salford, which was within close proximity of the well-established Salford Borough Gardens, Regent Road, Salford, proprietor Mrs Ann Attenbury.[59] His training pedigree and "celebrity status" meant Martin 'was the star round which the Manchester men concentrated', and his athletes, Charles Mower, John Nevin and John White, who resided with Martin and his family, were strictly trained and promoted, becoming champions within the sport.[60]

In May 1861, Martin, as part of his promotion of the aforenamed pedestrians, sailed to America with the intention defeating his American counterparts.[61] On their arrival to the USA, the athletes entered competitions at the Fashion Race Course, Long Island, where their talent could not be matched and they remained undefeated. On 10 July, 1861, White and Mower competed in 'the great ten-mile foot-race' against two Cattaraugus Indian athletes, Bennett and Smith, who, according to the *New York Daily Tribune*, 'walked around with the imperturbable gravity of their race, and evidently viewed their two white competitors with complacency'.[62]   28-year-old native, Louis "Deerfoot" Bennett, who at 5ft 11½ and 11st 6lb overshadowed the British athletes, led the race from the start.[63] However, at the seventh mile, White, who had been 'running as light as an antelope', overtook the exhausted Bennett and claimed victory to 'the enthusiastic applause of the spectators' where Martin's techniques were congratulated, with reports stating White's focus and execution had 'certainly never been seen in this country'.[64]

[59] *Manchester Guardian*, May 27, 1858, 2; *Bell's Life*, October 17, 1858, 7; *Census Returns*, 1861 (RG 9/2923), St Bartholomew, Salford, 14 Walter Street, George Martin, Married, 34, 'trainer of pedestrians', b. Surrey, York House; Alice Martin, Wife, 32, b. Lancashire, Manchester; John Nevin, Boarder, 23, 'pedestrian', b. Middlesbrough; Charles Mower, 22, 'bricklayer', b. Norfolk, Denham; Salford Borough Gardens, Borough Inn 1861 (RG 9/2924); Rob Hadgraft, *Deerfoot: Athletics' Noble Savage: from Indian Reservation to Champion of the World* (London: Desert Island Books, 2007), 58.
[60] *Bell's Life*, June 17, 1860, 7; March 3, 1861, 6; *The Times*, October 10, 1861, 12; *Illustrated Sporting News and Theatrical and Musical Review*, March 29, 1862, 17.
[61] *Era*, May 12, 1861.
[62] *New York Daily Tribune*, June 11, 1861, 8.
[63] *The Times*, September 24, 1861, 10; October 9, 1861, 7; October 10, 1861, 12; October 15, 1861, 12; *Bell's Life*, September 15, 1861, 7.
[64] *The Times*, June 26, 1861, 12.

Although elated with his runner's success, Martin was impressed with Bennett, and encouraged the Indian to travel to Britain.[65] In July 1861, the Indian raced in costume around the decks of the *Great Eastern* and, on his arrival to Britain, began training under the watchful eye of Jack MacDonald, a solicitor, amateur runner and 'advisor' to Cambridge University athletes, 'who has been appointed by his [Bennett's] American backer to look after his interests'. [66]

Figure 2. John Nevin, George Martin and Charles Mower with Champion's Belt and Championship Cup. *Illustrated Sporting News and Theatrical and Musical Review*, March 29, 1862, 17. (c) British Library Board (Mic.A.2580-2585)

---

[65] *The Post Standard*, November 10, 1997, page unknown; John Lucas, 'Deerfoot in Britain: An Amazing Long Distance Runner, 1861-1863', *Journal of America Culture*, 6, no. 3 (1983): 13.

[66] *Bell's Life*, September 8, 1861, 6; *The Racing Times*, December 9, 1861, 389; Peter Lovesey, *The Official Centenary of the AAA* (London: Guiness Superlatives Ltd., 1979), 15; Alfred Rosling Bennett, *London and Londoners in the Eighteen-Fifties and Sixties* (Gloucestershire: Dodo Press, 2009), 351.

Many sporting men had come to view the 'Red Jacket', as illustrated below;

> We do not remember to have seen for a long time past such an array of vehicles arriving at these grounds, and within the enclosure between 2,000 and 3,000 spectators were assembled, including many gentlemen who are not frequently in the habit of visiting courses set apart for foot racing. In short, all grades were present, including officers belonging and not belonging to the police; pedestrians (including the champion); pugilists, represented by the ex-champion; wrestlers of considerable note; the bar was represented by the presence of a barrister instead of a felon; the Turf by several connected with it, not omitting pigeon-shooters, as well as a considerable number of "publicans and sinners".[67]

A 'marketing genius ahead of his time', Martin, aware of the interest surrounding Deerfoot with both the sporting and British public and press, approached Bennett after his "ten-mile champion" success, and proposed a tour of the athlete around the United Kingdom.[68] Martin planned and financed the show, entitled the "Deerfoot Circus" which, by the same principle of Seward's 1849 arena, would see Bennett and several professional athletes compete in sporting feats as part of a travelling exhibition. The tour was arranged and Deerfoot plus various famed pedestrians including 'six-mile champion' Teddy "Young England" Mills, 'four-mile champion' John "Milkboy" Brighton, 'mile champion' William "Crowcatcher" Lang, and 'English champions' Mower, William "American Deer" Jackson, Stapleton and Andrews, agreed to compete every day, except Sunday, in four-mile displays whilst other athletes; pedestrians, jumpers, boxers, and horsemen; partook in 'all kinds of old English sports'.[69]

Whilst the circus was being constructed, Martin continued to promote Bennett. As ten-mile Champion, the Indian was required to race any man who wished to challenge his title, and Martin announced these events within the pages of *Bell's Life*.[70] Deerfoot's limits were challenged and he was subjected to many sporting trials, with the

---

[67] *Scotsman*, September 10, 1861, 3; *Bell's Life*, September 22, 1861, 7.
[68] Rob Hadgraft, *Deerfoot: Athletics' Noble Savage: from Indian Reservation to Champion of the World* (London: Desert Island Books, 2007), 127.
[69] *Bell's Life*, May 11, 1862, 7; *Scotsman*, August 18, 1862, 1.
[70] *Bell's Life*, September 29, 1861, 6.

conclusion that distance running was his forte.[71] However, not satisfied with his pedestrian dominance, Bennett challenged 'champion swimmer of England', Frederick Beckwith, 'to swim 20 lengths of Lambeth Baths, for £50', but this was ultimately forfeited one week before its execution due to the Red Jacket's demanding schedule.[72]

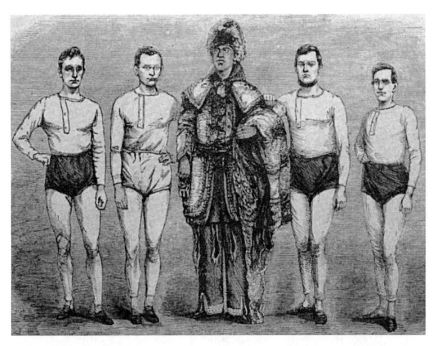

Figure 3. Celebrated peds. Left to right, Edward "Teddy, Young England" Mills, John "The Milkboy" Brighton, Louis "Deerfoot" Bennett, William "Crowcatcher" Lang, and Samuel Barker of Billingsgate. *Illustrated Sporting News and Theatrical and Musical Review*, **May 10, 1862, 38.**
(c) British Library Board (Mic.A.2580-2585)

In December 1861, Martin travelled to Cambridge University where, in the presence of the Prince of Wales, he watched Deerfoot overcome Lang, Brighton and Barker in a six-mile contest.[73] Doubts about the legitimacy of these events had started to surface; *The Racing Post* suggested, 'the pedestrians whom Deerfoot has "beaten" have been hired to play their part in the farce like any other actor', this view being confirmed when Edwin "Young England" Mills reported that his non-

---

[71] *Scotsman*, October 15, 1861, 3; Bell's Life, November 10, 1861, 7.

[72] *The Times*, October 7, 1861, 10; *Bell's Life*, September 29, 1861, 3; October 20, 1861, 6; *Manchester Guardian*, October 28, 1861, 4.

[73] *John Bull*, December 7, 1861, 773.

start at the Cambridge race was due to his reluctance to 'play second fiddle to the red 'un...the consequence being that they [Martin and MacDonald] would not allow him to start at all'.[74] Nonetheless, visitors of both sexes still travelled, and paid, to see the 'star runner' which Martin used to his advantage.[75]

Martin was known as the 'wizard of pedestrianism' or the 'wizard of the North', according to Sears, 'for his innovative ideas and promotional abilities', examples of which are clearly demonstrated through Deerfoot's competitions.[76] Martin had stakes in photographs of the Indian which were hung in public houses all over Britain, lithographs produced in *Illustrated Sporting News and Theatrical and Musical Review*, and the operetta "Deerfoot", which became a musical hit.[77] As part of the racing "show", Martin would parade Bennett in native clothing with 'wolfskin cloak', 'buckskin moccasins' and around his head 'one eagle-feather, the symbol of victory and power', his racing apparel being 'tights, and wearing a girdle richly ornamented with floss silk and feathers, and also a slight belt, to which several small bells were attached'.[78] Deerfoot would present his war-cry, a 'yell so shrill, ear-splitting, and protracted' when he defeated his opponents and, as Hayes describes;

> ...when Martin thought he [Deerfoot] had exercised his legs enough, he used to run into the middle of the course, stretch out his arms, shout out some gibberish, which passed for Cherokee or Iroquois, and try to stop the wild man who used to act the part to perfection and take a lot of catching and holding.[79]

---

[74] *The Racing Post*, December 9, 1861, 389; *Licensed Victuallers' Mirror*, December 8, 1891, 581.

[75] *Scotsman*, October 2, 1861, 3; April 2, 1862, 3; John Lucas, 'Deerfoot in Britain: An Amazing Long Distance Runner, 1861-1863', *Journal of America Culture*, no. 3 (1983): 14.

[76] *Era*, September 22, 1861, 9; *Bell's Life*, July 2, 1864, 4; *Sports Quarterly Magazine*, no. 6 (1978): 12-14; Edward Seldon Sears, *Running Through the Ages* (North Carolina: Macfarlane & Co., 2001), 139.

[77] *Bell's Life*, September 22, 1861, 7; June 22, 1862, 2; *Scotsman*, April 1, 1862, 1; *Birmingham Daily Post*, September 18, 1862, 8.

[78] *The Times*, October 3, 1861, 7; *Penny Illustrated Paper*, October 19, 1861, 11; Warren Library Association, *Warren Centennial: An Account of the Celebration at Warren, Pennsylvania* (Pennsylvania: Warren Library Association, 1897), 121.

[79] *John Bull*, April 19, 1862, 256; Matthew Horace Hayes, *Among Men and Horses* (London: T. Fisher Unwin, 1894), 18.

The performance element of the races added to their entertainment value and when the 'Deerfoot Travelling Race Course' opened in May 1862, Martin continued to present the native in a similar manner.

> G. Martin wishes to inform the public that, having received so many application for Deerfoot to run at various parts of the country, and so few places being enclosed where a race can take place, Martin has, at an enormous expense, built a travelling race course, twelve feet high, and nearly a quarter of a mile in circumference, so that a race can take place in any town where an even piece of ground can be selected.[80]

'Mr Martin's *monstre* canvas race course, 1,000ft in circumference' contained a 220 yard portable track for these demonstrations, which was transported by road to each venue, whilst the athletes themselves travelled by rail. The tour regularly attracted 4,000-5,000 spectators from all backgrounds, including 'a large proportion of ladies, noblemen, any officers, and a great number of military'.[81] The races started each evening at six, with admission from five for the prices of 1s within the amphitheatre and 6d in stand, where there were also 'seats for ladies'.[82] However, as the weeks continued Martin began to struggle financially and trouble with the law ensued.

'Tales emerged of heavy drinking and the occasional brawl, and as the weeks went by the reputation of Martin and Deerfoot, in particular, took a pounding'.[83] Martin was prosecuted for assault and ordered to face one month's imprisonment or pay a £3 fine, the latter being chosen, with Bennett also being charged for strangling a spectator.[84] Within the crowds, pick-pocketing occurred which led to confrontations in court, and members of the "circus" staff were tried

---

[80] *Bell's Life*, 11 May 1862, 7.

[81] *Illustrated Sporting News and Theatrical and Musical Review*, May 17, 1862, 75; *Era*, May 18, 1862, 14; *Bell's Life*, May 18, 1862, 7.

[82] *Scotsman*, August 18, 1862, 1.

[83] Rob Hadgraft, *Deerfoot: Athletics' Noble Savage: from Indian Reservation to Champion of the World* (London: Desert Island Books, 2007), 133.

[84] *Manchester Guardian*, January 12, 1863, 3; *Penny Illustrated*, January 17, 1863, 43; *Lancaster Gazette, and General Advertiser for Lancaster, Westmorland, Yorkshire &c.*, January 17, 1863, 6.

for robbery.[85] Martin's athletes, being concerned with the growing number of illegalities, presented as witnesses against their manager, and on the 23 October 1862, William "American Deer" Jackson, with the support of his fellow performers, effectively sued Martin for lack of pay and poor living conditions. Throughout the hearing, and in the presence of numerous reporters, Jackson announced that the matches were fixed with Martin 'working' them in the Indian's favour and, as a result, interest in the extravaganza subsided, concluding on 10 September 1862, only five months after its launch.[86] Due to the negative attention surrounding Deerfoot, in May 1863, the Indian returned to America with 'upwards of a thousand pounds as the fruits of his running labours', becoming the wealthiest man in his reserve.[87] Deerfoot always maintained that his races were legitimate and, before his death in 1896, he insisted that his training was the same, if not more intense, than all of Martin's athletes, he 'ran and walked at least forty miles a day...his trainer watched with a watch in one hand and a whip in the other...he had no rest...only at night'.[88]

Martin's reputation was severely damaged with news reports emerging which discussed his 'dishonourable character' and 'disgraceful shams and frauds upon the public', with County Court Judge, Mr J.F. Fraser, announcing 'I trust that you (addressing the reporters) will convey my strong opinion of such disgraceful affairs'.[89] Still, Martin continued to work as a trainer and backer at his new home in Garratt Lane, Tooting, near to Mr John Garratt's 'Copenhagen Grounds, Garratt-Lane, Wandsworth', where he constructed, witnessed and held articles of agreements for races against his pedestrian athletes.[90] Undefeated, in November 1863, Martin returned

---

[85] *Hull Packet and East Riding Times*, June 13, 1862, 6; *Bedford Times*, cited in Rob Hadgraft, *Deerfoot: Athletics' Noble Savage: from Indian Reservation to Champion of the World* (London: Desert Island Books, 2007), 133.

[86] *John Bull*, October 25, 1862, 685; *Scotsman*, October 25, 1862, 3; *Bell's Life*, October 26, 1862, 7; *New York Clipper*, October 28 1862, 284; *Standard*, November 7 1862, 3; Matthew Horace Hayes, *Among Men and Horses* (London: T. Fisher Unwin, 1894), 18.

[87] *Scotsman*, May 20, 1863, 3; John Lucas, 'Deerfoot in Britain: An Amazing Long Distance Runner, 1861-1863', *Journal of America Culture*, 6, no. 3 (1983): 16-17.

[88] Warren Library Association, *Warren Centennial: An Account of the Celebration at Warren, Pennsylvania* (Pennsylvania: Warren Library Association, 1897), 122-123; *Washington Post*, July 19, 1908, 15.

[89] *John Bull*, October 25, 1862, 685; *New York Clipper*, October 28, 1862, 284; *Standard*, November 7, 1862, 3.

[90] *Bell's Life*, December 22, 1861, 6; July 19, 1863, 7.

to Manchester where he undertook a new business project which contributed to his "celebrity" which was maintained for years to come.

Table 1. The "Deerfoot Circus" Schedule 1862[91]

Month	Date	Location	Month	Date	Location
May	7	Tunbridge Wells	June	1	Burslem
	8	Reigate		2	Macclesfield
	9	Guildford		3	Chesterfield
	10	Aldershot		4	Retford
	12	Windsor		5	Doncaster
	13	Harrow		6	Pontefract
	14	St Albans		7	Goole
	15	Hertford		9	Hull
	16	Hitchin		10	Grimsby
	17	Bedford		11	Louth
	19	Northampton		12	Lincoln
	20	Rugby		13	Horncastle
	21	Leamington		14	Boston
	22	Coventry		16	Newark
	23	Birmingham		17	Nottingham
	24	Walsall		18	Derby
	30	Dudley		19	Leicester
	31	Wolverhampton		20	Stamford
				21	Peterborough
July	8	Ramsgate	August		
	9	Dover		1	Workington
	10	Folkstone		2	Cockermouth
	11	Hastings		4	Maryport
	12	Chichester		5	Carlisle
	14	Southampton		6	Kendal
	15	Bath		7	Bradford
	16	Cheltenham		8/9	Halifax/Harrogate
	26	Birkenhead		11/12	York/Scarborough
	28	St Helens		13/14	Malton/Darlington
	29	Lancaster		15/16	Durham/Sunderland
	30	Ulverston		18/19	Newcastle/Edinburgh
	31	Whitehaven		20/21	Glasgow/Stirling
				22/23	Perth/Dundee
September	1	Manchester		25/26	Montrose/Aberdeen
	2/10	Ireland		28/29	South Shields/Ripon
				30	Leeds

---

[91] Sources: *Bell's Life in London and Sporting Chronicle*, May 11 1862, 7; May 18 1862, 7; May 25, 1862, 7; June 1, 1862, 6; June 8, 1862, 7; June 17, 1862, 7; June 22, 1862, 22; July 13, 1862, 7; July 27, 1862, 7; August 3, 1862, 6; August 10, 1862, 7; August 17, 1862, 7; *John Bull*, September 13, 1862, 581; Rob Hadgraft, *Deerfoot: Athletics' Noble Savage: from Indian Reservation to Champion of the World* (London: Desert Island Books, 2007), 131.

In the mid-1860s, pedestrianism started to decline, and 'this triple role of promoters, layers, and backers…could only have one conclusion, namely, the loss of confidence from the public and the ultimate collapse of the whole series of promotions'.[92] However, Martin, not deterred by the failure of his previous endeavours, retired as a trainer and backer of pedestrians and announced his intention to develop the grounds attached to the Royal Oak Hotel, his new establishment on Oldham Road, Newton Heath.[93] Location was perfect; Miles Platting railway station was nearby, omnibuses and trams stopped within 200 yards of the ground, and it was less that half a mile from the renowned Copenhagen Running Grounds attached to the Shears Hotel, proprietor Thomas Hayes, with whom Martin had prior connections. Sixteen-acres of land were enclosed, with Martin spending £2000, approximately £145, 000 by today's monetary value, to ensure the ground would be 'first class'.[94]

In February 1864, Martin advertised his grounds within the pages of *Bell's Life*, informing the public of its imminent opening.[95] The ground boasted and 651 yard circular track, quarter of a mile straight course, circular 750 yard rabbit course, wrestling arena, bowling green, quoits ground, trotting course and grandstand, all within the fenced enclosure capable of holding 20,000 people with ease. Further amenities included a shower-bath with soap, towels and brushes which could be used by the public for the sum of one penny, and a portable dressing room, with carpets and fitting, where athletes could 'strip by the fireside opposite the starting post'.[96] Reports in the *Manchester Guardian* claimed Martin had created 'one of the most superior sporting arenas in England, if not the world', with the *Illustrated Sporting News and Theatrical and Musical Review* insisting that Martin was 'the right man at the right place…we trust Mr Martin will receive that support which he deserves'.[97]

---

[92] Charles Lang Neil, *Walking: A Practical Guide to Pedestrianism for Athletes and Others* (London: C. Arthur Pearson Ltd., 1903), 19; David A. Jamieson, *Powderhall and Pedestrianism* (London: W. & A.K. Johnston Ltd, 1943), 104.
[93] *Bell's Life*, November 28, 1863, 7.
[94] *Bell's Life*, February 22, 1857, 7; *Era*, February 22, 1857, 9; November 28, 1863, 7; April 24, 1864, 14.
[95] *Bell's Life*, February 27, 1864, 7.
[96] *Illustrated Sporting News and Theatrical and Musical Review*, April 9, 1864, 54; April 23, 1864, 77.
[97] *Manchester Guardian*, April 18, 1864, 4; *Illustrated Sporting News and Theatrical and Musical Review*, April 23, 1864, 77.

The ground officially reopened on the 17 April, 1864, to crowds of over 3,000 spectators, with the first event, comprehensively promoted within the sporting press, being the 'great mile race for £25 a side' between 'celebrated "clippers"' Siah Albison and James "Treacle" Sanderson.[98] In conclusion of the athletic events music played which 'greatly enlivened the proceedings' and the *Era* reported that the Royal Oak would, 'no doubt be the finest enclosed pedestrian ground in the kingdom'.[99] With the Copenhagen Grounds being within the locality of the Royal Oak, Martin and Hayes, as proprietors of the attached public houses, worked in conjunction with each other to ensure profits. Spectators migrated from stadium to stadium and their sporting entertainments became day-long affairs.[100]

Martin followed the same principles as previous successful publicans such as William Sharples, proprietor of The Star Inn, Bolton, who provided a concert hall with dancing, acrobats, clowns, waxworks, live exhibits and ornamental gardens, regularly filling to its 1,500 capacity, and the famed Mr Rouse, of the Eagle Tavern, City-Road, London, who provide entertainments such as the T.Cooke's Circus, "Cockney Sportsmen", and grand concerts within the Grecian Saloon and Olympic Temple, 'capable of containing about fifteen hundred people', as well as 'ornamental pleasure grounds...most tastefully laid out in parterres of flowers and gravelled walks, relieved by beautiful fountains'.[101] Martin's grounds featured ornamental gardens with statues and sculptures, pianists and singers, aeronauts and photographers, as well as "live exhibits", such as Tonawanda Indian, "Steeprock", who resided in a wigwam in the centre of his newly constructed arena, and in September 1865, the Gypsy King, Queen and tribes who were displayed in a similar fashion.[102]

Martin wanted to provide the pedestrian society with a truly magnificent spectacle and through his promotional skills, he publicised the first annual competition for the 'Great Mile Championship', a contest which continued in his memory after his

---

[98] *Era*, April 17, 1864, 14.

[99] *Era*, April 24, 1864, 14.

[100] *Bell's Life*, June 11, 1864, 7; *Era*, July 30, 1865, 14.

[101] *Eagle Tavern/Grecian Theatre, City Road: Playbills and Illustrations, 1829-1899,* Bishopsgate Institute Archives (London Collection Manuscripts/72); Robert Poole, *Popular Leisure and the Music-Hall in Nineteenth-Century Bolton* (Lancaster: University of Lancaster Press, 1982), 51-55.

[102] *Era*, March 13, 1864, 14; September 3, 1865, 1; *Manchester Guardian*, September 6, 1865, 1.

death. Six champion "clippers" were invited to compete for 'a silver cup weighing 76oz (which immediately becomes his absolute property), in addition to £110 in money', those athletes being Mills, Sanderson, Lang, Nuttall, Stapleton and Albison.[103]

The first competition was held on the 25 June 1864, in the presence of over 20,000 spectators where, according to the *Sheffield & Rotherham Independent*, 'all the London Deerfoot exhibitions…were completely cast into the shade'. Entrance fees equated over £600, and the 'rush for admission was so great that the gates were burst through, and thousands gained admission for free'. Martin took the role of starter and referee and introduced the athletes to the crowds, who paraded around the arena in their colours before being numbered and placed into their starting positions. The race was fast, with the winner, Edward "Teddy" Mills, completing the mile in four minutes twenty seconds, to the thunderous applause of the audience. [104] The following year, on the 19 August 1865, the second instalment of the 'One Mile Champion' was organised, this time for twelve months claim to a 'magnificent gold cup' plus 'one half of the admission money taken at the gates', where, once more, Martin took position as starter and referee. [105] Upwards of 15,000 people witnessed the race between Mills, Sanderson, Lang, Stapleton, Neary, Mower, Richards, Albison, McKinstray and Nuttall, which resulted a dead-heat between William "Crowcatcher"

Figure 5. 'Royal Oak Park One Mile Champion Cup'. *Illustrated Sporting News and Theatrical and Musical Review*, **August 5, 1865, 344.**
(c) British Library Board (Mic.A.2580-2585)

---

[103] *Bell's Life*, May 13, 1865, 7.

[104] *Sheffield & Rotherham Independent*, June 27, 1864, 3.

[105] *Bell's Life*, August 19, 1865, 8; *Manchester Guardian*, August 21, 1865, 4; Bob Phillips, 'The Ancient Art of Mile Pacemaking', *Official Journal of the British Milers' Club*, 3, no. 16 (2004): 30.

Lang and William "the Welshman" Richards, 'time *four minutes seventeen and a quarter seconds* – the quickest time on record'.[106]

Although the grounds were in excellent condition, Martin was not; his physique, which had previously been praised, had become rotund and he looked older than his father-in-law Holden, who was nearly 30 years his senior.[107] In September 1865, reports spread that Martin, 'the energetic and spirited proprietor', had been suffering from 'mental afflictions' and was unable to officiate in his 'present state'.[108] And on the 7 September 1865, Martin was hospitalised at Wye House, a private asylum, 'for the care and treatment of the insane of the higher and middle classes', for 'over attention to business and excitement'.[109]

The Victorian asylum was viewed negatively, as were the lunatics themselves. According to Cambridge County Council, the 1845 Lunacy Act and County Asylum Act 'fundamentally changed the treatment of mentally ill people from that of prisoners to patients…one of the great moves towards compassionate social reform'.[110] The Acts were concerned with the lack of "pauper" asylums; county ran institutions, hospitals, workhouses and prisons; which had a long history of mistreatment of inmates and overcrowding.[111] During the nineteenth century 'charitable hospitals' opened which provided the upper and middle class lunatics, for a fee, refuge from the county asylums, and it was common for these private asylums to be discussed as "retreats" where families could commit 'disturbed relatives' for a period of respite.[112] Ultimately, these private institutes were expensive

---

[106] *Bell's Life*, August 19, 1865, 8; *Preston Guardian*, August 26, 1865, 2; *Penny Illustrated*, August 26, 1865, 206.

[107] *Bell's Life*, May 13, 1865, 7.

[108] *Bell's Life*, September 16, 1865, 7; October 21, 1865, 7.

[109] Post Office, *Post Office Directory of the Counties of Derby, Leicester, Rutland and Nottingham* (London: Kelly & Co. 1876), 36; *Notice of Admission*, George Martin, September 1865, Derbyshire Record Office (Q/Asylum).

[110] Cambridge County Council, *General Introduction: A History of County Asylums* (Cambridge: Cambridge Council, 2011), 3.

[111] Joan Lane, *A Social History of Medicine Health, healing and Disease in England, 1750-1950* (London: Routledge, 2001), 99.

[112] William Parry-Jones, 'Asylums for the Mentally Ill in Historical Perspective', *Psychiatric Bulletin*, no. 12 (1988): 407-408; David Wright, 'Getting Out of the Asylum: Understanding the Confinement of the Insane in the Nineteenth Century', *Social History of Medicine*, no. 10 (1997): 137.

and if patients could not afford their hospitalisation they would be admitted into state-funded establishments.[113]

Figure 4. Wye House Asylum, Buxton, 'for the care and treatment of the insane of the higher and middle classes'. Post Office, Post Office Directory of the Counties of Derby, Leicester, Rutland and Nottingham (London: Kelly & Co. 1876), 36.

Wife, Alice, committed Martin for his continued rambling and refusing to sleep. Friend, and ex-athlete, Teddy Mills stated 'he refuses food; and also refuses to see his wife saying that she wants to kill him', with John Parke insisting, 'he declares he is going to make his racing grounds into a paradise and invite the French King, Victoria and all the Royal Family. He is going to lay the Atlantic Cable and have it completed in a month and he is going to invite the moon down into his gardens and make £100,000 a month', and acute mania was certified.[114] However, less than a week after his admission Martin was discharged, said to have 'recovered by the authority of Alice Martin'.[115]

---

[113] John K. Walton, 'Lunacy in the Industrial Revolution: A Study of Asylum Admissions in Lancashire, 1848-1850', *Journal of Social History*, no.13 (1979): 6.
[114] *Medical Certificate*, George Martin, September 1865, Derbyshire Record Office (Q/Asylum).
[115] *Notice of Discharge or Removal of a Lunatic from a Licensed House*, George Martin, October 3, 1865, Derbyshire Record Office (Q/Asylum).

On the 21 October, 1865, 38-year-old Martin died at St Martins Workhouse Hospital, Middlesex, cause of death being 'cerebral disease' due to mania.[116] His death at such a young age shocked the sporting community and there was concern that the grounds would never be the same again.[117] The following obituary was presented in the pages of *Bell's Life* on 28 October 1865, the publication which for so many years had supported the notorious entrepreneur;

> We regret to announce the death of Mr G. Martin, the enterprising proprietor of the above extensive sporting area, which sad event took place as St Martin's, London, at half-past two a.m., Oct 21. For several years he was well known as a professional pedestrian, and his name is familiar throughout the three kingdoms as the party who introduced Lewis Bennett (alias Deerfoot) to these shores, with what success our readers are well acquainted. In the estimation of the late George Martin all other sports sunk into comparative insignificance when place in juxtaposition with pedestrianism, and his last effort in that pastime was made at his own grounds several months ago, when, in a race of 100 yards, over five hurdles, for £25 a side, he was defeated by Mr W. Booth of Manchester, by three quarters of a yard, after an excellent race. As judge of foot racing pace, allotting starts in handicaps, or as timekeeper, poor Martin had few equals – certainly no superior – and his decease has caused a vacancy which it will be difficult to supply. Within a short period he planned, laid out, and completed the Royal Oak Park Grounds, Manchester, upon which he lived to see some of the fastest races ever known brought to issue; but a short time ago he became mentally afflicted, and, after having made his escape from a private asylum at Buxton, Derbyshire, he subsequently proceeded to London, and died as above stated. Mr Martin was only 39 years of age, and he leaves a widow and a large family to mourn his loss.[118]

Martin left little money for his wife and family, with creditor, wine and spirits merchant Joseph Fildes, reclaiming the majority of Martin's £2000 estate.[119] After his death his family and pedestrian friends continued his legacy, sharing the responsibilities of proprietor, referee,

---

[116] *Death Certificate*, George Martin, October 21, 1865 (DYC 866274); *Manchester Guardian*, October 23, 1865, 4; *Leeds Mercury*, October 24, 1865, 9.

[117] *Bell's Life*, November 4, 1865, 7.

[118] *Bell's Life*, October 28, 1865, 7.

[119] *Will and Probate*, (G 62/21); *Manchester Guardian*, November 10, 1866, 2.

starter, stakeholder and timekeeper at the establishment until its eventual sale in September 1866.[120]

Although the Royal Oak Park Grounds are now a thing of the past, it is important to note that without the entrepreneurial vision and dedication of men, such as Martin, pedestrian amusements and competitions in Britain's industrial cities would have been unable to survive. Martin laboriously promoted the sport through good times and bad, becoming an inspiration to a new generation of sporting entrepreneurs, and he truly deserved the title 'wizard of pedestrianism'.

---

[120] *Manchester Guardian*, August 25, 1866, 8; *Bell's Life*, December 8, 1866, 7.

11

Entrepreneurial Pugilists of the Eighteenth Century

Dave Day

During the eighteenth century the English economy underwent an accelerated structural transformation in which industry came into greater prominence. Industrialisation and urbanisation led to reductions in both the time to indulge in ludic activities and the space to participate in them,[1] although in developing urban areas it was insufficient working-class spending power that limited access to sports as powerful economic influences acted to change traditional pursuits.[2] A combination of increasing population growth and rapid urbanisation created an environment for the enterprising to exploit and the entrepreneurial response from leisure providers in many of the emerging large urban communities, especially London, was dynamic.[3] Gough's illuminated Amphitheatre, or artificial Marble Green House, in Long Lane, Aldergate Street, presented a variety of curious paintings of fruit and flowers in 1743, together with representations of regimental soldiers in battle dress and a plan of the battlefield at Dettingen, all under a branch of lights and twenty eight Pier glasses about nine feet high, for the entrance money of six pence per person.[4] Professional anatomy teachers lectured to anyone who bought a ticket and there were anatomical waxwork exhibitions from the beginning of the eighteenth century at venues such as Rackstrow's public museum in the Strand.[5]

Sporting entrepreneurs like George Smith at the Artillery Ground promoted foot racing[6] and cricket, although the difficulties he faced

---

[1] Joseph Maguire, 'Images of Manliness and Competing Ways of Living in Late Victorian and Edwardian Britain', *British Journal of Sports History*, 3, No.3 (1986), 267.

[2] Wray Vamplew, *Industrialisation and Popular Sport in England in the Nineteenth Century*, (Leicester: University of Leicester, The Centre For Research into Sport and Society, 1998), 24-27.

[3] Neil Tranter, *Sport, Economy and Society in Britain 1750-1914* (Cambridge: Cambridge University Press Economic History Society, 1998), 7.

[4] *Daily Advertiser*, October 24, 1743.

[5] Alan W. Bates, '"Indecent and Demoralising Representations": Public Anatomy Museums in Mid-Victorian England', *Medical History*, 52 (2008), 3.

[6] *Daily Advertiser*, October 24, 1743.

were reflected in one advert in July 1744 announcing that since a recent match had been attended by disorder he would in future be charging each spectator six pence and establishing a ring of benches holding up to 800 people to accommodate gentleman. No-one, except those appointed to keep order and the players, would be permitted within this ring. Swimming and bathing was advertised at the Peerless Pool, behind the bowling green in Old Street, which had been converted in 1743 by jeweller William Kemp into a pleasure bath where gentlemen could safely learn to swim. It was 170 feet long and 100 broad, encompassed by a wall, with a gravel bottom and sited in the middle of a grove. Waiters attended to teach gentlemen to swim if required. There was also a large fishpond and skating in the winter for a guinea per annum or two shillings a time for bathing.[7] Thomas Higginson, who kept the Fives Court in St. Martin's Street, near Leicester Fields, offered Fives, Racquets or Hand Fives for tuppence a game doubles, thruppence and fourpence for singles. He also offered tennis at his new court in Windmill Street facing the Hay Market while another court was available in High Holborn, near the *Bull and Gate Inn*, where there were also two billiard tables.[8]

The rougher sports of the lower classes were also contained and packaged for financial gain and it is this process, particularly the provision for boxing in London and the men involved in making that happen, that occupies the following discussion. Eighteenth-century popular culture was marked by a disorderly and undisciplined nature and a high level of physical violence was evident both in daily life and in recreational activities.[9] At the boarded house in Mary-Bone-Fields in July 1721 there was a match between a wild panther and twelve dogs for £300, a bear was baited and a bull turned loose in the gaming place with fireworks all over him and bull dogs after him, while a dog was drawn up with fireworks about him and an ass baited on the same stage.[10] Combat sports such as wrestling, had been practised by the upper as well as the lower classes in the sixteenth century and although their personal involvement had diminished during the course of the seventeenth century the aristocracy gradually rediscovered an interest in those popular sports practised by their

---

[7] *Daily Advertiser*, July 4, 1744.

[8] *London Daily Post and General Advertiser*, December 6, 1743; *Daily Advertiser*, December 28, 1743.

[9] Joseph Maguire, 'Images of Manliness and Competing Ways of Living in Late Victorian and Edwardian Britain', *British Journal of Sports History*, 3 No.3 (1986), 266.

[10] *Weekly Journal or British Gazetteer*, July 15, 1721.

social inferiors. [11]   On December 27 1681 a boxing match was performed before the Duke of Albemarle, between his footman and a butcher,[12] and in March 1705 the Spanish Ambassador staged a boxing match between his footmen and those of his gentlemen 'for the diversion of his lady'.[13] By 1742 boxing was 'as regular an exhibition as we now see at any of the public places of amusement' and it was being 'patronised by the first subjects in the realm, and tolerated by the magistrates',[14] although the level of violence which accompanied many contests did have legal consequences.   When Richard Teeling, a Hackney coachman, was committed for the murder of another coachman in 1725 the Jury found him guilty of manslaughter because it had been a boxing match agreed between them and he was condemned to be "Burnt in the Hand" with an "M" for murder.[15]

These early eighteenth century boxing matches generally took place at facilities associated with inns or in the open air. In 1724, supporters of boxing often met at John Spenser's, *The Black Dog* at Kentish Town,[16] and in September 1732 a boxing match was fought on the bowling green at Harrow on the Hill between John Faulconer, carpenter, and Bob Russel, an alehouse keeper, where a large crowd was contained by a rope around the green.[17] There were obvious problems in such open air contests however. A boxing match in an open field by Islington between Tom Romain a pipe maker and Jack Stareabout a butcher in 1738 ended in confusion when the butchers, recognising that their man was being beaten, interrupted the contest and a 'general skirmish ensued about the stakes and by-betts'.[18]

There were some specialist facilities even at the end of the seventeenth century such as Preston's Amphitheatre or Royal Bear garden situated

[11] Christopher Johnson, '"British Championism": Early Pugilism and the Works of Fielding', *The Review of English Studies*, 47 No.187 (1996), 331-352.

[12] *True Protestant Mercury or Occurrences Foreign and Domestick*, December 28, 1681.

[13] *Daily Courant*, March 28, 1705.

[14] An Amateur of Eminence *The Complete Art of Boxing According to the Modern Method* (London, 1788), 47.

[15] *Daily Post*, June 28, 1725; July 2, 1725; *Parker's Penny Post*, July 14, 1725; Punishments at the Old Bailey: Branding (Burnt in Hand). http://www.hrionline.ac.uk/oldbailey/his...

[16] *Original London Post or Heathcote's Intelligencer*, August 14, 1724.

[17] *Daily Journal*, September 20, 1732.

[18] *London Daily Post and General Advertiser*, August 1, 1738.

in Coppice Row near Hockley in the Hole, Clerkenwell,[19] where the diversions included wrestling, boxing, cudgelling, fighting at back-sword, quarter-staff, and bear-baiting.[20] The Amphitheatre was 150 or 200 feet square boarded in with benches all round, one above the other, for the spectators to sit at different prices and under which were dens for the bears and bulls to be baited. In the middle of the area was a large stage for the human fighters, men who included James Figg, Ned Sutton, James Stokes and John Broughton.[21]

James Figg

Oxfordshire man James Figg is credited with being the first person to commercialise boxing and to develop it as a 'business' when in 1719, with the help of his patron, the Earl of Peterborough, he set up a School of Arms in Tottenham Court Road where his amphitheatre attracted the patronage of the upper classes. Among his acquaintances he included Prime Minister Sir Robert Walpole, essayist Jonathan Swift, poet Alexander Pope, and William Hogarth, the artist, and both he and his facility contributed to the popularity of pugilism throughout the first half of the century. Figg was six foot tall, 185 pounds, athletic, very strong, tough and courageous. He was an accomplished wrestler and swordsman and he became acknowledged as the best boxer in England. Described as 'more of a *slaughterer*, than a neat, finished pugilist', Figg fought sparingly and remained unbeaten in a career which spanned eleven years but he could not unambiguously be identified as a boxer since his business card, engraved by Hogarth, emphasised his prizefighting skills. He was best known as a teacher,[22] proving so successful that he was able to relocate to larger premises.

It was from among the younger members of the aristocracy and gentry that Figg drew most of his clientele and this universal support for the activity was reflected in the novels of Fielding which abound with exponents of boxing and of other combat sports.[23] Fielding, like many of his contemporaries, recognised an association between boxing and

[19] *A discourse upon the character and consequences of priestcraft, betwixt a Merry Andrew, a religious church-man, and Mr.Hickeringill.* (London, 1705), 28.

[20] *The works of Monsieur Voiture, ... compleat: containing his Familiar letters to gentlemen and ladies. Translated by Mr. Tho. Brown.* (London, 1705).

[21] *Gazetteer and New Daily Advertiser,* January 11, 1788.

[22] Fleischer, N. *The Heavyweight Championship: An Informal History of Heavyweight Boxing from 1719 to the Present Day,* (London: Putnam & Co., 1949), 4.

[23] Christopher Johnson, '"British Championism": Early Pugilism and the Works of Fielding', *The Review of English Studies,* 47(187) (1996): 331-252.

nationalism as epitomised by the contest between Whitaker, a student of Figg's, and di Carni, a Venetian, in 1733 which resulted in a victory for Whitaker after he employed the 'English peg in the stomach, quite a new thing to the foreigners'.[24] Figg seems to have been one of the first entrepreneurs to appreciate the value of publicity and advertising and he immediately capitalised on the interest surrounding this event by announcing that he had an even more capable fighter who he would match against the winner. A week later 'very near as great and fine a Company as the Week before' watched Peartree defeat Whitaker in only six minutes.[25]

Edward Sutton and James Stokes

Over the course of his career Figg fought Ned Sutton on a number of occasions and Sutton was involved in establishing another amphitheatre in conjunction with prizefighter James Stokes during the 1720s. Based in Islington Road the venue advertised boxing matches at the start of 1727,[26] and they remained a feature of this amphitheatre until 1735.[27] Thomas Allen ("Pipes") and John Gretton, cabinet maker, fought for two hundred pounds in May 1730,[28] and appearing in June that year were Whiteacre, Allen, Taylor and one Thomas Day, who had previously kept his own boxing school until arrested for 'Robbing on the Highway'.[29] John Broughton fought 'Pipes' for considerable sums in both 1730 and 1731,[30] and again in May 1732 when these men of 'the first rank well known in London for their bravery and great

---

[24] Randy Roberts, 'Eighteenth Century Boxing' *Journal of Sport History* 4 No.3 (1977), 248-249; By all forms of self-defense I mean the ability to use foil, backsword cudgel, and quarter-staff, as well as the fist. That Figg was a master of all these forms of self-defense can be seen by his calling card which described him as "Master of ye noble science of defense...teaches gentlemen ye use of ye small sword, backsword, and quarterstaff at home and abroad"; Boulton, *Amusements of Old London*, pp. 4, 73-74; Pierce Egan, *Boxiana; or Sketches of Ancient and Modern Pugilism; From the Days of the Renowned Broughton and Slack, To the Heroes of the Present Milling Era* (Leicester, England: Vance Harvey Publishing, 1971 [first published in 1812]), 2-25, gives a more nationalistic account of the bout.

[25] Capt. John Godfrey, *A Treatise Upon the Useful Science of Defence.* (London Printed for the Author, by T. Gardner in the Strand, 1747); Randy Roberts, 'Eighteenth Century Boxing', *Journal of Sport History*, 4(3) (1977): 249-250; *Egan, Boxiana*, pp. 40-42.

[26] *Weekly Journal or British Gazetteer*, July 29, 1727; August 19, 1727.

[27] *Daily Gazetteer (London Edition)*, July 11, 1735.

[28] *Daily Post*, May 27, 1730.

[29] *Original Weekly Journal*, March 12, 1720.

[30] *Read's Weekly Journal or British Gazetteer*, October 10, 1730; April 3, 1731.

skill' boxed for fifty pounds.[31] In 1733 Sutton himself, having previously retired, returned to fight Holmes, lured by the prospect of fighting for the whole box.[32] Sutton and his family added to the unsavoury reputation of the prize fighting fraternity by their subsequent behaviour. In 1730 Sutton was taken into custody and carried to the county gaol of Surrey for wounding several women in the Mint with his sword, in particular one woman who has received a dangerous wound in her thigh.[33] Elizabeth Ward (better known as Bess Sutton, wife of the prizefighter) was tried in 1749 for robbing Richard Brookland, a sailor, of 51 six-and-thirty shilling pieces, and a three pound twelve shilling piece, at her house in Axe-and-Bottle-Yard, Southwark, for which she was transported.[34]

By 1731 Stokes had also decided to retire and concentrate on teaching, his pupils being 'equal in birth and fortune' to any in England,[35] and on his commercial enterprise where he included a number of different attractions such as a boxing match between boys in May 1730,[36] and contests featuring female boxers although women boxers had been appearing at Hockley in the Hole since 1722.[37] Elizabeth Stokes was heavily involved in her husband's enterprises and in 1728 when Stokes accepted a challenge from Knott he had to agree to fight without his wife being his second.[38] Later that year Mary Barker challenged Elizabeth, the English championess, to a fight with weapons and special seating was provided for women.[39] In October Anne Field also challenged Elizabeth, this time to a boxing match,[40] and following her defeat, which she attributed to having been plied with drink before the contest, Anne reissued her challenge.[41] In 1730, Elizabeth was challenged by four women who had come to London specifically to fight her and even though she was intending to retire she agreed to fight them one after the other at her husband's.[42] In 1732 a Stokes's advert noted that the European Championess Mrs. Stokes had fought

[31] *Read's Weekly Journal or British Gazetteer*, April 29, 1732.

[32] *Daily Post*, June 5, 1733.

[33] *Grub Street Journal*, August 27, 1730

[34] *Penny London Post or The Morning Advertiser*, April 7, 1749.

[35] *Daily Advertiser*, August 2, 1731.

[36] *Weekly Journal or British Gazetteer,* May 9, 1730.

[37] *London Journal (1720)* June 23, 1722; August 31, 1723.

[38] *Weekly Journal or British Gazetteer,* May 18, 1728.

[39] *Weekly Journal or British Gazetteer,* August 24, 1728.

[40] *Weekly Journal or British Gazetteer,* October 5, 1728.

[41] *Weekly Journal or British Gazetteer,* November 23, 1728.

[42] *Daily Journal*, June 22, 1730.

forty five times, the last before the Duke of Larvain and several British Noblemen, and still remained unbeaten.[43]

Boxing continued to sit alongside other entertainments. In May 1731, bull baiting, bear baiting, an ass and a bull dressed with fireworks, and a pair of cocks fighting for ten shillings preceded 'Pipes' against Broughton for 100 guineas.[44] On the 6th June 1732 Stokes advertised that his firework bull would be turned loose amongst the gamesters and anyone quitting before all the combustibles were discharged would forfeit five shillings. The ground was railed ten feet deep to prevent danger and raised two feet higher for the better prospect of the gentlemen. The meaner sort of people that Mr. Stokes lets in gratis are desired not to come into the Game-Place because they affront the gentlemen.[45] In July Stokes presented a new opera called Rule a Bear and have a Bear or The Way to Tame a Shrew and announced that he had also purchased a wolf from France, the 'beautifullest creature' seen in England'.[46]

Thomas Sibblis
In 1730, Thomas Sibblis from Worcestershire, late scholar of James Figg, having received 'some Invectives' from Stokes on account of his erecting a drinking booth and hanging up a sword in the field near Stokes's amphitheatre challenged Stokes who agreed to fight 'this herculean Champion whose huge trunk of mortality would affrighten any Thing but myself'.[47] A year later an advertisement for a contest between Edwards and Broughton at Figg's Great Room noted that Figg had now retired and taken a house in Poland Street near Great Marlborough Street, in order to teach gentlemen,[48] and it appears that Sibblis took over the facility, subsequently referred to as Mr. Sibblis's Great Room (Late Mr. Figg's) In Oxford-Road, where he was busy promoting Broughton against Birch in November 173[49] and Broughton against Charles Raventon in June 1733, when he also advertised himself in a prizefighting challenge, at the particular desire of several persons of quality, as citizen and dyer, Professor of the said science.[50]

---

[43] *Daily Post,* June 6, 1732.
[44] *Daily Post,* May 3, 1731.
[45] *Daily Post,* June 6, 1732.
[46] *Daily Post,* July 3, 1732.
[47] *Daily Journal,* August 25, 1730.
[48] *Daily Advertiser,* June 15, 1731.
[49] *Daily Journal,* November 28, 1732.
[50] *Daily Post,* June 5, 1733; June 9, 1733.

George Taylor

In 1734, while still in his early twenties, George Taylor acquired the amphitheatre from Sibblis and he enjoyed considerable success as a manager and showman. Known as George the Barber, Taylor had made his first appearances as a combatant in his teens fighting at Figg's amphitheatre, alongside Boswell, Smallwood, and Broughton, who was the only man to beat him, partly, it was believed because Taylor lacked 'Bottom'.[51] His advertisements were graphic and he used the press to publish challenges from fighters. Taylor charged an expensive 2s. 6d. for entrance, and a day's takings of £150 was not uncommon with two thirds normally going to the winner.[52] Taylor also ran an academy where gentlemen were taught self-defence and he may also have modelled at the St. Martin's Lane Academy, where Hogarth taught. At the start of the 1740s Taylor had successful fights against Boswell and Stephenson,[53] and his business was flourishing, but Broughton left him in 1742 and a year later, opened a much more comfortable amphitheatre. Taylor tried to respond in 1744, declaring that his facility had been commodiously altered for the better entertainment of gentlemen at a very large expense,[54] but he was eventually forced to close and fight for Broughton. After a few years he left to become landlord of *The Fountain Inn*, Deptford but he later decided to fight again, losing to Tom Faulkner in August 1758, and he died a few months later.[55] Like other pugilistic entrepreneurs his contacts had always included gentry, nobility and artists and it was Hogarth who produced the designs for his tombstone.[56]

John Broughton

The best remembered of the boxing professors and entrepreneurs was John (Jack) Broughton, a pupil of Figg's, who appeared at Taylor's booth in Tottenham Court Road and fought at both Stokes's amphitheatre and at Sibblis's establishment in the 1730s.[57] Broughton, who was considered champion from the mid-1730s until 1750, was, like Figg, a powerful man (196-200 pounds and 5-10½ inches/6ft),

[51] Capt. John Godfrey, *A Treatise Upon the Useful Science of Defence*. (London, Printed for the Author, by T. Gardner in the Strand 1747).

[52] An Amateur of Eminence *The Complete Art of Boxing According to the Modern Method*. (London, 1788), 48

[53] *General Evening Post*, March 4, 1740.

[54] *Daily Advertiser*, March 12, 1744; April 23, 1744.

[55] Dennis Brailsford, 'Taylor, George (c.1710–1758)', Oxford Dictionary of National Biography, Oxford University Press, 2004

[56] *The Genuine Works of William Hogarth; with Biographical Anecdotes*. Gentleman's Magazine, (1818:Aug.) 139-140.

[57] *Daily Journal*, November 23, 1734.

muscular enough for sculptor John Michael Rysbrack to use his biceps as the models for a statue of Hercules, but he also brought method into boxing by introducing scientific moves and more technical punching.[58] Patronised by the Duke of Cumberland, Broughton was apparently an intelligent and courteous man and it was under his influence that boxing became a specialised activity which became increasingly popular. His contribution to boxing was significant, not only for his development of the science but for his introduction of rules and for the success of his amphitheatre.

In 1743 Broughton drew up a set of rules which essentially governed boxing until 1838 and he used the money he earned from fighting, along with help from wealthy patrons, to open an amphitheatre,[59] dedicated to the Manly Art of Boxing, and structured so as to 'prevent the gentry's being incommoded by the populace'. Fighters were vetted as to their ability while their payments were determined by agreement between them or decided by the gentlemen present. Broughton justified himself as manager of this enterprise, citing his invincibility and esteem within the boxing community and emphasising that he had sufficient physical presence to ensure the 'Preservation of Decency and Decorum'. He also wished to open an Academy at the Amphitheatre for those wishing to be taught boxing and he offered to provide Mufflers to avoid black eyes, broken jaws, and bloody noses. Gentlemen could have a course of lessons at their own house and anyone who contributed towards the Amphitheatre would be admitted free of charge to public classes.[60]

Broughton's New Amphitheatre was situated virtually adjacent to Taylor's premises and Taylor responded by contracting Stevenson, James, and Smallwood under articles not to fight on any stage but his as well as publishing an advertisement criticising Broughton on a number of counts and accusing him of swindling his fighters. Broughton replied that since he had contributed £400 of his own money to supplement the £80 raised by subscription it was only reasonable that he should take a third part of the money collected at

---

[58] Randy Roberts, Eighteenth Century Boxing, *Journal of Sport History* 4 No.3 (1977), 250-251; John Durant, *The Heavyweight Champions* (New York: Hastings House, 1971), 4.

[59] Edward D. Krzemienski, 'Fulcrum of Change: Boxing and Society at a Crossroads', *The International Journal of the History of Sport*, 21, No.2 (2004), 162–164.

[60] John Broughton, (January 1 1742-3). *Proposals for Erecting an Amphitheatre For the Manly Exercise of Boxing*, 3-4.

the door. In the end all the 'principal amateurs of the science' gave their support to Broughton so that Taylor and his boxers eventually agreed to abandon their Booth and to only fight for Broughton on condition that he made good the loss they sustained by the forfeiture of their articles.[61] The Amphitheatre prospered and by the time Taylor beat Slack in January 1750 receipts sometimes amounted to three hundred pounds.[62]

Following his retirement in 1744, Broughton had devoted his time to running an academy and giving private lessons. Godfrey believed that Broughton would forever remain unbeaten because he would 'scarce trust a Battle to a waning Age',[63] but Broughton took the stage again on 11 April 1750 and suffered his first defeat at the hands of Jack Slack, who made an estimated six hundred pounds on the fight.[64] Although it has been suggested that the Broughton's Amphitheatre was closed down following his defeat under pressure from Cumberland who reputedly lost £10,000 on Broughton, it was still operating in 1752 with William Willis fighting Thomas Falkener, the Cricket-Player from Kent, and Slack defeating Lee the Chairman.[65] One 1752 diary entry emphasises the centrality of boxing during this period.

> Tuesday morning, got up at eight, drank tea, hurried away to *Broughton's* Amphitheatre, paid a Crown for my seat, *Tom boy* a very good second, tolerable battle enough. One O'Clock went to *Dolley's*, dined and had half a pint of Gill as usual, gave an account of the battle to the gentlemen in the back room. Mr. *Gripes* eat three pound of beef steaks, had a good deal of discourse in the back room about *Broughton, Slack*, the *Barber*, and others, they allow me to be a very good judge. Eight O'Clock got home, had fresh tea made by Mrs. *Butters*, went to coffee house, talked a good deal about the battle at *Broughton's*, had half a Pint of Red Port, and went home to bed.[66]

---

[61] An Amateur of Eminence *The Complete Art of Boxing According to the Modern Method.* (London, 1788), 58-63.

[62] Thomas Fewtrell, *Boxing Reviewed; Or, The Science of manual Defence, Displayed on Rational principles.* (London, 1790), 85.

[63] Capt. John Godfrey, *A Treatise Upon the Useful Science of Defence.* (London, Printed for the Author, by T. Gardner in the Strand, 1747).

[64] *Whitehall Evening Post or London Intelligencer*, January 30, 1750; *London Evening Post*, March 13, 1750; *London Evening Post*, April 10, 1750.

[65] *Daily Advertiser*, February 4, 1752; *London Daily Advertiser*, February 11, 1752.

[66] *The General review, or, Impartial register; being a faithful representation of the civil, military, commercial and literary transactions of the present time.* (London, 1752), 238.

However, there was considerable opposition to these specialist facilities with one author arguing that 'If only the "populace of distinction" would withdraw their support from those Amphitheatres that are the "vile seminaries of insolence and disturbance", the magistracy would soon suppress them', [67] and by 1754 they had closed,[68] public boxing matches were driven out of London and boxing did not revive until the 1780s.[69] Later commentators argued that it was the behaviour of the boxing professors themselves that led to this decline as they had become a distinct and noxious class of beings in society.[70] There were some regrets though.

> I cannot but lament the cruelty of that law, which has shut up our Amphitheatres: and I look upon the professors of the noble art of Boxing as a kind of disbanded army, for whom we have made no provision. The mechanics, who at the call of glory left their mean occupations, are now obliged to have recourse to them again, and coachmen and barbers resume the whip and the razor instead of giving black eyes and cross-buttocks. Broughton employs the muscle of his brawny arm in squeezing a lemon or drawing a cork. His Amphitheatre itself is converted into a Methodist Meeting-house! The dextrous use of the fist is a truly *British* exercise and the sturdy *English* have been as much renowned for their Boxing as their Beef; both which are by no means suited to the watry stomachs and weak sinews of their enemies the *French*. To this nutriment and this art is owing that

---

[67] *A hint on duelling, in a letter to a friend. The second edition. To which is added, The bruiser, or an inquiry into the pretensions of modern manhood. In a letter to a young genttleman.* (London, 1752), 37.

[68] Ken Sheard, Boxing in the Western Civilizing Process, In Dunning, E., Malcolm, D. and Waddington, I. (Eds.) (2004). *Sport Histories: Figurational Studies of the Development of Modern Sports*, Routledge, 20.

[69] Randy Roberts, Eighteenth Century Boxing, *Journal of Sport History* 4 No.3 (1977), 253-254; Lardner, *The Legendary Champions*, 6; Joseph Abbott Liebling, *The Sweet Science* (New York: Viking Press 1958), 2; John Boyton Priestley, *The Prince of Pleasure and His Regency, 1811-20* (New York: Harper and Row, Pub., One. 1969), 47; Christopher Johnson, 'British Championism': Early pugilism and the works of Fielding. *The Review of English Studies*, 47, No. 187 (1996), 331-352.

[70] Thomas Fewtrell, *Boxing Reviewed; Or, The Science of manual Defence, Displayed on Rational principles.* London (1790), 43-44; An Amateur of Eminence, *The Complete Art of Boxing According to the Modern Method.* (London, 1788), 79.

long-established maxim, that one *Englishman* can beat three *Frenchmen*.[71]

In his retirement Broughton ran an antiques business and a furniture warehouse as well as continuing to teach boxing, charging 5s. a lesson or 1 guinea if required to stand up to his students in 1787, the same year that it was reported that Mendoza had adopted a new blow from Broughton.[72] When he died on 8 January 1789 newspapers observed that his 'skill in boxing will ever be recorded in the annals of that science',[73] while his entrepreneurial talents were reflected in his leaving an estate believed to have been worth upwards of £7000.[74]

The first half of the eighteenth century clearly witnessed significant developments in boxing in London driven by entrepreneurs who used their knowledge of the activity, their business acumen and their aristocratic contacts to develop facilities in which they controlled the fighters and the direction of the sport itself. They clearly formed a tightly knit community. When Thomas Allen (Pipes) was buried on May 12 1738 the coffin of this man 'famous for his art and bravery in boxing who had latterly been Gallery Door-Keeper to Drury-Lane Play-House' was carried by Broughton, Peartree, Taylor, Stevenson, Boswell and Thomas Dimmack, six of the most celebrated boxers of the age, an example of the 'innate generous love of valour for which Englishmen are so justly distinguished'.[75]

The popularity of boxing does not appear to have survived the passing of these men and the closing of their amphitheatres and it was another thirty years before the activity regained the same degree of support among the gentry and nobility. This has led some historians to conclude that the closing of Broughton's amphitheatre retarded the development of boxing since it became an illegal activity which was forced to compete with legal activities like cricket and racing, which could establish permanent venues, advertise, charge for admission and pay reliable performers a steady income.[76] For others, however, the closure of the amphitheatres prevented boxing from becoming merely

[71] *The connoisseur. By Mr. Town, critic and censor-general* London, 1755-1756. Vol.1.No. 30. 177-180.

[72] *World (1787),* December 27 1787.

[73] *St. James's Chronicle or the British Evening Post,* January 8, 1789; *Bath Chronicle,* January 15, 1789.

[74] Tony Gee, 'Jack Broughton' Oxford Dictionary of National Biography.

[75] *Common Sense or The Englishman's Journal,* May 13, 1738.

[76] Dennis Brailsford, *Bareknuckles: A Social History of Prizefighting,* (Cambridge: Lutterworth Press, 1988), 13-14.

an exhibition controlled by a few showmen since it was clearly in the interests of entrepreneurs and the fighters themselves to control the activity and extend their careers by exhibiting in easily controlled facilities rather than engaging in full-blooded contests in the open air. The argument here is that it is unlikely that boxing would have developed as a cult and national pre-occupation in the way that it did during the Regency period had it remained confined to the towns and cities.[77]

Whichever position one adopts on this issue there is no doubting the impact that these individuals, and their collective community, had on the development of boxing in this period and, ultimately, on the development of modern sport. Eighteenth century industrialisation brought with it the concept of achievement through improved performance and the expansion of interest in pugilism was combined with a growing appreciation of the importance of appropriate training and instruction, the roots of which had appeared when Figg took responsibility for one fighter's 'Instruction and proper Diet' in 1725.[78] By the time the Amphitheatres were being closed it was being argued that an expanding competitive programme for bruisers would lead gentlemen to 'keep champions in training, put them in sweats, diet them, and breed up the human species with the same care as they do cocks and horses.' Tellingly, the author believed that, as a result, this 'branch of gaming would doubtless be reduced to a science',[79] something which is a familiar concept within our contemporary sporting landscape.

---

[77] Ken Sheard, Boxing in the Western Civilizing Process, In Dunning, E., Malcolm, D. and Waddington, I. (Eds.) (2004). *Sport Histories: Figurational Studies of the Development of Modern Sports*, Routledge, 21.

[78] *London Journal (1720)*, January 16, 1725.

[79] *Connoisseur (Collected Issues)*, August 22, 1754.